LONELY PLANET'S
WONDERS
OF THE WORLD

101 GREAT SIGHTS AND HOW TO SEE THEM ON ANY BUDGET

© Eric Lafforgue / Lonely Planet

Contents

Introduction 004

AFRICA 006
Mt Kilimanjaro 008
Tanzania
Lalibela 010
Ethiopia
Pyramids of Giza 014
Egypt
Ngorongoro Crater 018
Tanzania
Kolmanskop 022
Namibia
Great Zimbabwe 024
Zimbabwe
Victoria Falls 028
Zimbabwe/Zambia
Tsingy de Bemaraha 030
Madagascar
Abu Simbel 034
Egypt
Okavango Delta 038
Botswana

NORTH AMERICA 042
Yosemite Valley 044
USA
New York Harbor 048
USA
Haida Gwaii 052
Canada
Antelope Canyon 056
USA
Grand Canyon 058
USA
Hawai`i Volcanoes
National Park 062
USA
Redwoods 066
USA
The Blue Hole 070
Belize
Mesa Verde 072
USA
Calakmul 076
Mexico
Lake Louise 078

Canada
Smithsonian
Institution 082
USA
Niagara Falls 086
Canada/USA

SOUTH AMERICA 090
Amazon Rainforest 092
Peru/Brazil
Salar de Uyuni 096
Bolivia
Caño Cristales 100
Colombia
Iguazú Falls 102
Brazil/Argentina
Galápagos Islands 106
Ecuador
Moai, Easter Island 110
Chile
Antarctica 112
Machu Picchu 116
Peru

Marble Caves 120
Chile
Angel Falls 124
Venezuela
Tikal 126
Guatemala

**ASIA & THE
MIDDLE EAST** 130
Grand Palace 132
Thailand
Burj Khalifa 136
United Arab Emirates
Temple Mount 140
Israel & the Palestinian
territories
Hang Son Doong 144
Vietnam
Taj Mahal 146
India
Gunung Mulu National
Park 150
Malaysia

Mt Everest 154
Nepal
Naqsh-e Jahan Sq 156
Iran
Angkor Wat 160
Cambodia
The Great Wall 164
China
Door to Hell 168
Turkmenistan
Golden Temple 170
India
Terracotta Army 174
China
Petra 178
Jordan
Forbidden City 182
China
Halong Bay 186
Vietnam
Sakura 188
Japan
Meghalaya Tree

©Pete Seaward/Lonely Planet

©Jonathan Gregson/Lonely Planet

Bridges	192	Norway/Iceland		The Netherlands		**Nemrut Dağı**	306	**Trolltunga**	342
India		**Hermitage Museum**	226	**Giant's Causeway**	266	Turkey		Norway	
Dead Sea	196	Russia		Northern Ireland		**Meteora**	308	**Bay of Kotor**	344
Jordan/Israel & the		**Cappadocia**	230	**Louvre**	270	Greece		Montenegro	
Palestinian territories		Turkey		France		**St Basil's Cathedral**	312		
Taktshang Goemba	200	**Pompeii**	234	**Colosseum**	272	Russia		**OCEANIA**	348
Bhutan		Italy		Italy		**Matterhorn**	316	**Great Barrier Reef & the**	
Ghats of Varanasi	202	**Alhambra**	238	**Blue Lagoon**	276	Switzerland		**Daintree Rainforest**	350
India		Spain		Iceland		**Sagrada Família**	318	Australia	
Temples of Hampi	206	**Stonehenge**	242	**Stari Most**	280	Spain		**Stewart Island**	354
India		England		Bosnia & Hercegovina		**Skara Brae**	322	New Zealand	
Himeji Castle	210	**Davit Gareja**	244	**Acropolis**	284	Scotland		**Uluru**	356
Japan		Georgia		Greece		**Schloss**		Australia	
Zhāngyè Dānxiá		**Geirangerfjord**	248	**British Museum**	288	**Neuschwanstein**	326	**Lord Howe Island**	360
Geopark	212	Norway		England		Germany		Australia	
China		**Mont St-Michel**	252	**Ephesus**	290	**Sintra**	328	**Milford Sound**	362
Punakha Dzong	216	France		Turkey		Portugal		New Zealand	
Bhutan		**Aya Sofya**	254	**Sistine Chapel**	294	**CERN**	332		
Borobudur	218	Turkey		Italy		Switzerland		**Index**	366
Indonesia		**Bordeaux Wine**		**Grand Canal**	298	**Klementinum**	336	**Acknowledgements**	368
		Region	258	Italy		Czech Republic			
EUROPE	222	France		**Plitvice Lakes**	302	**Széchenyi Baths**	338		
Northern Lights	224	**Rijksmuseum**	262	Croatia		Hungary			

Introduction

The wonders of the world have exerted a fascination for humans ever since we could point and murmur 'Wow! That's quite something.' The first list of awe-inspiring sights was the Seven Wonders of the Ancient World, compiled by various Hellenic writers. These had quite a Mediterranean bias with the Temple of Artemis, the Colossus of Rhodes and the Statue of Zeus. The Greeks spoke of these places as 'places to be seen' ('Tá eptá thaumata tís oikouménis') so perhaps this was one of the world's earliest bucket lists.

Only the oldest of those seven original wonders still stands: the Great Pyramid of Giza (see p14), which was constructed at around 2500 BC. The pyramids are now more than 4500 years old but they are pre-dated by plenty of natural wonders: Niagara Falls is thought to be 12,000 years old, Mt Everest about 60 million years old and Uluru, Australia's great red monolith, shows all of its 600 million years on its eroded surface.

Lonely Planet's collection of 101 wonders includes both natural and human-made sights across the world. We have selected, with the help of our destination editors, places that represent the best and most extraordinary 'places to be seen'. There are sights that most people on Earth have heard about – the modern Seven Wonders perhaps – including the Taj Mahal, Angkor Wat and the Great Wall of China. But we also feature less famous sights that cannot fail to captivate: the entwined tree bridges of Meghalaya in India, the intricate and astounding Islamic architecture of Naqsh-e Jahan in Iran, and our cover star, the massive Buddhist temple of Borobudur in central Java, with Mt Merapi volcano smouldering in the distance. We've added museums with remarkable collections of wonders too, such as the Rijksmuseum in the Netherlands and the British Museum in London.

© Justin Foulkes / Lonely Planet

The great carved heads of moai on Easter Island

See India's Taj Mahal at dawn from the water

Victoria Falls, a chasm between Zambia and Zimbabwe

The aurora borealis pulsates over Norway

The planet's natural wonders are no less awesome: giant trees in California, cascading lakes in Croatia, multi-coloured hills in China, great waterfalls, the world's biggest cave, and such natural phenomena as the wave of cherry blossom (*sakura*) that sweeps across Japan each spring, and the light show of the auroras across the planet's northern and southern extremities.

Why do these wonders enthral? As Thomas Rockwell, Creative Director of San Francisco's Exploratorium – the city's museum of science, art and human perception – observes, most people spend only a tiny fraction of their lives in formal learning (our school days). But everything outside of the classroom is an opportunity to learn. These wonders tell us more about ourselves and our planet. They demand our engagement and our attention. It's impossible to resist being immersed in them for a moment or more – which

is a fantastic feeling. 'Many things that we think are wonderful make us stand back and look at the whole world,' says Thomas Rockwell.

That sort of experience sounds expensive, doesn't it? Not necessarily. The second purpose of this book, after inspiring you to enjoy each of our 101 great wonders in person, is to explain how you can visit them, whatever your budget. Thanks to Lonely Planet's unique resources – our network of travel experts and 45 years of experience – we've compiled a guide to each wonder that recommends the best times to visit each of them, how to get there, and where to stay and eat, however deep your pockets. Two sample itineraries cover short and longer trips so you can start to make travel plans based on the time and funds you have available. And our guidebooks and website offer the next detailed steps in exploring Lonely Planet's wonders of the world.

NORTH ATLANTIC OCEAN

Canary
Islands
(SPAIN)

MOROCCO

TUNISIA

ALGERIA

LIBYA

MAURITANIA

MALI

NIGER

CABO
VERDE

SENEGAL

CHAD

THE GAMBIA

BURKINA FASO

GUINEA-BISSAU

GUINEA

BENIN

NIGERIA

SIERRA
LEONE

CÔTE
D'IVOIRE

TOGO

LIBERIA

GHANA

CAMEROON

Gulf of Guinea

EQUATORIAL
GUINEA

SÃO TOMÉ AND
PRINCIPE

GABON

CONGO

Africa

ANGOLA

NAMIBIA

SOUTH ATLANTIC OCEAN

Kolmanskop ✪

Mediterranean Sea

Pyramid of Giza ✪

EGYPT

**Abu Simbel
Temples** ✪

Red Sea

The
Gulf

Arabian
Sea

SUDAN

ERITREA

Lalibela ✪

DJIBOUTI

Somaliland

CENTRAL
AFRICAN
REPUBLIC

SOUTH
SUDAN

ETHIOPIA

SOMALIA

DEMOCRATIC
REPUBLIC OF
CONGO

UGANDA

KENYA

RWANDA

BURUNDI

✪ ✪ **Mt Kilimanjaro**
Ngorongoro Crater

TANZANIA

SEYCHELLES

INDIAN OCEAN

COMOROS

Mayotte
(FRANCE)

MALAWI

ZAMBIA

**Victoria
Falls** ✪

MOZAMBIQUE

ZIMBABWE

✪ **Tsingy de
Bemaraha**

**Okavango
Delta** ✪

✪ **Great
Zimbabwe**

MADAGASCAR

MAURITIUS

BOTSWANA

ESWATINI

LESOTHO

SOUTH
AFRICA

TANZANIA

Mt Kilimanjaro

Its name is as exotic sounding as the thought of its summit's equatorial glaciers. To see this geographic phenomenon is a trip worth taking. And to stand atop the continent of Africa is a dream worth fulfilling.

The stars above are still bright and spinning slowly as you make your push to the summit of mighty Kilimanjaro (5896m). Your head torch lights your path and illuminates each and every one of your exhausted breaths in the cold air. The fatigue in your legs has as much to do with the lack of oxygen as it does with the previous week's efforts. After all, Kilimanjaro is not only one of the world's loftiest volcanoes, but its highest free-standing mountain – from base to summit it's an incredible 5100m. This means you've trekked for miles, first past cultivated farmlands, then through lush rainforests, before even reaching the mountain's stunning alpine meadows. Now you're walking on what looks like a lunar landscape, and glaciers are calling. It must be said that the change of habitat and scenery is one of the most captivating parts of a Kili climb. That and reaching Uhuru Peak for sunrise, of course.

Even if you've travelled to Mt Kilimanjaro National Park with no plans to make an ascent, just seeing the dramatic glacier-topped mountain rising out of the African plains is an incredible reward in itself. Spotting an elephant or buffalo in the lower rainforests is another highlight.

Travel

International
Dar es Salaam's Julius Nyerere International Airport is the main international air hub for Tanzania, but it's worth flying on to Kilimanjaro International Airport for access to the mountain itself. The airport sits between the towns of Arusha and Moshi, which are both hubs for Kili climbs.

Regional
Moshi and Arusha, both 50km from Kilimanjaro International Airport, can be reached by taxi. These cities are the main departure points for treks, and where they can be organised. Reaching the trailhead will be organised by your operator, and the length of the journey will depend on which route you are taking up the mountain.

Stay

Shoestring
Hibiscus This cosy B&B in Moshi has spotless, nicely decorated rooms, all with fans and most with a private bathroom, plus a pleasant garden and meals on request. *(Rooms from TSh70,000/US$30; www.thehibiscusmoshi.com)*

Midrange
Karama Lodge On a forested hillside just southeast of Arusha, Karama offers 22 rather lovely stilt bungalows, each with a veranda and views to Kilimanjaro. *(Rooms from TSh265,000/US$115; http://karama-lodge.com)*

Flush
Mt Meru Game Lodge Bordering a private wildlife sanctuary that has zebras, ostriches and monkeys, Mt Meru is a wonderful option. Stunning rooms are decked out in soothing wood and white linen. *(Per person US$275; www.mtmerugamelodge.com)*

Eat

Shoestring
Khan's Barbecue An institution, Khan's is an auto-spares shop by day and the best-known roadside barbecue joint by night. This is a great place to experience Arusha like a local. *(Meals TSh9000/US$4)*

Midrange
Peppers Part Indian restaurant, part sports bar, Peppers serves up delicious meals on its pleasant terrace overlooking the football pitch in Moshi. *(Mains from TSh16,000/US$7)*

Flush
Blue Heron Sit on this Arusha-based restaurant's leafy veranda or out on the lawn tables to enjoy anything from paninis and soups to beef tenderloin and various creative specials. *(Mains up to TSh25,000/US$11; www.facebook.com/pizzaheron)*

Timing

Mt Kilimanjaro can be climbed year-round, but the best conditions are typically from late June to October, and from late December to early March, just after the short rains and before the long rains.

During November and March/April, it's more likely that paths through the forest will be slippery and that routes up to the summit, especially the Western Breach, will be covered by snow.

The striking jewellery crafted by Maasai women – different styles and pieces denote different ages and social status.

A herd of elephants with majestic Mt Kilimanjaro in the background.

Trekkers set out on their ascent of Mt Kilimanjaro.

Best value itineraries

3–4 days
After landing at Kilimanjaro International Airport, head north into the region of West Kilimanjaro. This remote and surprisingly little-visited corner of northern Tanzania is a gem and comes complete with a couple of terrific tented camps, a fabulous world of Amboseli-like plains and light woodlands, and a sprinkling of Maasai *manyattas* (traditional homesteads). There are wildlife-watching options on foot, on horseback and in traditional 4WD vehicles, as well as cultural encounters with local Maasai. Besides elephants, zebras, cheetahs, warthogs and lesser kudus to keep you company, there are rather resplendent views of the mighty Mt Kilimanjaro.

7–10 days
Fly into Kilimanjaro International Airport and then explore either Arusha or Moshi for a couple of days while getting over the worst of your jetlag. On day three head to the trailhead of the Machame route with your licensed guides. This particular trail up Kili is a wonderful alternative to the standard (and busy) Marangu trail. Machame's more gradual ascent includes a spectacular day contouring the southern slopes before approaching the summit via the top section of the Mweka route. As it's usually a six- or seven-day return, it also means you're less likely to be hit by altitude sickness.

①

ETHIOPIA

Lalibela

The astounding rock-hewn churches of Lalibela represent the apogee of ancient Ethiopia's monument construction, and to explore them is to embrace the nation's remarkable past.

Descending into Lalibela's subterranean world isn't an opportunity to just contemplate the past, it's a chance to physically touch, smell and hear it. It is history living today as it did almost a millennium ago. It is also Christianity in its purest sense. As you navigate the passageways and grottoes, your fingers caressing the roughly hewn stone walls, you'll encounter traditional, cross-wielding priests who float through the shadows like the clouds of incense and the scent of beeswax candles. You'll follow the resonating chants echoing from dark recesses, only to find yourself standing in a beam of sunlight, in front of a towering masterpiece, frozen in stone. Step inside to witness age-old religious ceremonies and to admire the remarkable artistry involved in creating these places of worship.

This medieval world, which includes 11 fantastically sculpted churches, was carved down into the volcanic rocks that underlie Lalibela during the 12th and 13th centuries. Each of the churches is unique in both its style and scale: Bet Medhane Alem, which is the largest rock-hewn church in the world, is surrounded by 34 towering columns; while Bet Giyorgis is a 15m high, three-tiered plinth in the shape of an ornate cross. Incredible.

Travel

International
The majority of travellers arrive in Ethiopia by air at Addis Ababa's Bole International Airport, which is on the south side of the capital. For those who have time and a spirit of adventure, it's possible to enter Ethiopia overland via Sudan, Kenya, Djibouti, Somaliland and (since 2018) Eritrea.

Regional
Ethiopia Airlines links Addis Ababa with Lalibela twice daily; the flights are scenic and short (45 minutes). There are also daily flight arrivals from Aksum, Gonder and Bahir Dar. There is a single bus service between Lalibela and the capital each day (in both directions), which takes two days (overnighting in Dessie).

Stay

Shoestring
Asheton Hotel This classic budget-traveller haunt offers older whitewashed rooms – don't be fooled by the intricately carved doorways, as what lies within is far simpler. *(Rooms from Birr300/US$11)*

Midrange
Old Abyssinia Lodge Wood furnishings, many with ornately carved traditional designs, inhabit large stone-walled rooms that come with good-sized bathrooms. The balconies have wonderful views. *(Rooms from Birr1550/US$55)*

Flush
Hotel Maribela This intimate, light-filled option sits on a ridge and faces out over the surrounding valleys and mountains. The balconies, some with daybeds and cushions, are perfect. *(Rooms from US$65; www.hotelmaribela.com)*

Eat

Shoestring
Unique Restaurant This basic but cosy restaurant serves the usual mix of Ethiopian and *faranji* (foreigner) dishes. It's the kind of place you'll hesitate to enter but then find yourself staying to take cooking classes. *(Mains from Birr40/US$1.50)*

Midrange
Ben Abeba One of Ethiopia's coolest restaurants, this Ethio-Scottish-owned jumble of walkways, platforms and fire pits sits on the edge of the ridge for 360-degree views. The food is tasty – especially the goat burger on traditional bread. *(Mains from Birr45/US$1.65; www.benabeba.com)*

Flush
XO Lalibela With a classier dining area than most here (but with no views), XO Lalibela serves up a fresh, modern menu of roast chicken, burgers, fajitas and paninis. *(Mains from Birr55/US$1.97)*

Timing

High season runs from January to March, when the highlands are dominated by sunny skies and warm days. This period is good for wildlife watching and Ethiopia's most colourful festivals, including Timkat and Leddet.

If trekking in the Simien Mountains is of interest, the shoulder season months of October to December are perfect – the landscape is green, wildflowers are in bloom, skies are blue and there are fewer visitors.

Lalibela's masterpiece, Bet Giyorgis. The church's perfectly proportioned shape required no internal pillars.

A priest blesses pilgrims at the entrance to Bet Giyorgis.

Inside the church light filters in and illuminates the ceiling's large crosses. Books and paintings are on display, including an exquisite 16th-century canvas of St George slaying the dragon.

Best value itineraries

7 days
After a day revelling in the chaos of Addis Ababa, fly north to palm-fringed Bahir Dar for a day. Spend the next day at Lake Tana, exploring some of the lake's centuries-old island monasteries. Next it's a three-hour bus journey to Gonder to wander the extensive ruins of crenulated 17th-century castles. Fly on to Aksum where pre-Christian tombs underlie splendid 1800-year-old stelae (obelisks). Now hop south by plane to Lalibela to tour the astounding rock-hewn churches and myriad tunnels. Finish with a flight back to Addis Ababa.

9–10 days
Spend a full day in Addis Ababa, long enough to sample its museums and fine restaurants, then fly to Gonder, one of the country's most monument-rich historic towns. Then it's on to Simien Mountains National Park for Ethiopia's best trekking and fine wildlife watching. It's another short flight to Lalibela, then plan on a minimum of two days exploring the rock-hewn church masterpieces. Next head north to Mekele, en route to a couple of nights in the Danakil Depression. Fly from Mekele back to Addis Ababa.

1

EGYPT

Pyramids of Giza

Their perfect shape, impeccable stonework and hulking mass have ensured that the Pyramids of Giza have not only withstood the test of time, but have also inspired billions of people since they rose out of the desert in the 26th century BC.

These three pyramids – the last surviving wonder of the ancient world – have been part of your life for as long as you can remember, rousing childhood wonder from the first time you saw a picture of them. But, despite the familiarity, seeing them in person for the first time is truly unforgettable. Your initial glimpse is as exciting as it is surprising, seeing the tips of them rising above Cairo's skyline as you look out from a taxi. Somehow we all imagine a foray across desert to reach them, yet the frenetic city parades right to their doorstep.

But that is forgotten the second you step out of the taxi and proceed through the gates. Laid out before you is that timeless image of them standing alone, towering over a hundred metres into the blue sky with nothing but sand as a backdrop. Unbelievably, it's not long before you find yourself climbing up the Great Gallery inside (yes, inside) Khufu's Great Pyramid. As you get down on all fours to crawl into the Queen's Chamber, you can't help but ask yourself a simple question: 'Is this really happening?'

Travel

International
Cairo International Airport, which is the country's main entry point, is 20km northeast of the city centre. Given the instabilities in Libya and northern Sinai, entering Egypt by land is less of a recommended option than in the past.

Regional
Ramses Station is Cairo's main train hub, linking the capital to Alexandria, Upper Egypt, and the historical treasure troves of Luxor and Aswan. Buses are another option and arrive into the city's Cairo Gateway and Go Bus stations. Once in the city, the most efficient way to reach the Pyramids is via metro to Giza, then a taxi, microbus or bus.

Stay

$ Shoestring
Pension Roma Run by a French-Egyptian woman with impeccable standards, this place brings dignity, even elegance, to the budget-travel scene. *(Rooms from LE160/ US$9; www.pensionroma.com.eg)*

$$ Midrange
Hotel Longchamps The comfortable, stylish rooms are spacious, well maintained and come with full mod-cons. Bathrooms are generously sized and modern. The greenery covered, peaceful rear balcony is a major bonus. *(Rooms from US$84; www.hotellongchamps.com)*

$$$ Flush
Steigenberger Hotel El Tahrir From the vast, modern, minimalist lobby with casual bar to the contemporary-styled rooms, the Steigenberger is a soothing oasis right in the city's heart. Service is stellar and it's excellent value. *(Rooms from US$116; www.steigenberger.com)*

Eat

$ Shoestring
Abu Tarek This ever-expanding place holds Cairo's unofficial 'best *kushari*' title. The nation's staple dish comprises noodles, rice, lentils, chickpeas, fried onions and tomato sauce. (Kushari *from LE10/US$0.66)*

$$ Midrange
O's Pasta Squeeze (there are only five tables) into O's for Red Sea calamari pasta doused in spinach and cream sauce, or pecan-basil-pesto chicken pasta. *(Mains from LE68/US$3.80)*

$$$ Flush
Sabaya Delicious Lebanese food in a sumptuous but relaxed atmosphere. There are plenty of grilled-meat mains at Sabaya, but the mezze here is the real star of the show. *(Mains from LE145/US$8.10)*

Timing

The best time to visit is from October to February, when Egypt's 'winter' provides a warm and largely sunny climate (it rains at times, particularly on the Mediterranean). That said, be prepared for a real chill at night in unheated hotels.

The spring shoulder season (March to May) brings occasional dust storms, while the scorching heat of summer (June to August) can linger into September and early October.

The pyramids from left to right: Menkaure, Khafre and the Great Pyramid of Khufu.

The Sphinx, whose nose was hammered off some time between the 11th and 15th centuries, according to accounts of early Arab travellers.

One way to approach the iconic site is by camel.

Best value itineraries

4 days
Start with the magnificent Egyptian Museum, then hop the metro to Coptic Cairo to marvel at the Coptic Museum, the churches and Manial Palace. On day two, it's the main show: the Pyramids of Giza. Afterwards dive into Islamic Cairo to hit the Museum of Islamic Art, then stroll past the many monuments on Sharia Al Muizz Li Din Allah. End the day haggling in Khan Al Khalili market. On day three walk from the Mosque-Madrassa of Sultan Hassan to the Mosque of Ibn Tulun, taking in the dervish theatre of the Museo Mevlevi and the Gayer-Anderson Museum. On your last day, cafe-hop in leafy Zamalek, visit some art galleries and end atop the Cairo Tower for a final view.

8 days
After exploring Cairo and the Pyramids of Giza, take an express train to Alexandria. Explore the stunning Bibliotheca Alexandrina and visit the Alexandria National Museum. On the following day indulge in Alexandrian nostalgia: ride the creaking streetcar, touring Pastroudis and other cafes where the city's literati once sipped coffee. On the third day add a day trip to Rosetta and the mouth of the Nile. The day after, head to El Alamein to spend an afternoon on the beach in Sidi Abdel Rahman.

1

© Jonathan Gregson / Lonely Planet

TANZANIA

Ngorongoro Crater

Seemingly cut off from the outside world, this vast, unbroken volcanic caldera is the stomping ground for an incredible variety of iconic African wildlife.

It may be a long and bumpy road to the Ngorongoro Crater, but all the knocks are forgotten the second you crest the lofty rim and look down into what feels like a forgotten world. Concealed by the steep volcanic walls is a pristine wilderness comprised of sweeping savannah, pockets of acacia woodland and glistening lakes and swamps. Binoculars quickly turn black specks into herds of distant buffaloes and reveal the true scale of this 264 sq km unbroken caldera.

Once on the crater floor the focus is brought closer to home, as you scan the surrounding grasses for lurking lions and prowling hyenas. With large numbers of wildebeest, zebras, gazelles and buffaloes, these dominant predators are never short of sustenance. Excitement builds when your guide suddenly halts proceedings, whips out some binoculars and two simple words fill the air: 'black rhino'. Moments later, you're close enough to hear the prehistoric-looking creature's every breath. Pure safari gold.

The remainder of the day will follow a similar pattern, with dramatic sightings of elephants, lion prides and hippo pods causing your heart to race.

Travel

International
Julius Nyerere International Airport in Dar es Salaam is Tanzania's main international air hub, but Kilimanjaro International Airport, which sits between the towns of Arusha and Moshi, is the best option for accessing Ngorongoro Crater and the rest of the country's famed northern safari circuit.

Regional
There's no public transport to the crater. If you aren't travelling on an organised safari and don't have your own vehicle, the easiest thing to do is hire one in Karatu, where most lodges charge from US$160 per day for a 4WD, including fuel and driver, but excluding entry and vehicle fees.

Stay

$

Shoestring
Simba A Public Campsite Ngorongoro's only public campsite, it rests up on the crater rim and has basic facilities. *(Camping US$47.20; www.ncaa.go.tz)*

$$

Midrange
Rhino Lodge This small, friendly lodge, run in conjunction with the Maasai community, is arguably the best-value option. The rooms are simple and tidy, and the balconies have fine forest views. *(Half-board from US$145; www.ngorongoro.cc)*

$$$

Flush
Ngorongoro Crater Lodge This is the place to go for the full Ngorongoro experience of knock-out views and no-expense-spared indulgence. This eclectic rim-top lodge (actually three separate lodges) has every luxury you could want. Few spaces lack crater views (even the toilets have them), and the rooms are sophisticated and intimate, with abundant use of wood. *(All-inclusive per person US$1715; www.andbeyond.com)*

Eat

$

Shoestring
Mwahingo Canteen Located at the Ngorongoro Conservation Area headquarters, Mwahingo Canteen is the only non-lodge option. It serves traditional Tanzanian fare: chicken, pilau, and beans and rice. *(Mains from TSh2500/US$1)*

$$$

Flush
Ngorongoro Wildlife Lodge This lodge, like most of the others on the rim, allows non-guests to visit for lunch. The thing that sets this one apart is its crater views, which are spellbinding. *(Lunch US$35; www.hotelsandlodges-tanzania.com)*

Timing

There is no wrong time of year to visit the incredible confines of the Ngorongoro Crater. However, if you'd like to time your visit to the flows of wildlife elsewhere, there are a few key things to keep in mind: a million wildebeest congregate in the southern Serengeti between January and March; the wildebeest migration reaches full flow towards Kenya between May and July; and in October, thousands of elephants flood into Tarangire National Park.

The vast grasslands of the Ngorongoro Crater are home to a range of wild animals: some are prey, others are predators.

Maasai men wearing their traditional red *shuka* robes.

A glimpse inside the luxurious Ngorongoro Crater Lodge.

Best value itineraries

3–5 days
After a full day exploring the Ngorongoro Crater, set out on a rewarding trek in the nearby Crater Highlands. A fantastic option is the steep climb up the ashen sides of the conical volcano Ol Doinyo Lengai, which sits just outside the Ngorongoro Conservation Area. Some other great hikes include walking the Ngorongoro Crater rim, trekking from Olmoti to Empakaai or from Empakaai to Lake Natron. If you have more time, these three can be strung together into an excellent four-day trip: start at Nainokanoka ranger post to make it three days or extend it one day to climb Ol Doinyo Lengai.

7–10 days
Fly into Kilimanjaro International Airport. Starting at Arusha, spend your time exploring a few of the region's world-class parks. A great wildlife-watching combination could include Tarangire National Park (fantastic for elephants in October), Lake Manyara National Park (known for its tree-climbing lions), Ngorongoro Crater and Serengeti National Park (famous for the 'Great Wildebeest Migration'). Or start with a week-long climb up Kilimanjaro (the continent's highest mountain), before embarking on a three-day safari to Ngorongoro Crater and either the Serengeti, Lake Manyara or Tarangire.

NAMIBIA

Kolmanskop

On the south coast of Namibia, within the infamous Sperrgebiet (Forbidden Area), is a ghost town quite unlike any other. Diamonds were its future, but they certainly didn't last forever.

Given that this abandoned mining town is being digested spectacularly by the Namib Desert, it seems fitting that it was named after an early Afrikaner trekker whose ox cart succumbed to the grip of the same sands here well over a century ago.

Although Kolmanskop's demise as the headquarters for Consolidated Diamond Mines was a drawn-out affair – starting after WWI and ending in 1956 when the last person turned out the lights – you'd never know it while exploring today. You'll see the odd children's toy poking from the sand in some houses, furniture still in place in others, and the skittles/bowling alley and theatre don't look too much the worse for wear.

Yet the most captivating aspect is the buildings and homes that are inundated by the unstoppable flow of sand. As you climb through blown-out windows and walk on dunes that march down faded hallways and spill into bedrooms, you'll find yourself struggling to believe what you're seeing – it's just that surreal and beautiful.

Things can get spooky if the wind sends swirling, ghostly clouds of dust through the shafts of light that cut sharply through the darkness in some houses.

Travel

International

If not driving yourself up from South Africa, the most straightforward access to Namibia's southern coastal city of Lüderitz (the leaping-off point for Kolmanskop) is to start by flying into Windhoek, the country's capital (there are a few direct flights from Europe each week, with many others arriving via Johannesburg). You can then catch one of the local Air Namibia services south to Lüderitz Airport, which is 8km from town.

Regional

Kolmanskop is only a 15-minute drive from Lüderitz, just off the main B4 highway. Tour agencies sell tours to Kolmanskop or you can drive yourself so long as you have arranged a permit beforehand.

Stay

$

Shoestring

Hansa Haus Guesthouse This lovely, family-run guesthouse in an early 20th-century German-style house has wooden floors, white linen and sea breezes (especially on the upstairs terrace). *(Rooms from N$552/US$37)*

$$$

Flush

Lüderitz Nest Hotel This upmarket hotel occupies a jutting peninsula in the southwest corner of town, complete with its own beach. Each room is stylishly appointed with modern furnishings and faces the sea. Amenities include a pool, sauna, kids' playground, car hire, terraced bar and a collection of gourmet restaurants. *(Rooms from N$1320/US$90; www.nesthotel.com)*

Eat

$

Shoestring

Garden Cafe The garden setting, white-wood furnishings and filled rolls add up to one of the best little haunts in town. The baked treats are also highlights. *(Light meals from N$25/US$1.70)*

$

Shoestring

Diaz Coffee Shop The cappuccinos are strong, the pastries are sweet and the ambience is all very Munich. The food, such as hot wraps or chicken shawarma, is delicious. Come evening, it's an oyster and wine bar. *(Mains from N$45/US$3)*

$$

Midrange

Barrels A wonderfully festive bar-restaurant accented by occasional live music, Barrels offers rotating daily specials highlighting fresh seafood and German staples. Portions are hefty and the buffet is great value. *(Buffet N$150/US$10)*

Timing

The months from May to October are the prime time to visit. Daytime temperatures are moderate and skies are dry, with nights cool (sometimes surprisingly so). If you're planning to take in a wildlife safari, this time is also best as wildlife will be congregating around the few remaining waterholes. Heavy rains can occur in November and some tracks will be impassable come December. Humidity and high temperatures can make days unpleasant between January and April.

 Scenes reminiscent of a Dalí painting are commonplace in Kolmanskop.

 The eerie view from the veranda of one of the mine manager's houses.

 The rare Namib wild horses have adapted to the harsh desert conditions.

Best value itineraries

3–4 days

Fly into Lüderitz from Windhoek and spend your first day soaking up its novel atmosphere and surreal German art nouveau architecture. On day two make your trip to the ghostly remains of Kolmanskop, either as part of a tour or independently. If you have your own transport, you can continue driving east and try to catch a glimpse of the wild desert horses that inhabit the area immediately west of the town of Aus. Without transport you can spend the rest of the day (and the following one) enjoying the coastal scene, taking part in an oyster tour or cruising on the schooner *Sedina*.

8–10 days

From Windhoek, drive west to Swakopmund for a day or two of desert adventures, whether dune boarding, skydiving or quad biking. Then head south to Sesriem to check out Deadvlei and the dunes of Sossusvlei in Namib-Naukluft National Park. After a day of further explorations in the park, spend a day driving south to Lüderitz. The following day make your trip to Kolmanskop, then continue east to Aus and south to the Fish River Canyon, one of the largest chasms in the world. From here it's a full day's drive back north to Windhoek or south to Cape Town.

ZIMBABWE

Great Zimbabwe

The sophisticated ruins of Great Zimbabwe inspired a modern nation, and also turned the early European historians' perception of ancient Africa on its head.

Although it's the largest ancient structure in sub-Saharan Africa, Great Zimbabwe feels intimate. The stone complexes and enclosures from the 11th to 14th centuries are never overwhelming in size, enabling focus on finer details that might otherwise be overlooked. At times, such as when taking the Ancient Path to the Hill Complex, you'll even need to squeeze through crevice-like passages. And following the towering, mortar-less stone walls of the Parallel Passage in the Great Enclosure, as they curve round a blind bend, only invites further exploration. But there are still moments of grandeur, such as the Conical Tower and the views of the ruins from the royal enclosures.

The site's splendour actually led 19th-century European historians to refuse to believe it was African in origin. Yet this medieval city of 10,000 to 20,000 people was the capital of a Bantu civilisation that ruled over much of southern Africa. It traded ivory and gold with places as far away as Arabia and China. Great Zimbabwe is so important in local culture that when the new nation won independence in 1980, it took its name from this historic site.

Travel

International
Harare International Airport, located 15km southeast of Harare city centre, is served by Emirates, South African Airways, FastJet, British Airways, Air Zimbabwe, Ethiopian Airlines and Kenya Airways. From town, regular buses and *combis* (minibuses) run the gauntlet to Masvingo (four hours), the main access point for Great Zimbabwe.

Regional
Combis run frequently between Masvingo and Great Zimbabwe (30 minutes). You'll be dropped off at the Great Zimbabwe Hotel entrance, from where you can walk through the grounds to the Great Zimbabwe main gate – about 800m.

Stay

$ Shoestring
Great Zimbabwe Family Lodges Inside the main gate and within plain sight of the Great Zimbabwe complex is this very basic, but convenient option. *(Camping US$7, dorm beds US$10, rooms from US$30)*

$$ Midrange
Norma Jeane's Lakeview Resort This wonderful hilltop lodge is 8km from Great Zimbabwe on a sprawling garden property that overlooks Lake Mutirikwi. *(Camping US$13, self-catering cottages per person from US$50; www.normajeanslakeview.com)*

$$$ Flush
Great Zimbabwe Hotel Built in 1905, this hotel has famously hosted the likes of Princess Di and Nelson Mandela. Now it's a little generic, with motel-style rooms, but it's comfortable and only a short walk to the ruins. *(Rooms from US$147; www.greatzimbabwehotel.com)*

Eat

$ Shoestring
Moira Jane's Blue Bird Cafe A genuine reason to stop by Masvingo is this attractive little cafe that does steak rolls, toasted sarnies and 10 different kinds of burgers. *(Meals from US$3)*

$$ Midrange
Great Enclosure Restaurant At the Great Zimbabwe Hotel, this typical tourist hotel-restaurant serves reasonably priced food, both buffet and à la carte. *(Mains from US$7; www.greatzimbabwehotel.com)*

$$$ Flush
Norma Jeane's Book ahead for a fantastic set-course dinner (often featuring delicious home-style roasts) served among very British surrounds and magnificent gardens. *(Set-course meals from US$16; www.normajeanslakeview.com)*

Timing

There is no wrong time of year to visit Great Zimbabwe, but if you'd like to include some wildlife watching on safari, the best time is during the height of the dry season (July to September). The sun is generally out between April and October, though the rainy season (November to March) is still beautiful, with only sporadic rain and dramatic afternoon electrical storms.

The Hill Complex of the Unesco World Heritage–listed Great Zimbabwe.

A view from within the Hill Complex.

The ruins of the city, which covered an area of approximately 80 hectares, are connected by winding paths and passages.

Best value itineraries

6–8 days
Starting in Harare, drive down to Masvingo to see Great Zimbabwe. With your history itch scratched, make your way southeast to Gonarezhou National Park. It's the nation's second-largest park, and certainly one of its most scenic, with iconic sandstone Chilojo Cliffs, rivers, sandveld flood plains and forests of baobabs, mopane and palm trees. Here you'll find an abundance of elephants, plus giraffes, buffaloes, zebras, lions, leopards, cheetahs, hyenas, wild dogs and 453 different bird species. Next drive north to Chimanimani National Park, which is a hiker's paradise. Complete the loop with a drive back to Harare.

7–10 days
Fly into Victoria Falls and spend some time enjoying the scenic sites and the plethora of activities. Next hop a bus to elephant-haven Hwange National Park, where you can enjoy a day or two on safari. Continue your journey eastward to the charming city of Bulawayo, with its tree-lined avenues, parks and colonial architecture. Depending on the time available, you can then either take a day trip to nearby Matobo National Park or overnight there – it's famous for rhinos and rock formations. Move on by bus to Masvingo, the access point for Great Zimbabwe, before completing your journey in Harare.

ZIMBABWE/ZAMBIA

Victoria Falls

Officially classed as one of the world's Seven Natural Wonders, the planet's largest waterfall has the capability to inspire moments of both jaw-dropping awe and sheer delight.

Sparkling in the African sun like cut diamonds, large water droplets seemingly defy gravity and dance in the air before your disbelieving eyes. Caught in the intense updraft caused by the might of the Zambezi River plummeting over 100m into the shadows immediately below you, these balls of wonder eventually make bids for freedom – one by one – and fly off in various directions, some splattering into your ever-widening smile. Be warned, you may giggle like a school child.

This Victoria Falls experience – standing on the edge of the precipice opposite the falls – is one that illustrates that this natural world wonder is marvellous on so many levels, both small and large. Its sheer scale is indeed hard to fathom, with up to 550 million litres of water flowing over the mile-wide chasm every minute. The permanent mist thrown up not only creates a constant rainbow, but also a rainforest for you to explore. Walking beneath its thick canopy provides discrete windows to views of the falls beyond, each unique and beautifully framed by the lush vegetation.

More staggering views of Victoria Falls are available from optional activities, such as flights in a helicopter, microlight or hot-air balloon.

© Peter Unger / Getty Images

Travel

International
Plenty of flights arrive at Victoria Falls Airport, which is 18km southeast of the falls in Zimbabwe. On the Zambian side, Harry Mwanga Nkumbula International Airport in Livingstone is the main arrivals point. The majority of flights into both these airports come from Johannesburg.

Regional
From Victoria Falls (town) in Zimbabwe, it's a few minutes' walk to the majesty of the falls (just walk towards the mist). On the Zambian side, blue taxis ply the 11km route between the falls and Livingstone. Most travel agencies and hotels in Victoria Falls and Livingstone charge about US$25 for transfers between the two towns.

Stay

 $

Shoestring
Victoria Falls Backpackers The eclectic mix of rooms is scattered among the well-tended garden property, which has a pool, a bar and plenty of quirky touches. *(Camping/dorm beds US$10/18; www.victoriafallsbackpackers.com)*

 $$

Midrange
Olga's Guesthouse In Livingstone, Olga's offers large clean rooms with tiled floors, teak furniture and slick bathrooms a few feet away. Profits support local disadvantaged youth. *(Rooms from US$40; www.olgasproject.com)*

 $$$

Flush
Victoria Falls Hotel Built in 1904, the oldest hotel in Zimbabwe oozes elegance and sophistication. It occupies an impossibly scenic location, looking across manicured lawns (with roaming warthogs) to Batoka Gorge and Victoria Falls Bridge. *(Rooms from US$423; www.victoriafallshotel.com)*

Eat

 $

Shoestring
Cafe Zambezi Bursting with local flavour (hungry for mopane caterpillars?), this Livingstone favourite also has authentic wood-fired pizza and delicious eggplant-and-haloumi burgers. *(Mains from US$6)*

 $$

Midrange
Lookout Cafe Enjoy views of the Zambezi River while tucking into a burger or crocodile kebab on this Zimbabwean option's open-air deck or grassy lawn terrace. *(Mains from US$12; www.thelookoutcafe.com)*

$$$

Flush
Stanley's Terrace High tea is served to a postcard-perfect backdrop of the gardens, with polished silverware, elegant cakes and three-tiered trays of finger sandwiches. *(High tea US$15; www.victoriafallshotel.com/stanleys-terrace)*

Timing

For the best vistas of the falls, travel between July and September – this period also offers lovely weather. The whitewater below the falls, which includes numerous Grade V rapids, is at its most epic for rafting when the water level is low, so the months between July and December are best. If you'd like to swim in the natural Devil's Pool, which sits dramatically on the precipice of the falls, you'll need to travel in October or November.

Enjoy magnificent views of the Eastern Cataract from the Knife Edge Bridge, on the Zambia side of the falls.

The scale of Victoria Falls, and the chasm separating Zimbabwe and Zambia, is clear from the air.

Around 625 million litres of water gush over the edge of the falls every single minute.

Best value itineraries

3 days
Spend your first day gazing slack-jawed at one of the world's greatest natural wonders, taking in the numerous vantage points from both the Zimbabwean and Zambian sides of the falls – the stroll over the historic Victoria Falls Bridge is also a highlight. Line up whitewater rafting on the mighty Zambezi for morning two, then enjoy the rest of the day (and the following day) taking your pick of the other adrenaline-inducing activities available: bungee jumping, bridge swing, zipline, gorge swing, flying fox, abseiling and jet boating. Set aside one evening for a scenic sunset cruise on the upper side of the falls, which offers possible encounters with elephants, hippos and other wildlife.

7–10 days
Fly into Maun, Botswana, which is the visitor hub for the Unesco World Heritage–listed Okavango Delta. Explore some of Africa's most pristine wilderness in a *mokoro* (dugout canoe), perhaps flying into a remote camp for some safari luxury, before eventually moving north by bus to Kasane. With Chobe National Park and some of the world's largest elephant herds now on your doorstep, enjoy cruises on the Chobe River and wildlife drives. From here it's a short hop across the border into Zimbabwe and on to Victoria Falls.

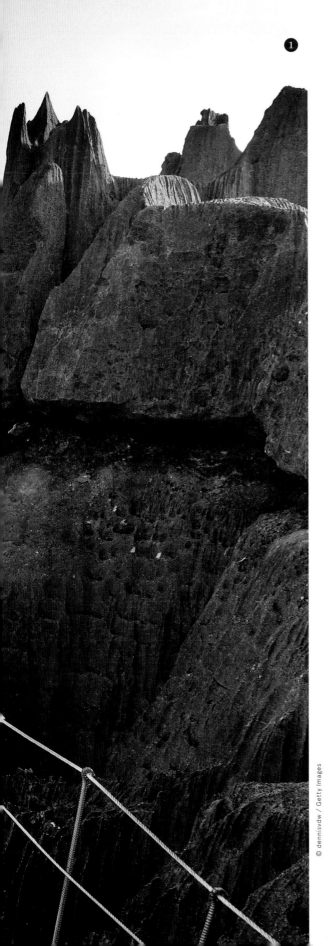

1

© dennisvdw / Getty Images

Tsingy de Bemaraha

On an island known for its wildlife, it's the astonishing landscape that takes centre stage in this national park – and you may well still see a lemur or two.

Shaped by wind, rain and time, the limestone karst formations in Tsingy de Bemaraha are far from ordinary. Instead of the forces of nature blunting the rocky landscape (as is the norm), they have carved innumerable razor-sharp pinnacles, some climbing hundreds of metres into the air. Though a dazzling spectacle, they are formidable to navigate. So much so that the Malagasy name for this area means 'the place where one can't walk'. Yet, with the aid of guides, walkways and a via ferrata system of fixed cables, ladders and bridges, it's possible to do just that.

The ascent into the most phenomenal section of the landscape at Grans Tsingy is as tense as it is exciting – you squeeze through tight crevices, crawl through caves and clip your harness on to the safety cables to make vertical climbs. When pulling yourself on to the summit, elation joins the mix of emotions. The views over the surreal landscape are otherworldly, as are the crossings of the swaying suspension bridges, which connect the upper sections of *tsingy* over precipitous drops. The distant forests below are home to 11 species of lemur, so keep an eye out.

Travel

International

International flights land at Ivato Airport, 20km north of Madagascar's capital, Antananarivo. Air Austral, Air France, Corsair and Air Madagascar all fly into the country from Paris, while Kenya Airways, South African Airways and Turkish Airlines link the island with the world beyond, via Nairobi, Johannesburg and Istanbul respectively.

Regional

Bekopaka is the gateway town for the park, but it takes some getting to – it's at least a seven-hour drive by 4WD from Morondava, the nearest town with an airport. If you don't fly to Morondava from Antananarivo, hire a 4WD or catch a *taxi-brousse* (bush taxi) for the bumpy 16-hour journey.

Stay

$ Shoestring

Le Relais des Tsingy The dorms and thatch-roofed bungalows are fairly standard, but the views from this property are outstanding. *(Dorm beds from Ar15,000/US$3.50, bungalows Ar40,00/US$12; www.tsingy-de-bemaraha.com)*

$$ Midrange

Tanankoay This super-friendly hotel with a lovely garden offers everything from camping to spacious en-suite bungalows. *(Camping Ar5000/US$1.50, rooms from Ar45,000/US$13; www.tanankoay.com)*

$$$ Flush

Le Soleil des Tsingy Set in a 200,000 sq metre garden, with a pool and views over the surrounding wilderness, these beautifully appointed bungalows are spacious, as are their terraces. *(Rooms from US$103; www.soleildestsingy.com)*

Eat

$ Shoestring

Tanankoay The restaurant at this hotel serves excellent food in the evening – although it must be said that the packed lunches are rather sorry looking. *(Three-course meal Ar22,000/US$6.50; www.tanankoay.com)*

$$ Midrange

Le Grand Hôtel du Tsingy du Bemaraha This hotel-based restaurant, which is set in expansive grounds, offers various breakfast and buffet options. *(Buffet Ar50,000/US$14.50; www.legrandhotel-du-tsingy.com)*

$$$ Flush

Le Soleil des Tsingy Set next to the infinity pool, the restaurant of this top hotel mixes local and European selections. In the morning, expect out-of-the-oven croissants and fresh fruit. Pizza is an option at the snack bar. *(Two-course meals from US$12.75; www.soleildestsingy.com)*

Timing

April to June and September to October are best, with warm days and fewer visitors than the peak months of July and August.

If you do travel in high season, when guides and harnesses are in short supply, be sure to arrange both the day before – this also allows you to depart at about 5am to avoid congestion on the via ferrata.

Cyclone season (January to March) is to be avoided.

1 One step at a time on a swaying suspension bridge.

2 A Decken's sifaka, one of many lemur species which inhabit the canyon forests.

3 Madagascar's national bird is the giant coua.

4 Take to the river to approach the limestone spikes and spires of Tsingy de Bemaraha.

Best value itineraries

7 days

After a day in Antananarivo, fly west to Morondava from where you'll meet your 4WD and driver. Revel in the sight of Africa's most iconic tree while winding along the Allée des Baobabs as you head north towards Belo-sur-Tsiribihina, the halfway point to Parc National des Tsingy de Bemaraha. Once in the park, take two days to absorb the grandeur of the Grands and Petits Tsingy before returning south to Morondava to catch your flight back to the capital.

14 days

Descend down the Tsiribihina River by boat for 2½ days from Miandrivazo, which is a day's drive from Antananarivo, to Belo-sur-Tsiribihina. From there your 4WD and driver will take you north to Parc National des Tsingy de Bemaraha. After two days of wild exploration, it's then a day's drive through scorched landscape down to Réserve Forestière de Kirindy, home to the elusive fossa and the giant jumping rat. Make sure you go on a night walk. On your way to Morondava, stop at the iconic Allée des Baobabs. After a day in the seaside town of Morondava, head down to the fishing village of Belo-sur-Mer for a couple of days. You can then drive on to Tuléar for your flight to Antananarivo.

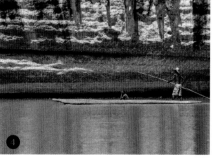

EGYPT

Abu Simbel

While the moving of the Abu Simbel complex to Lake Nasser, stone by stone, was a modern marvel, the temples represent ancient history at its brilliant best.

When walking up the steps of the Great Temple of Ramses II, Abu Simbel's ultimate treasure, tripping over is a distinct possibility. With four colossal statues of the pharaoh of all pharaohs looming large, you certainly won't be looking anywhere but up. Way up.

Longing to linger outside is natural, but the prospect of what lurks in the shadows will eventually pull you towards the dark. As you cross the threshold into the hypostyle hall, your focus jumps between the vulture-filled ceiling, eight huge Osiride statues of Ramses II and the reliefs on the walls. The latter tell of the pharaoh's victories in combat, such as the Battle of Kadesh in 1274 BC (in what is now Syria), where Ramses inspired his army to overcome the Hittites.

Next, follow the shadows deeper into the temple's vestibule and sanctuary. Hewn out of a mountainside in the 13th century BC, this temple was designed to allow the first rays of sunlight to breach the interior – illuminating the statues of Ramses II and the sun god Ra-Horakhty in the back of the sanctuary – on 21 February and 21 October every year, the dates of the pharaoh's birthday and coronation day. Ingenious.

Travel

International
Abu Simbel's airport can be reached with regular EgyptAir flights from the international air hub of Cairo. These flights travel via Aswan, the tourism hub of southern Egypt. Access to Aswan for Abu Simbel is also possible by both bus and ferry from Wadi Halfa in Sudan, as well as by sleeper train from Cairo.

Regional
The vast majority of visitors to Abu Simbel arrive on an organised tour from Aswan. All the hotels, cruise ships and travel agencies in Aswan can arrange tours. Independent travellers can access Abu Simbel via a four-hour bus journey from Aswan, which leaves daily at 8am.

Stay

Shoestring
Tuya Hotel Overlooking Lake Nasser, this hotel's comfortable rooms are painted in strong Nubian colours and all are equipped with clean bathrooms. There is free shuttle service to the temple, just a kilometre away. *(Rooms from €35/US$40; www.facebook.com/Tuya-Hotel)*

Midrange
Eskaleh Part Nubian cultural centre with a library dedicated to Nubian history, part wonderful ecolodge in a traditional mud-brick house, Eskaleh is by far the most interesting place to stay or eat in Abu Simbel. It's also a destination in its own right, and a perfect base for a visit to the temples. *(Rooms from €65/US$75; www.facebook.com/eskaleh)*

Eat

Shoestring
Tuya Cafe A simple but reliable place near the temple of Abu Simbel that serves breakfast for early arrivals, and local cuisine in a lovely garden or the boldly painted rooms inside. *(Mains from LE23/US$1.25)*

Flush
Panorama Restaurant & Bar One of Aswan's best restaurants, with mezze, tagines, kebabs, Red Sea fish, curries and some Italian dishes. Its 360-degree view of the Nile, Aswan and the desert is spectacular at sunset, glittering at night. *(Mains from LE140/US$7.80)*

Timing

The best time to visit Abu Simbel and Egypt is between October and February, when the weather is warm and predominantly sunny. If you can manage it, visit on 22 February or 22 October, the two days that the sunrise pierces the sanctuary (the phenomenon occurs a day later since the complex was moved in the 1960s to save it from the floodwaters caused by the building of the High Dam).

The four statues of seated Ramses II at the Great Temple are about 20m in height; the smaller statues represent his foes.

Interior design, Abu Simbel-style.

Take a *felucca* (sailboat) along the Nile River from Aswan.

The Temple of Philae is near Aswan, to the north of Lake Nasser and Abu Simbel.

Best value itineraries

4–6 days
Spend four days sailing up the Nile to Aswan from Luxor on a budget-friendly *felucca* (a small, traditional sailing boat) or a luxurious *dahabiyya* (a large, shallow-bottomed sailing barge); the quicker option is to find a taxi to take you there, stopping at interesting temples on the way. From Aswan you can visit the temples at Abu Simbel, perched on the edge of Lake Nasser.

10 days
After exploring Cairo and the Pyramids of Giza, continue to the necropolis of Saqqara. Next head south on the sleeper train to Aswan, where you can soak up Nubian culture and make the side trip to the awesome temples of Abu Simbel. Sail back down the Nile from Aswan to Edfu on a *felucca*, or take a taxi stopping at various temples along the way, continuing on to Luxor. Visit the vast temple complex of Karnak, and Luxor Temple on the Nile's east bank, and then hang out on the west bank for a few days – there is so much to see here. For a great day out from Luxor, take a boat or drive to the sacred site of Abydos, visiting the Ptolemaic temple at Dendara on the way.

© Peter Seaward / Lonely Planet

© jsanchez_bcn / Getty Images

1

BOTSWANA

Okavango Delta

One of the world's few inland deltas, the Okavango is the place where the dramatic death of its eponymous river spawns an incredible profusion of life and proffers unparalleled safari experiences.

You'd envisioned your African safari in the continent's most pristine wilderness to be a heart-racing affair, with your binoculars pulled, your eyes scanning for movement and your guide blazing a trail across the grasslands in an open-sided 4WD in chase of creatures large and small. Yet your eyes are closed, you're lying near horizontal and you're moving at less than a mile an hour. And you're enraptured.

The Okavango, a unique inland delta, is a water world unlike any other. Each year it welcomes (and eventually consumes) floodwaters from the Angolan highlands. At the height of the flood it swells to almost 20,000 sq km in size. Islands are formed, vegetation erupts and an incredible concentration of animals descends. Although traditional safari drives play their part here, there is nothing like gliding along the reed-lined channels in a *mokoro* (dugout canoe). With your eyes almost at water level, you feel the scale of the surroundings grow, and encounters with elephants, giraffes and antelopes become all the more special. In the moments in between, when you look up to the deep blue sky and you close your eyes, all you can hear is a magnificent chorus of African birdsong. Welcome to the Okavango.

Travel

International
No European or North American airline flies directly into Botswana, so most travellers fly into Johannesburg or Cape Town (both of which are served by international and domestic carriers) and then hop on a connecting flight to Maun in Botswana to access the Okavango Delta.

Regional
Maun is the main gateway to the Okavango Delta and is Botswana's primary tourism hub. If you are planning a *mokoro* day trip or a multiday bush-camping expedition from Maun, you will be transported to/from the Eastern Delta by 4WD. The only way into and out of the Inner Delta for most visitors is by light aircraft. This is an expensive extra, but the pain is alleviated if you look at it as two scenic flights. Chartered flights to the lodges typically cost about US$200 per leg. A *mokoro* or 4WD vehicle will meet your plane and take you to the lodge.

Stay

Shoestring
Xakanaxa Campsite In the Moremi Game Reserve, Xakanaxa occupies a narrow strip of land surrounded by marshes and lagoons. The wildlife here is prolific and campers are frequently woken by elephants or serenaded by hippo grunts. *(Camping per person P260/US$25)*

Flush
Kwetsani Camp The five rooms – elevated high above the water – feature striking, contemporary looks, with whites and steely greys. The camp manager is a top-class photographer who can help elevate your photography in just a few days. *(All-inclusive per person from US$985; www.wilderness-safaris.com)*

Eat

Shoestring
Wax Apple Cafe Handy for Maun airport (a 100m walk away), Wax Apple has a lovely atmosphere and serves tasty baguettes and wraps, with the odd local dish on the short-but-sweet menu. *(Light meals from P32/US$3)*

Midrange
Hillary's This homely place in Maun offers a choice of wonderfully earthy meals, including homemade bread, filter coffee, baked potatoes, soups and sandwiches. *(Mains from P85/US$8)*

Timing

Generally, the best time to visit the delta is from July to September or October, when the water levels are high and the weather is dry, with warm days and mild nights. Tracks can get extremely muddy and trails are often washed out during and after the rains (November to March), particularly in the Moremi Game Reserve where areas can be inaccessible, even with a state-of-the-art 4WD.

Cameras and binoculars at the ready for superb photo opportunities and wildlife sightings.

A giraffe runs and an oxpecker takes flight in the Moremi Game Reserve.

High water levels in the summer months draw myriad animals to the Okavango Delta.

Best value itineraries

3–4 days
Starting in Maun, head out to the Okavango Delta, either by *mokoro* or charter plane. If you're pinching your pennies, there's no shortage of budget camping trips to choose from. If you have more to spend, this is certainly the time to play with it – aim for a couple of nights in one of the safari-chic tented camps in the Inner Delta or the adjacent Moremi Game Reserve. The latter contains some of the densest concentrations of wildlife on the continent.

10–14 days
Fly into Maun, take a scenic flight to get a sense of the delta, and then pick up your pre-booked 4WD. Drive into Moremi Game Reserve, with a couple of nights at either Xakanaxa Campsite, Savuti Campsite or Linyanti Campsite. Spend a couple of nights recharging the batteries in Kasane, with a sunrise and a sunset foray along the Chobe Riverfront. Drive to Gweta and stay overnight, long enough for an encounter with meerkats, then plan a night by the Boteti River in Makgadikgadi Pans National Park. With some hard driving, you could make a dash for the Central Kalahari Game Reserve, camping in Deception Valley and Motopi on your way back to Maun.

© Peter Adams / Getty Images

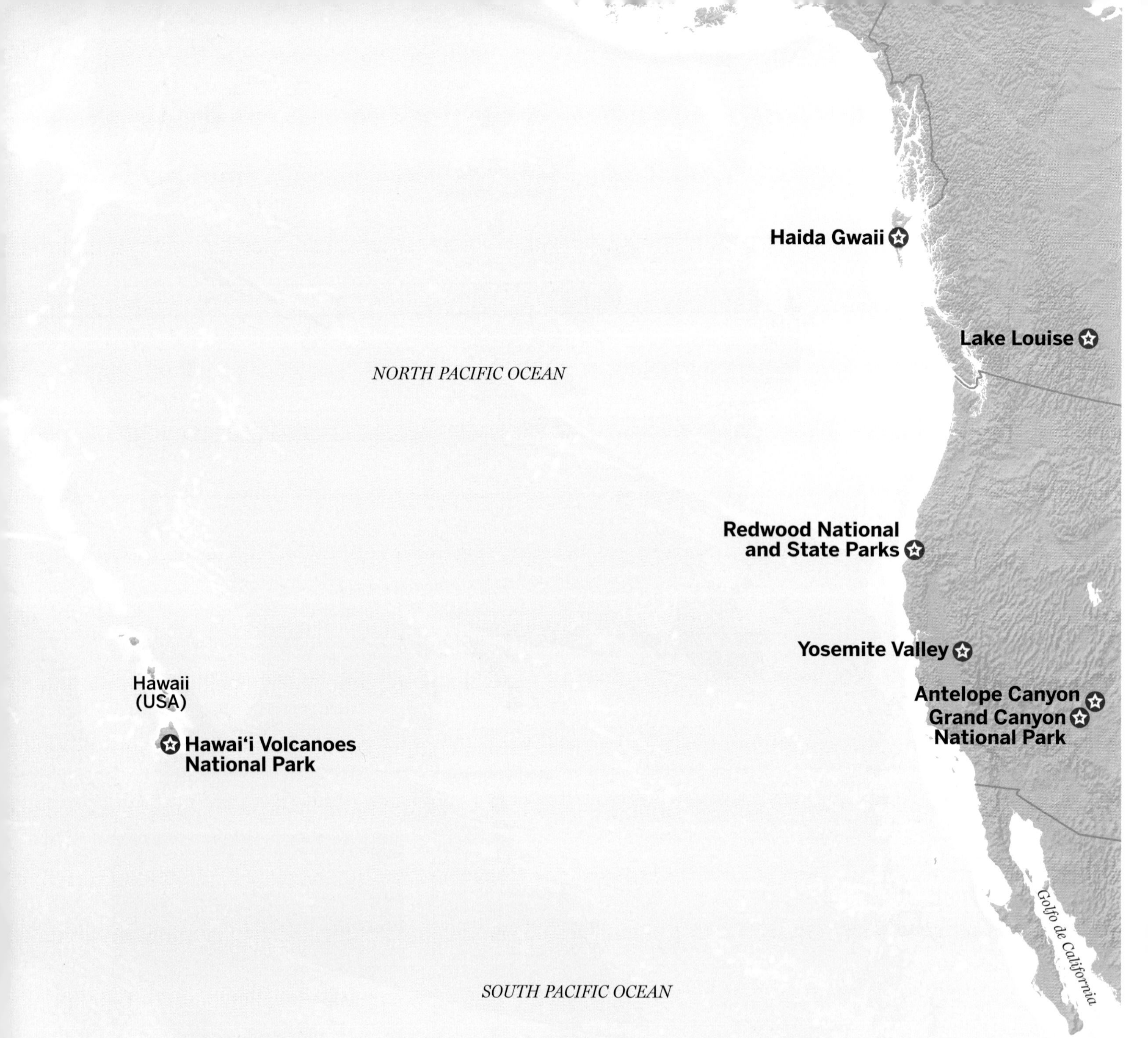

Haida Gwaii ✪

Lake Louise ✪

NORTH PACIFIC OCEAN

Redwood National
and State Parks ✪

Yosemite Valley ✪

Hawaii
(USA)

Antelope Canyon ✪
Grand Canyon ✪
National Park

✪ Hawai'i Volcanoes
National Park

SOUTH PACIFIC OCEAN

Golfo de California

North America

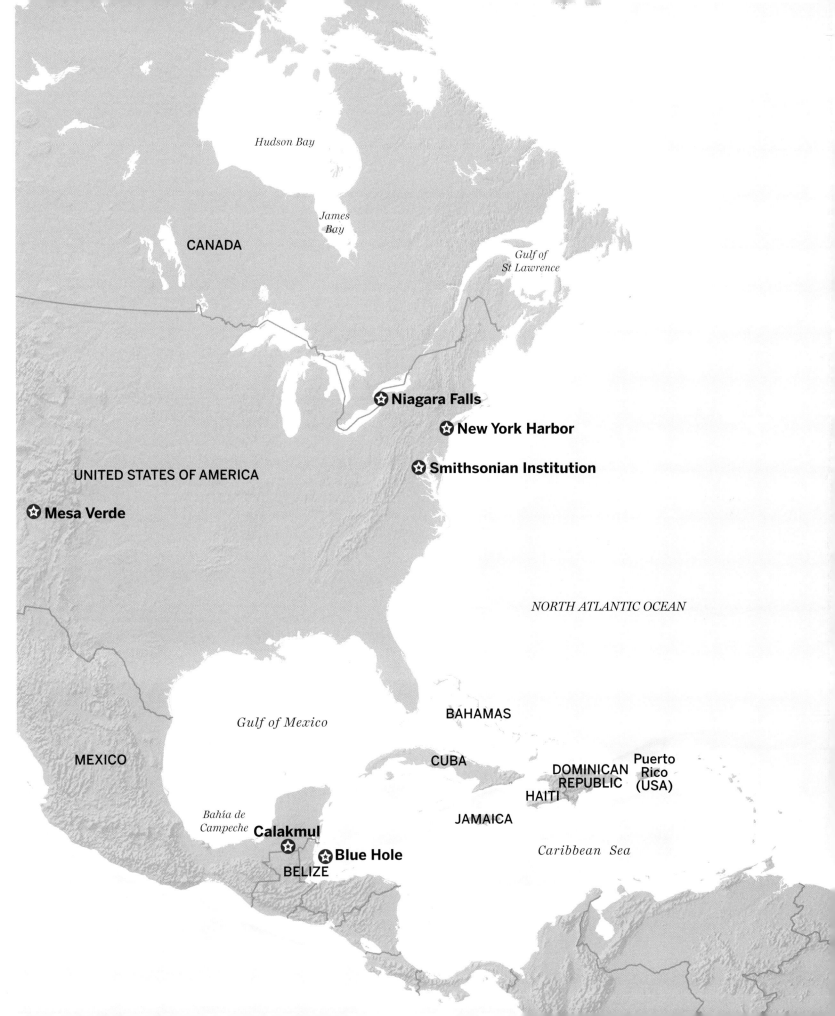

USA

Yosemite Valley

Yosemite Valley is a glorious tableau of wildflower-strewn meadows and thunderous waterfalls hemmed in by some of the most majestic chunks of granite on earth.

At the core of Yosemite National Park, Yosemite Valley serves up the landscape's greatest hits. A visit here is like being transported into an Ansel Adams photo. At the edge of the picture is the granite monster of El Capitan, whose sheer face draws world-class climbers. Hang out in the meadow below and you'll see the ant-size figures – and maybe even hear them – as they grapple with El Cap's ledges.

At the picture's other side, haughty Half Dome rises over 2500m above the valley floor. This mountain is the park's spiritual centrepiece and likewise sends out a siren call to climbers. In the middle of the scene Yosemite Falls drops from a dizzying height. It's the tallest cascade in North America and it roars with an urgent force. Bridalveil Fall also steals some of the focus. Gusts blow it from side to side and it'll soak you as you hike to its base. An endless array of trails scatters throughout the valley, which remains the poster-child for nature's grandeur.

Travel

International

San Francisco International Airport is the main hub; it lies 200 miles (322km) to the east. Oakland, Sacramento and San Jose International Airports also serve the region and are roughly the same driving distance to the valley.

Regional

Yosemite is accessible by public transport. Greyhound buses and Amtrak trains serve Merced, where they are met by Yosemite Area Regional Transportation System (YARTS) buses. These travel to Yosemite Valley several times daily. In the park, free shuttle buses are a good way to get around.

Stay

Shoestring

Upper Pines Campground This campground is big and busy. Each campsite has space for your tent or RV and contains a fire ring, picnic table and food locker. Book ahead from mid-March to November. *(Sites from US$26; www.nps.gov/yose)*

Midrange

Half Dome Village Hundreds of units squish together beneath towering evergreens. There are tent cabins and motel-style rooms, but book one of the cosy wood cabins decorated with vintage posters. *(Cabins from US$225; www.travelyosemite.com/lodging/dining/half-dome-village)*

Flush

Majestic Yosemite Hotel The finest of Yosemite's lodging options dazzles with soaring ceilings and atmospheric lounges with huge stone fireplaces. Rooms have star mountain views. *(Rooms from US$480; www.travelyosemite.com/lodging/the-majestic-yosemite-hotel)*

Eat

Shoestring

Degnan's Kitchen It mixes modern decor with deli-style sandwiches, pizzas, doughnuts and other baked goodies, with an emphasis on locally sourced produce. *(Mains from US$6; www.travelyosemite.com/lodging/dining/yosemite-village)*

Midrange

Half Dome Village Pizza Deck A chatty après-hike hangout by the late afternoon. Try a speciality pizza like the Hog Heaven (pepperoni, bacon, sausage). *(Pizzas from US$9; www.travelyosemite.com/lodging/dining/half-dome-village)*

Flush

Mountain Room Restaurant Window tables at this casually elegant eatery offer a killer view of Yosemite Falls. Plates of strip steak, grilled pork mole and local mountain trout woo diners. *(Mains from US$21; www.travelyosemite.com/lodging/dining/yosemite-valley-lodge)*

Timing

In April and May, Yosemite's waterfalls are gushing and spectacular. It's a great shoulder-season time to visit, with crowds on weekends only.

High season is June to August, though temperatures in the valley can soar above 90°F (32°C).

Winter arrives by mid-November and peters out in early April. Cross-country skiing, downhill skiing and other winter sports abound. Roads in the valley are ploughed, but some highways will close.

Dawn breaks over Cathedral Peak and Upper Cathedral Lake on the John Muir Trail.

Half Dome and the Merced River are names that resonate in Yosemite's climbing and hiking history.

You'll spot only black bears in Yosemite, not grizzlies, but exercise caution and stow food out of their reach.

Best value itineraries

3 days

Stay in Yosemite National Park for the duration. Check out the Tunnel View lookout to drink in vistas of the valley, with Half Dome front and centre and Bridalveil Fall plunging in the distance. Spend the rest of the day strolling the crowd-free Yosemite Valley Loop trails. Next day, experience mind-altering views hiking the drenched Mist Trail to Vernal Falls and Nevada Falls. On day three, head to Glacier Point, stopping en route for a leisurely walk to vertigo-inducing Taft Point and the Fissures. Then continue past Wawona to the park's South Entrance to take a gander at the giant sequoias of Mariposa Grove.

9 days

After the waterfalls and granite monoliths in Yosemite, continue the outdoor action in Sequoia and Kings Canyon National Parks. Tour the groves of ancient trees, ethereal caves and the show-stopping river canyon. After two days make a break for San Francisco, a hilly beauty spread between ocean and bay. Jump aboard a cable car, hop a ferry to Alcatraz, cross the Golden Gate Bridge and fork into the city's slew of chowhound restaurants for the next three days. For the finale, enjoy the vineyards of the Napa Valley. The trip is around 520 miles (837km) total.

1

© Tetra Images / Getty Images

USA

New York Harbor

New York City covers an enormous amount of ground, but a sparkling selection of iconic sights huddles around the harbour.

The Statue of Liberty raises her hand as the local superstar. Hop on the ferry, sail out to Lady Liberty and prepare to pinch yourself as you climb up inside the monument, peer out from her crown and see the world's most famous skyline spreading out before you. Ellis Island floats nearby, America's most famous gateway, where you'll hear the stories of some of the 12 million immigrants who passed through the site.

The Brooklyn Bridge rears up to the east. Though the poetic span looks magnificent from the water, the real thrill is crossing it on foot under its crisscrossed cables as you soak up the soul-stirring views. The harbour's backdrop is a roll call of architectural big shots, including crazy-tall One World Trade Center and the neo-Gothic Woolworth Building. Perhaps the most harbour-y marvel of all is the Staten Island Ferry. Board one of the hulking orange commuter boats and behold cinematic vistas of the luminous skyline, Verrazano-Narrows Bridge and the Statue of Liberty. And get this: the 25-minute ride is free, proving that wonders never cease.

Travel

International
Three airports serve as entry points: John F Kennedy International Airport, LaGuardia Airport and Newark Liberty International Airport. All have bus and/or train transport into the city that takes roughly one hour.

Regional
Amtrak trains link Washington DC, Philadelphia and Boston to NYC's Penn Station multiple times daily. Once in NYC, the subway is the main way to get around. The popular bike-share programme Citi Bike provides excellent access throughout the core areas. Ferries depart for Staten Island at downtown's southern tip. Ferries to Liberty and Ellis Islands depart from nearby Battery Park.

Stay

$ Shoestring
Club Quarters World Trade Center This chain hotel keeps things affordable with clean, modern rooms at reasonable prices. *(Rooms from US$180; www.clubquartershotels.com/new-york/world-trade-center)*

$$ Midrange
Gild Hall The property's entrance leads to a library and wine bar exuding hunting-lodge chic. Rooms fuse Euro elegance and US comfort with glass-walled balconies. *(Rooms from US$229; www.thompsonhotels.com/hotels/gild-hall)*

$$$ Flush
Greenwich Hotel Nothing about Robert De Niro's hotel is generic. Each of the 88 individually designed rooms has aged-wood floors and bathrooms with opulent Carrara marble or Moroccan tiling. *(Rooms from US$650; www.thegreenwichhotel.com)*

Eat

$ Shoestring
Arcade Bakery This little treasure in the vaulted lobby of a 1920s office building trades in beautiful, just-baked goods, including artful sandwiches and superb almond croissants. *(Mains from US$10; www.arcadebakery.com)*

$$ Midrange
Da Mikele It channels *la dolce vita* in Tribeca with its weeknight *aperitivo* (5pm–7pm) and light, beautifully charred pizzas good enough to make a Neapolitan weep. *(Pizzas from US$17; www.luzzosgroup.com/about-us-damikele)*

$$$ Flush
Locanda Verde The buzzy brasserie showcases modern, Italian-inspired fare such as house-made rigatoni with rabbit genovese or grilled swordfish with eggplant caponata. *(Mains from US$27; www.locandaverdenyc.com)*

Timing

Summers can be scorching, though the season also brings a lineup of festivals and free outdoor concerts. Winters are cold and not without blizzards. Spring or autumn offer the best weather in which to explore.

In the evenings, 'dress to impress' remains the rule at many restaurants, bars and venues, so bring at least one evening dress or long-sleeved shirt, pair of trousers and smart shoes.

The Statue of Liberty, a gift from France, has graced New York Harbor since 1886.

The city lights at full wattage, seen from the cobblestoned waterfront area of Dumbo.

Hot, hot summers in NYC demand plenty of iced tea and ice-cream stops.

Best value itineraries

3 days
After a day of cruising the harbour highlights, spend the following day in Midtown and work your way north, visiting the Empire State Building, Times Square, Broadway and the Museum of Modern Art. On the third day, make a break for Central Park to escape the urban madness with meadows and rowing boats, then head next door to the Upper East Side, where the Metropolitan Museum of Art and Guggenheim Museum offer vast halls full of treasures. In the evening seek out a jazzy bar in the East Village.

7 days
It's tough to leave the city that never sleeps, but after three whirlwind days in NYC change it up with a trip to Philadelphia. Rich history meets small-town charm here. There's Independence Hall, the Liberty Bell, a burgeoning food, art and music scene, and the famed cheesesteak sandwich to bite into. A couple of days should do it, then move on to Washington DC. Wander around the Smithsonian Institution's troves, Capitol Hill's political sights and the Mall's iconic monuments. It's 95 miles (153km) from NYC to Philly, and 140 miles (225km) from Philly to DC, all easily doable by Amtrak train.

Haida Gwaii

The beguiling and unspoilt islands, known as 'Canada's Galápagos' for their unique wildlife, offer a lost world of Haida culture and superb natural beauty.

You have to make an *effort* to reach Haida Gwaii. The dagger-shaped archipelago of some 450 islands lies off British Columbia's northern coast, remote and sparsely populated and not exactly brimming with transport options. But you know it's worth the trek the moment you step into the mist-veiled scene. Colossal spruce and cedars cloak the wild landscape, their clean scent lingering wherever you go. Bald eagles and bears roam the ancient rainforest, while sea lions and orcas patrol the waters. Visit one of the starkly beautiful beaches and you'll feel how nature ramps up its power out here: strong winds blow, the surf pounds and flotsam drifts in from across the Pacific.

The islands' real soul, though, is the resurgent Haida people. Gwaii Haanas National Park provides an immersion into the culture. Local guides take you by kayak or inflatable boat to age-old villages where hot springs bubble up and weathered totem poles stare eerily out to sea – places so hushed it seems as if you're the first person ever to set foot on the land.

Travel

International
Vancouver International Airport is the closest hub. It has flight connections to Haida Gwaii's main airport at Sandspit (on Moresby Island) and its smaller airport at Masset (on Graham Island). The other option is to drive 1500km from Vancouver to Prince Rupert in northern British Columbia and catch the ferry to Haida Gwaii. The boat takes eight hours and docks at Skidegate Landing (on Graham Island).

Regional
Ferries link Graham and Moresby Islands. There's no public transport on the islands, so you'll need a car, which you can rent on site or bring over on the ferry.

Stay

$

Shoestring
Premier Creek Lodging This friendly lodge has eight beds in a hostel building at the back; and 12 rooms in the main building that range from singles to spacious studios with views, kitchens and porches. (*Dorms from C$30/US$23, rooms C$50/US$38; www.qcislands.net/premier*)

$

Shoestring
Golden Spruce Motel Urs, the owner of the simple yet comfortable Spruce, gives a warm welcome and runs a good breakfast cafe. (*Rooms from C$76/US$58; www.goldenspruce.ca*)

$$

Midrange
North Beach Cabins Tucked into the dunes of beautiful North Beach are six cosy escapes. You're totally off the grid, with only fabulous views and endless sandy strolls to entertain you. (*Cabins from C$100/US$76; www.northbeachcabins.com*)

Eat

$

Shoestring
Moon Over Naikoon This tiny community centre–cum–bakery is housed in an old school bus in a clearing about 6km from Masset. The baked goods and coffee are brilliant. (*Snacks from C$3/US$2.30*)

$$

Midrange
Charters Restaurant The numbers are small: six tables, three entrées. But the pleasure is great: simply delicious food, such as seafood fettuccine and fresh local halibut. (*Mains from C$15/US$11*)

$$

Midrange
Haida House The Haida-run restaurant cooks up excellent, creative seafood and other dishes with island accents, such as Haida favourites with berries. (*Mains from C$20/US$15; www.haidahouse.com*)

Timing

The best weather is from May to September. July and August are the warmest months, while May gets the most hours of sunshine.

Be prepared for rain year-round, though it is generally short lived. The east coast of the islands is drier than the west coast.

Download a free copy of the Haida Gwaii Visitors Guide (www.gohaidagwaii.ca), which has all kinds of useful trip-planning information.

The drama of Peel Inlet is typical of landscapes along Haida Gwaii's west coast.

Remote Rennell Sound is prime hiking and surfing territory.

Bald eagles, here perched on a totem pole at Haida Gwaii, are a common sight in the skies above.

Best value itineraries

5 days
It's such a lengthy journey to reach Haida Gwaii, and so unhurried once you arrive, you'll need at least five days to give it its due. Spend a day at the Haida Heritage Centre and browsing local shops and galleries. Allow a few days to explore the islands' windswept beaches and hike the rainforest trails. Then tour remarkable Gwaii Haanas National Park for as long as your budget allows.

14 days
After your Haida Gwaii travels, take the ferry to Prince Rupert. From there, hop on the ferry to Port Hardy on Vancouver Island. Book ahead as it only sails a few times per week. The 15-hour journey plies the Inside Passage, lauded for its fjord-like scenery and whale sightings. From Port Hardy, drive southeast. Stop in Nanaimo for a spin through the Old City Quarter, and in Chemainus for a look at the little community's many murals. Your next stop is Victoria, BC's pretty capital, 500km from Port Hardy. Enjoy a few days of great restaurants, breweries and bohemian shops, then ferry to Tsawwassen (1½ hours) for some time in Vancouver. The city's gob-smacking sea-to-sky nature and first-rate foodie scene are a perfect way to end the trip.

©Markus Thompson / 500px

USA

Antelope Canyon

Wind and water have carved a cathedral of red-hued, swirling sandstone, where light and shadow play hide and seek.

Unearthly in its beauty, Arizona's Antelope Canyon is certainly in the running for the title of world's most-famous slot canyon. You know the type: impossibly narrow, deep gorges etched like wrinkles into the face of the earth. Antelope is particularly prized for its magical lighting, a symphony of shapes and textures that are a photographer's dream. Ready the camera, because when sunbeams fall through the canyon's openings and strike the wavy walls, they spark a heavenly red-gold-pink-tangerine glow.

The canyon lies on Navajo land and is a sacred space. Guides take you either to the Upper Canyon, known as *Tsé bighánílíní* ('the place where water runs through rocks') or the Lower Canyon, called *Hasdestwazi* ('spiral rock arches'). The latter wins the prize for eye-popping formations, though they hide in a surreal underworld reachable only via steep staircases and tight rock passages. Meanwhile, the Upper Canyon offers easy access at ground level and it's pretty darn photogenic in its own right. Alas, the antelopes that once grazed around the canyon's rim and gave it its name vanished ages ago.

Travel

International
Phoenix Sky Harbor International Airport and Las Vegas' McCarran International Airport are each about 275 miles (443km) from Page, the closest town to the canyon. You'll need a car to make the trip.

Regional
Antelope Canyon is about 7 miles (11km) from Page. The site is on Navajo land and the only way to visit is on a guided tour. See www.navajonationparks.org for details.

Stay

Shoestring
Lake Powell Motel The sweet and simple lodging was originally constructed to house Glen Canyon Dam builders. Four units have kitchens. A fifth smaller room is held for walk-ups. *(Rooms from US$139; www.lakepowellmotel.net)*

Midrange
Best Western View of Lake Powell Hotel Perched on the edge of a hill overlooking Glen Canyon Dam, the property provides modern guestrooms, a swimming pool with a spectacular view and free breakfast. *(Rooms from US$180; www.bestwestern.com)*

Flush
Lake Powell Resort This bustling hotel offers beautiful vistas and a lovely little pool perched in the rocks above the lake. Rates for lake-view rooms with tiny patios are worth the extra money. *(Rooms from US$199; www.lakepowell.com/lodging/lake-powell-resort)*

Eat

Shoestring
Big John's Texas BBQ Cheerfully occupying a former petrol station, it's a friendly place to feast on pulled-pork sandwiches and ribs. Live music lets loose several evenings of the week. *(Mains from US$13; www.bigjohnstexasbbq.com)*

Midrange
Bonkers Impressive murals of local landscapes cover the walls inside. The restaurant is open for dinner only and serves good steaks, seafood and pasta dishes. *(Mains from US$18; www.bonkerspageaz.com)*

Midrange
Blue Buddha Sushi Lounge The food and drinks at this ultra-cool hideaway hit the spot after a hot and dusty day of exploring. There's steak and seafood, too. *(Mains from US$20; www.bluebuddhasushilounge.com)*

Timing

Lighting conditions are best around mid-morning between April and September – the peak season – but the other months bring smaller crowds and a more intimate experience.

During peak season it's wise to reserve a tour as far in advance as possible.

The Upper Canyon is more accessible, while the Lower Canyon involves climbing steep staircases.

Marbled rust reds and oranges find their complementary colour in Arizona's bright blue skies.

Tour company guides will steer you towards the best photo angles.

Above ground visit a ranch and head out into the Sonoran Desert from Tucson.

Best value itineraries

3–4 days
Go canyon to canyon. After a day of photographing trippy rocks at Antelope Canyon, point your wheels towards the Grand Canyon. Pick a rim – the 125-mile (200km) drive is equidistant to either – and hang out for a few days. At the North Rim be sure to gawp at the view from Bright Angel Point, hike the Widforss and North Kaibab trails, and saddle up for a horseback ride. At the South Rim stroll the Rim and South Kaibab trails and hit the eye-popping overlooks of Hermit Rd.

10 days
After your three-day canyon excursion, rejoin town life again in groovy, outdoorsy Flagstaff. Walk downtown, loaded with ecofriendly restaurants, coffee shops and breweries. The next day continue south to Sedona, an otherworldly place of crystal shops, galleries and crimson buttes. Soak it up for a few days, then move on to Phoenix, Arizona's sprawling capital city, prime for terrific southwestern food and intriguing museums. Spend your remaining couple of days even farther south, taking in Tucson and its artsy 4th Avenue district, studying cacti at Saguaro National Park and gun-slinging in Tombstone. The jaunt is about 550 miles (885km) in total.

© Kris Davidson / Lonely Planet

Grand Canyon

The jaw-dropping, red-rock chasm of the Grand Canyon embodies the scale and splendour of the American West, captured in dramatic vistas and dusty trails.

The sheer immensity of the canyon is what grabs you first: it's a two-billion-year-old rip across the landscape that spans 277 miles (446km) in length and plunges up to 6000ft (1829m) in depth. There is nothing like arriving at the edge and taking it all in – the vastness, the crimson buttes, the long drop down. Sunrises and sunsets are particularly sublime, with the changing light painting the canyon in unbelievably rich hues of vermilion and purple.

You won't spend your entire time staring at the hole in the ground, though. You'll also saddle up a mule and ride down into said hole. Or you'll hoof it on trails that wind through sagebrush, over coyote tracks and past timeworn pictographs etched into the rocks. Even a short dip below the rim gives an appreciation for the canyon's staggering scale and awesome silence. Two locations are the gateways into the abyss: the South Rim, which is busier and stocked with psychedelic viewpoints, and the North Rim, prime for quiet hikes in the pine-scented air.

Travel

International
If headed to the South Rim, fly into Phoenix's Sky Harbor International Airport (230 miles/370km, 3½ hours) or Las Vegas' McCarran International Airport (273 miles/439km, 4½ hours). For the North Rim, fly into Las Vegas (266 miles/428km, 4½ hours). You can rent a car at the airports.

Regional
Regularly scheduled shuttle buses service the South Rim from the airports in Phoenix and Las Vegas, as well as from the towns of Sedona, Williams and Flagstaff. Getting to the North Rim is more of a challenge. A shuttle (mid-May to mid-November) runs from rim to rim, but otherwise the only way to reach the North Rim is by car.

Stay

Shoestring
Bright Angel Lodge The 1935 log-and-stone building has easy charm. Expect bright, handsome, simple rooms (fridge but no TV) only steps from the canyon rim. *(Rooms with/without bath from US$110/89; www.grandcanyonlodges.com)*

Midrange
Kachina & Thunderbird Lodges Don't be put off by the institutional-looking exterior. Inside are modern, comfortable rooms with fantastic views of the Rim Trail and canyon beyond. *(Rooms street-side/canyon-side from US$234/254; www.grandcanyonlodges.com)*

Flush
El Tovar The public spaces of the 1905 hotel ooze old-world national-park glamour. Some rooms are lovely, others are standard, but the location at the canyon's edge can't be beaten. *(Rooms from US$228; www.grandcanyonlodges.com)*

Eat

Shoestring
Bright Angel Bicycles & Cafe at Mather Point Fuel up on grab-and-go sandwiches, wraps, snacks and coffee, and then rent a bike. *(Mains under US$10; www.bikegrandcanyon.com)*

Midrange
Maswik Pizza Pub Hunker down for a slice or whole pie to enjoy over a Grand Canyon Pilsner. Veggies can chow on the pesto pie. *(Pizzas from US$18; www.grandcanyonlodges.com)*

Flush
El Tovar Dining Room Dark-wood tables are set with china and white linen at this classic restaurant. Breakfast favourites here include pancakes with prickly-pear syrup and blackened trout with eggs. *(Mains from US$20; www.grandcanyonlodges.com)*

Timing

High season is May to September, when it is very hot and many places to stay sell out. August brings monsoon rains.

March, April, September and October are the cooler shoulder months.

In winter, snowfalls bring frosted vistas, but also treacherous roads and trails. South Rim visitors slow to a trickle, while North Rim facilities close between mid-October and mid-May.

Views from both rims are equally stunning: the South Rim has more official overlooks, while the North Rim is quieter.

Descend deep below the rim for a closer look at a mind-boggling record of geologic time.

The emerald-green Havasu Falls are one of five stunning waterfalls within Havasupai tribal lands. Visitor numbers are limited.

Best value itineraries

3 days
Take in the South Rim sights, using Grand Canyon Village as your base. Check out the village's historic buildings and museums, then continue on the Rim Trail to Mather Point. Rent a bike and ride along the rim to the trailhead of the South Kaibab Trail and Yaki Point. The next day, wake up early and head down Bright Angel Trail. Hike and shuttle overlook-to-overlook along Hermit Rd, descend a little into the canyon on the Hermit Trail and shuttle back to the village. On your final day, hike the South Kaibab Trail to Cedar Ridge for a picnic lunch before returning.

9 days
After three days at the Grand Canyon drive northeast to immerse in Antelope Canyon (see p56), another unearthly beauty. Spend the night in Page. The next day, motor northwest to Bryce Canyon National Park, where golden-red-rock spires shimmer like trees in a magical stone forest. Zion National Park rises a short distance southwest, prime for vertigo-defying hikes in a landscape of sand, stone and sky. Allow three days between the parks. Continue southwest to Las Vegas and roll the dice for your last few days. The journey is about 500 miles (805km) in total.

© lucky-photographer / Getty Images

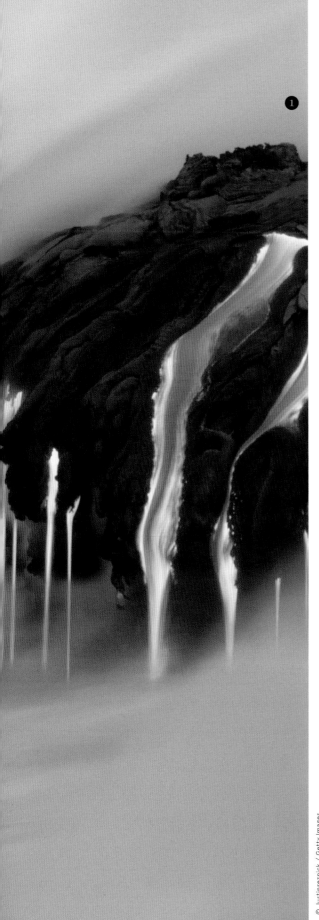

1

USA

Hawai'i Volcanoes National Park

Newly born earth churns in the chaotic realm of Pele, the Hawaiian goddess of volcanoes.

For more than 70 million years, volcanoes in the deep have been giving birth to the Hawaiian Islands. Today Hawai'i, also known as the Big Island, sits directly atop a 'hot spot' far beneath the earth's crust. It's still wildly active and the national park spotlights the fiery landscape that has bubbled up as a result.

Two volcanoes dominate the scene. Mauna Loa, the world's largest above-water volcano at 13,680ft (4170m), is so massive that you feel its presence more than see it. Kīlauea is the tricksy one that has been erupting for decades, most recently in 2018, when a colossal outburst spewed lava over its edges and into the sea. It changed the face of the volcano – and the park – dramatically. Several hiking trails take you into the thick of the primal terrain past apocalyptic lava deserts, steaming craters, sulphur smells and ancient petroglyphs pecked into the black flowing rock. But the park is ever changing, based on the whims of Madame Pele, who makes her home in the Kīlauea Volcano and shows off her power at will.

Travel

International
The park is on the Big Island of Hawai`i. Honolulu International Airport on O`ahu is the main gateway. From there, inter-island flights go to one of the Big Island's two primary airports: Hilo International Airport or Kona International Airport. The park is 30 miles (48km; 45 minutes) from Hilo and 95 miles (153km; 2¾ hours) from Kailua-Kona via Hwy 11.

Regional
The village of Volcano, a couple of miles east of the main park entrance, makes a fine base. There is no public transportation within the park, so you'll need to rent a car to see the sights.

Stay

Shoestring
Kilauea Hospitality Group Different properties within this group target different travellers. Volcano Hale is a bargain choice with its communal vibe and kitchen; Lokahi Lodge is a good basic option for families. *(Rooms with shared/private bath from US$65/125; www.volcano-hawaii.com)*

Midrange
Alii Kane Cottages The two small private cedar cottages – with slate floors, full kitchens, bathtubs and lofts – face off across the orchid-fringed grounds. *(Cottages from US$107; www.aliikanecottages.com)*

Flush
Volcano House Perched on the rim of Kilauea Caldera, Volcano House has long enjoyed its status as the park's only hotel. The 33 ecoconscious rooms are spacious, if plain. *(Rooms from US$285; www.hawaiivolcanohouse.com)*

Eat

Shoestring
Eagle's Lighthouse Café Hearty sandwiches, salads and ready-made wraps are served out of a small kitchen fronted by picnic tables serenaded by contemporary Christian music. *(Mains from US$5; www.eagleslighthouse.com)*

Midrange
Thai Thai Restaurant The chefs recognise that good Thai food doesn't have to set your tongue on fire. Dishes like the rich and peanutty 'Special Curry' are authentically flavoured and well portioned. *(Mains from US$15)*

Flush
'Ōhelo Café Combining local flavours with international flair, the portions may be small, but the execution is spot on. Don't miss the cauliflower appetiser and thin-crust margherita pizza. *(Mains from US$21; www.ohelocafe.com)*

Timing

● Clouds and rain are a fact of life (this is a rainforest after all), but August and September tend to have more clear days on average.

● Try to get an early start. The park is open 24 hours, but the tour buses and crowds start arriving from around 10am.

● Eruptions don't follow schedules; try to keep yours flexible enough to take advantage of short-notice viewing opportunities.

① Lava flowing from Kīlauea volcano steams, hisses and hardens as it hits the Pacific Ocean.

② Caves in Hawai`i Volcanoes National Park are typically lava tubes, such as Thurston Lava Tube, which is open to the public.

③ Halema`uma`u Crater in Kīlauea's summit caldera is the home of Pele, the Hawaiian goddess of fire and volcanoes.

Best value itineraries

3 days
Take at least a day to ramble around the park and hike its alien-looking moonscapes. Then spend a night or two in Hilo, taking time to drive part-way up Mauna Kea for stargazing after dark. After rolling up and down along the Hamakua Coast, amble the old sugar-plantation town of Honoka`a before dropping into ancient Waipi`o Valley. Giddy-up through Waimea (Kamuela), a Hawaiian cowboy town. In the quiet countryside of North Kohala, hike into Pololu Valley, circle around Mo`okini Heiau and relax in the quaint, artsy town of Hawi.

9 days
Follow the three-day itinerary and add an extra day to go to South Kona for manta ray adventures. Then fly to O`ahu, basing yourself in Kailua for five days. Check out the WWII memorials at Pearl Harbor in Honolulu and snorkel one morning at Hanauma Bay. Drive up the Windward Coast, stopping at panoramic beaches and to hike into the misty Ko`olau Mountains. Grab a 'shave ice' and mingle with surfers in Hale`iwa, dip your toes into the lagoons at Ko Olina and take a windy walk in Ka`ena Point State Park.

❶

© Phillip Bindeman / 500px

USA

Redwoods

The tallest trees on earth jab into the sky of Northern California, where you're guaranteed to get a crick in your neck from all the evergreen gazing.

Hidden away in the upper reaches of California's Pacific coast, Redwood National Park encompasses some of the world's loftiest and most ancient trees. We're talking *Sequoia sempervirens* – better known as the coastal redwoods – that tower up to 379ft (115m). They reach their phenomenal height by intertwining at the root, forming a network of mutual support that helps them stand tall through storms and other threats. The national park grows a massive stand of moss-draped beauties, but it's only the beginning.

Three state parks sprawl to the north and are managed jointly with the federal land. They are Prairie Creek Redwoods, Del Norte Coast Redwoods and Jedediah Smith Redwoods State Park, and together they compose an International Biosphere Reserve and World Heritage Site. To get in the thick of it, take a trail walk. Velvet humidity rises from the forest floor. The loamy soil springs underfoot. A sepulchral quiet reigns here and you're just a speck next to the 2000-year-old giants.

CHANDELIER
TREE

Travel

International
San Francisco International Airport is the main gateway; it's 330 miles (531km) south of Redwood National Park. It has connections to Humboldt County Airport, a small regional facility about 30 miles (48km) south of the park.

Regional
The park's attractions are scattered along a 60-mile (96km) stretch of US 101 and US 199 between Orick and Gasquet. Public transport is limited and the sights are most easily reached with your own vehicle. Crescent City, Klamath and Trinidad are practical towns to use as a base.

Stay

Shoestring
Hiouchi Motel Clean, straightforward motel rooms with owners who go out of their way to accommodate; they've even been known to offer to wash hiking gear – including socks! *(Rooms from US$65; www.hiouchimotel.com)*

Midrange
Historic Requa Inn A woodsy country lodge on bluffs overlooking the mouth of the Klamath River, this creaky and bright inn delivers charming, old-timey, carbon-neutral rooms. *(Rooms from US$119; www.requainn.com)*

Flush
Lost Whale Inn Set atop a grassy cliff, high above crashing waves and braying sea lions, this spacious, modern, light-filled B&B in Trinidad has stunning views out to the sea, and lovely gardens. *(Rooms from US$199; www.lostwhaleinn.com)*

Eat

Shoestring
Beachcomber Cafe Head here for the best breakfast in these parts, ranging from a hearty bowl of organic black beans with avocado and poached egg to delicious homemade muffins. *(Breakfast from US$4)*

Midrange
Trinidad Bay Eatery & Gallery It may resemble a run-of-the-mill diner, but the organic ingredients and menu of local-favourite dishes, such as red-curry-coconut scallops, guarantee a steady stream of customers. *(Mains from US$21; www.trinidadeatery.com)*

Flush
Larrupin' Cafe Moroccan rugs, chocolate-brown walls and gravity-defying floral arrangements create a moody atmosphere perfect for a lovers' tryst. It serves excellent mesquite-grilled seafood and meats. *(Mains from US$22; www.thelarrupin.com)*

Timing

June and July are the driest months and best for hiking and big views. August and September are also typically warm and pleasant. The other months are cooler and wetter, but less crowded.

Bring waterproof gear and be prepared for rain any time of year.

From December to April grey whales migrate off the coast. In early spring look out for mothers and calves.

1 Morning mist envelopes the trees in Redwood National Park.

2 The famous Chandelier Tree, whose trunk was carved out in the 1930s to allow cars to pass beneath.

3 The Redwood National Park extends down to a wild and rocky coast, often shrouded in fog.

4 Roosevelt bull elks call the redwood forests home.

Best value itineraries

3 days
There's a lot of ground to cover in Redwood National and State Parks, so take two days to commune with the trees. On day three, motor south and pit stop in Ferndale, a Victorian town where every building is a landmark. Afterward, drive on to Humboldt Redwoods State Park, California's largest redwood expanse. It boasts three-quarters of the world's tallest 100 trees. Exit Hwy 101 when you see the Avenue of the Giants sign and it'll take you through a magnificent 32-mile (51km) stretch of the park.

9 days
Once you've had your tree fix in the redwood parks, steer south to get on Hwy 1, a fabulous coastal drive that cuts a winding course on isolated cliffs high above the crashing surf. Stop for a day in Mendocino, an enchanting salt-washed village, and in Point Arena to putter around the shops and climb to the top of its lighthouse. Make a base in Bodega Bay and explore the endless nearby coves of Sonoma Coast State Beach. Swing by blustery and poetic Point Reyes National Seashore, then finish with a few days in hilly, beatnik San Francisco. The route covers 377 miles (607km).

© Panoramic Images / Getty Images

© Panoramic Images / Shutterstock

BELIZE

The Blue Hole

Submerge into the perfectly round, perfectly blue sinkhole off Belize's coast and see the mysterious ocean depths come to life.

In the 1970s, underwater pioneer Jacques Cousteau explored the Blue Hole and declared the dive site one of the world's best. Since then its image – a deep azure pupil with an aquamarine border surrounded by the lighter shades of the reef – has become renowned far and wide.

The hole forms a flawless circle on the surface, while its sheer walls drop more than 400ft (122m) straight down. Plunge into the chasm and you'll drift by a dense forest of ancient stalactites and stalagmites that hang from the walls. Swimming through these hulking features in the eerie blue glow of the water feels as though you've slipped into another, more primal world. A school of reef sharks and the occasional hammerhead – as well as plenty of invertebrates and sponges – keep you company as you descend further into the abyss. If you don't dive, don't worry: charter flights swoop over the Blue Hole, letting you experience its startling azure gleam from a bird's-eye view.

Travel

International
Philip Goldson International Airport, 11 miles (18km) northwest of Belize City centre, is the main hub. From there you can connect to a local airline and fly to Caye Caulker or San Pedro on Ambergris Caye (20 minutes), or take the ferry from Belize City to the cays (45 minutes to 1½ hours).

Regional
Caye Caulker (more laid-back and budget oriented) and Ambergris Caye (more developed and busy) are popular bases for exploring the Blue Hole. The only way to reach the natural monument is on a private vessel. Dive boats head out from both islands for the two-hour trip to the site.

Stay

$ Shoestring
Yuma's House Belize This fun and freshly painted hostel, with a palm shaded, hammock-strewn garden, is just steps from Caye Caulker's water-taxi dock. *(Dorms from BZ$38/US$19, doubles from BZ$90/US$45; www.yumashousebelize.com)*

$$ Midrange
Oasi Set around blooming gardens on Caulker, Oasi offers elegant apartments with woven tapestries and lovely wide verandas (hung with hammocks, of course). *(Apartments from BZ$190/US$94; www.oasi-holidaysbelize.com)*

$$$ Flush
Itza Lodge Located on Long Caye, Itza's thatched open-air dining room, kayaks and terrific dive shop are perks to go with its 24 hardwood rooms. *(Three-day resort packages from BZ$1470/US$730; www.itzalodge.com)*

Eat

$ Shoestring
Glenda's Cafe Glenda's serves traditional Belizean food in a clapboard house on Caye Caulker's west side. It boasts the best breakfasts in town, plus chicken with rice and beans for lunch. *(Mains from BZ$9/US$4.45)*

$$ Midrange
Caribbean Colors Art Cafe Browse the gallery's walls while sipping a coffee or smoothie, then sit down for a healthy breakfast, salad or sandwich in the thick of Caulker's scene. *(Mains from BZ$10/US$5; www.caribbeancolorsbelize.com)*

$$$ Flush
Hibisca by Habaneros At Caulker's poshest restaurant chefs prepare gourmet international food, combining fresh seafood, meat and vegetables with insanely delicious sauces. *(Mains from BZ$32/US$16; www.facebook.com/hibiscacayecaulker)*

Timing

The best time to go for good weather and water visibility is December to April – peak tourist season. Prices are highest mid-December to mid-January. May is a fine shoulder season; it still has decent weather, but crowds and costs lessen. Hurricanes are possible between August and October.

Due to the depth of Blue Hole dives, advanced scuba certification is typically required.

The Blue Hole was formed in what is the centre of Lighthouse Reef when sea levels were lower, up to 100,000 years ago.

Divers need to have more than 20 dives' experience and Advanced Open Water certification before venturing down into the Blue Hole.

Belize City is the global gateway, but your base will be the offshore cays.

Best value itineraries

4 days
Set aside one day to visit the Blue Hole and then stick around Caye Caulker or San Pedro on Ambergris Caye (whichever you choose for a base) for three more days. Outdoor activities abound in the area. Visit Shark Ray Alley to snorkel alongside a wriggling pile of nurse sharks and stingrays, and Swallow Caye Wildlife Sanctuary to watch manatees hovering in shallow waters. Take a golf-cart past mangrove swamps to off-the-grid Secret Beach, and kayak into the wilderness of Caye Caulker Forest Reserve. Head to Turneffe Atoll, the largest atoll in the Americas, alive with coral and fish including large rays.

7 days
If you have more time, keep your island base and make day trips to the mainland. Spend a day in the Belize District to visit Belize Zoo and commune with rescued tapirs, pacas and pumas. Check out the atmospheric Maya ruins at Altun Ha. It's also an easy trip to the eastern Cayo District, where you can go cave-tubing in the Nohoch Che'en Caves Branch Archaeological Reserve. Or head north to the extensive, jungle-encircled Mayan ruins at Lamanai, enjoying a peaceful boat ride on the New River along the way.

© Simon Velazquez / 500px

USA

Mesa Verde

A mysterious settlement of ancient houses hides in the pale cliffs of southwest Colorado, beckoning sure-footed types to investigate via steep ladders up the rock face.

More than 700 years after its inhabitants disappeared, Mesa Verde retains an air of eeriness. No one knows for sure why the Ancestral Puebloans left their elaborate cliff homes in the 1300s after living there for several centuries. Maybe drought or violence? Archaeologists are still looking for clues among the 600 dwellings tucked into the precipices. The sandstone structures are incredibly well preserved thanks to the dry, high-desert air – and they're wild to explore. You don't just walk into the buildings of Mesa Verde. You clamber up 32ft (9.8m) ladders set against sheer cliffs to reach the abodes, just like the ancients did. You also crawl through narrow tunnels and climb stone staircases as you take in the kivas, plazas, stone towers and painted murals.

It's all quite transporting: the elevation puts you next to the mammoth sky and every breath of whistling wind feels as if it carries the secrets of the departed. The National Park Service manages the sights, many of which are accessible only with a guide.

②

Travel

International
Denver International and Phoenix's Sky Harbor International Airports are the biggest hubs in the area, but they're both about 400 miles (644km) from Mesa Verde. They do have connections to Durango-La Plata County Airport, a regional facility that's 49 miles (79km) east of the park.

Regional
You'll need a car to get around. Mesa Verde's sights are spread out over several miles via switchbacking roads and there is no public transport. The town of Mancos makes a good base; it sits 8 miles (13km) to the east.

Stay

Shoestring
Mancos Inn & Hostel These homely digs could not be lovelier. There's a large, modern kitchen, a comfortable living room with games and a powerful telescope, and rooms with original art. *(Rooms without/with bathroom from USUS$60/75; www.mancosinn.com)*

Midrange
Far View Lodge Perched on a mesa top inside the park entrance, this Pueblo-style lodge has 150 Southwestern-style rooms, some with kiva fireplaces. Don't miss the sunset from your private balcony. *(Rooms from US$124; www.visitmesaverde.com)*

Flush
Willowtail Springs Set within 60 acres (24 hectares) of gardens and ponderosa forest, Willowtail Springs' cosy cabins feature warm decor, the owner's original art and kitchens stocked with organic goodies. *(Cabins from US$239; www.willowtailsprings.com)*

Eat

Shoestring
Absolute Baking & Cafe The screen door is always swinging open at this hot spot with giant breakfasts. Lunch includes lavender lemonade and local, grass-fed beef burgers. *(Mains from US$7; www.absolutebakery.com)*

Midrange
Millwood Junction Folks come from miles around to this steak and seafood joint, especially for Friday night's seafood buffet. It often doubles as a club, showcasing live music. *(Mains from US$8; www.millwoodjunction.com)*

Flush
Metate Room The Far View Lodge's upscale restaurant offers an innovative menu inspired by Native American food and flavours. Think prickly-pear pork belly and cold smoked trout. *(Mains from US$20; www.visitmesaverde.com)*

Timing

Late May, early June and September to mid-October are good times to visit, with cooler days and fewer crowds.

Mid-June to August is busiest. Daytime temperatures can get quite hot. Afternoon thunderstorms are common in July and August.

Many sites are closed from mid-October to mid-April.

Mesa Verde's elevation is above 7000ft (2135m), so you may get easily winded. Bring plenty of water.

There's a lot to see – Mesa Verde National Park occupies 81 sq miles of the northernmost portion of the mesa.

Visit the superb cliff palace on an hour-long ranger-led tour.

A marvel of adobe architecture, Taos Pueblo is one of the oldest continuously inhabited communities in the US.

Best value itineraries

3 days
Once you've completed your Mesa Verde marvelling, head east to mountain-beauty Durango, a graceful old mining town turned outdoors haven, where you can chill with a microbrew and bike ride. Motor north to Silverton, a hamlet ringed by snowy peaks. Continue north on the white-knuckle Million Dollar Hwy (US 550), where you'll pass larger-than-life alpine scenery en route to the enchanted village of Ouray. Loop through the mountains to Telluride. Glitterati mix with ski bums here, all surrounded by mastodon summits. The drive covers 157 miles (253km).

7 days
After Mesa Verde and Durango, and maybe even a jaunt up to Silverton as per the three-day itinerary, head southeast to New Mexico. Taos is a must, home to adobe architecture, quirky cafes, bohemians, hippies, alternative-energy aficionados and old-time Hispanic families. A short distance south, Santa Fe pops up. This chilli-laden foodie haven and art-fiend magnet is worthy of a couple of days. A short distance east, atomic-age secrets are revealed at Los Alamos, where the nuclear bomb was developed. The trip covers some 350 miles (563km).

© Justin Foulkes / Lonely Planet

MEXICO

Calakmul

Calakmul, which was possibly the largest city during Maya times, boasts massive pyramids hiding deep in the Mexican jungle.

From around AD 250, Calakmul was the Mayan place to be. It was the leading metropolis in the vast region known as the Kingdom of the Serpent's Head. More than 50,000 people lived in the hot spot, and remnants of their enormous stone buildings poke out of the rainforest canopy today. Climb up any of the sky-high pyramids, lungs burning and leg muscles quivering, and you'll get a feel for the scale. The pièce de résistance is 45m Estructura II, the tallest known Mayan structure, which unfurls views over the endless green jungle. Keep wandering the grounds and you'll pass tomb sites, stelae and thick-rooted trees growing over the ruins. Parrots and toucans squawk overhead, spider and howler monkeys call from the treetops, and occasionally a jaguar prowls from behind a pyramid.

Thanks to its middle-of-nowhere location, Calakmul remains awesomely untrammelled. Visitor numbers are a fraction of those at sites such as Tikal and Chichén Itzá. Plus most of Calakmul isn't even excavated yet, so you get to feel as though you're Indiana Jones exploring the lost world.

Travel

International
Mérida International Airport is the main hub in the region. Calakmul is a good 6½-hour drive to the south. From Mérida's city centre you can catch one of the many bus services to the city of Campeche and then onward from there to Xpujil or other regional towns.

Regional
Xpujil serves as a useful base for visiting Calakmul. There are no buses that run to the ruins, so you'll need to take a tour or hire a taxi. Both are easy to arrange in town. Taxis will wait while you explore the site for three hours or so, and then bring you back.

Stay

Shoestring
Hotel Maya Balam The best of a fairly basic lot in Xpujil, the Maya Balam is small and modern with tidy rooms, good wi-fi, a restaurant and friendly service. *(Rooms from MUS$540/US$30)*

Shoestring
Garra de Jaguar This spot has clean *cabañas* (cabins) arranged around a small grassy courtyard and an on-site restaurant. Rooms sleep two or four, and have private bathrooms. *(Doubles from MUS$800/US$40, quads from MUS$1200/US$60)*

Midrange
Hotel Puerta Calakmul Set in the jungle en route to the ruins, these 15 spacious bungalows are very tastefully decorated with polished concrete and wood. The howler monkeys are residents here. *(Cabañas from MUS$3000/US$150; www.puertacalakmul.com.mx)*

Eat

Shoestring
Genesis This very basic spot churns out *antojitos* (little bites, or snacks) plus sandwiches, hamburgers and tacos around the clock. It's a good spot to buy takeaway meals for Calakmul and other excursions. *(Mains from MUS$40/US$2)*

Midrange
Sazon Veracruzano It's as smart as you'll get in Xpujil. It offers a big menu of Mexican dishes with a focus on Veracruz, where the owners are from. Think *fajita la arrachera* (beef strips) and fried fish fillets. *(Mains from MUS$130/US$6.50)*

Timing

The dry months of November to March are the most pleasant for visiting Calakmul. During the rainy season access is often limited due to muddy roads.

Toucans, howler monkeys and other animals in the surrounding rainforest are most active during the morning and evening.

Take all water and snacks with you to Calakmul. Nothing is available en route to the site once you've turned off Hwy 186.

1 Imposing *stelae* (stone slabs) stand at the base of the 24m-high Estructura VII.

2 The temple pyramid of Estructura VII is found deep in the rainforest.

3 Mérida is a town steeped in colonial history, its streets lined with elegant and colourful buildings.

Best value itineraries

3 days
Give yourself at least two days to visit Calakmul. This will allow you a day to get there and visit the nearby bat cave at sunset, where some two to three million flying mammals swirl up in a tornado of wings, and another to drive to visit the extensive ruins. Both driving and walking distances at the site are substantial. Then head to colonial Mérida, the Yucatán Peninsula's lively cultural capital, to wander the narrow streets and browse the thriving markets and museums.

9 days
Follow the three-day itinerary, then stay in Mérida for another few days and use it as a base to seek out the superb ruins of Uxmal and the Ruta Puuc (Puuc Route), which meanders through rolling hills dotted with lonely Mayan sites sitting in dense forests. Next stop: Chichén Itzá, the most celebrated of all the Yucatán's Mayan sites, thanks to its mysterious 'time temples' based on the Mayan astronomical calendar. From here it's on to Tulum on the Caribbean coast, another spectacular Mayan site set beside a glorious beach. The journey is about 460 miles (740km) in total.

© mehdi33300 / Shutterstock

①

© BGSmith / Shutterstock

CANADA

Lake Louise

The bluer-than-blue water of Lake Louise in beautiful Banff National Park will make you rub your eyes in disbelief and strike out on inspired hikes.

Standing next to the serene, implausibly turquoise lake, with the smell of pine trees smacking your nose, the natural world feels (and is) tantalisingly close. Finely chiselled mountains surround you and hoist up a glistening glacier for your viewing pleasure. They reflect in the mirror-like water, which is so ethereally coloured you begin to wonder if Mother Nature has clicked on an Instagram filter. It's embarrassing, but you can't help sighing at the visuals almost everywhere you turn. No wonder this lake has captured the imaginations of mountaineers, artists and visitors for more than a century.

When you've finished gawping on the shimmering shore, hike up into the mountains beyond. Trails climb to alpine teahouses that reward with thick-cut sandwiches, cakes, hot chocolate and vistas of a certain lake. Then again, you can let the Lake Louise Gondola cable car do the huffing and puffing for you. It glides to a dizzying viewpoint above the water and offers a bonus of spotting grizzly bears roaming the slopes below.

Travel

International
The nearest airport is Calgary International Airport, 125 miles (200km) east of Lake Louise. Shuttle buses make the trip, but renting a car is the most convenient way to get there.

Regional
Lake Louise is reachable by shuttle from both Banff (a one-hour ride south) and Jasper (a four-hour ride north), although a car is easiest for getting around. The village of Lake Louise is 3 miles (5km) away from the lake itself. A free park shuttle covers the distance in summer.

Stay

$

Shoestring
HI-Lake Louise Alpine Centre The rustic, timber-and-stone hostel fills up fast with interesting travellers. Dorm rooms are fairly standard. Private rooms with lofts are great for families. *(Dorms from C$42/US$32, rooms from C$115/US$85; www.hihostels.ca)*

$$$

Flush
Deer Lodge The historic property dates from the 1920s. With its stone fireplace ablaze, it keeps a genuine alpine feel intact. Lodge rooms are small but quaint, while spacious Heritage rooms have smart, boutique-like furnishings. *(Rooms from C$250/US$190; www.crmr.com/deer)*

$$$

Flush
Moraine Lake Lodge Rooms and cabins offer mountain-inspired luxury with big windows, woodburning or antique gas fireplaces, soaking tubs and balconies overlooking the lake. *(Rooms from C$400/US$305; www.morainelake.com)*

Eat

$

Shoestring
Lake Agnes Teahouse The only way to reach it is via a 2.25 mile (3.4km) view-filled alpine hike upward. Homemade bread, soup, sandwiches and lake-water tea offer fuel for the jaunt back down. *(Lunch from C$7/US$5.35)*

$$

Midrange
Lake Louise Station Restaurant Eat in a beautifully restored railway station with turn-of-the-century ambience, and dig into the first-class Rocky Mountain sausage plate, maple salmon or bison burger. *(Mains from C$20/US$15; www.lakelouisestation.com)*

$$$

Flush
Fairview Lounge Along with sublime mountain views, it serves finger sandwiches, India's best orange pekoe and scones with Devonshire cream in an atmosphere heavy with *Downton Abbey*-era nostalgia. *(Tea service from C$46/US$35; www.fairmont.com/lake-louise/dining/afternoontea)*

Timing

July to September is the peak season, when trails are snow-free, making a full range of hikes available.

Arrive at Lake Louise before 10am or after 7pm to beat the rush, especially if you are driving. Car parks fill up fast.

About half of the local businesses close between October and April. The other half stay open and cater to the winter-sports crowd, who pile in between December and February.

❶

Give in to gawping at the impossibly clear blue waters of Lake Louise.

❷

Approach the lake on foot (bears permitting), by bike or on horseback, and explore the surrounding mountains, too.

❸

The annual Calgary Stampede attracts over one million visitors. Each year a First Nations Princess is crowned.

Best value itineraries

3 days
After a day of tea, scones and true-blue water at Lake Louise, hit the road north. Get on the Icefields Parkway, North America's highest and most spectacular road. Gape at the gothic, glacier-strewn Columbia Icefield and pull over to take an adrenaline-pumping walk on Athabasca Glacier. After 145 miles (230km) you'll reach Jasper National Park, which offers superb hiking, mountain biking and bear, elk and moose watching. Spend a couple of days in the charming, mountain-encircled town.

8 days
With Lake Louise and Jasper in the rear-view mirror, make your way south to mega popular Banff National Park. Allot a few days for hiking, paddling, hot-springs soaking and grizzly bear spotting. Zip over to nearby Yoho National Park. It may be small, but it packs a big wallop of looming peaks and crashing waterfalls. Wapta Falls and Lake O'Hara are worth the hike. The next day, take Hwy 1 eastward to cowboy-ish Calgary. Book a cool downtown boutique hotel and check out the excellent Glenbow Museum and kicking footwear at Alberta Boot Co.

© Justin Foulkes / Lonely Planet

USA

Smithsonian Institution

The world's largest museum and research complex stashes everything but the kitchen sink. Actually, it has that, too...

If America was a quirky grandfather, the Smithsonian Institution would be his attic. Rockets, Rodin sculptures, George Washington's sword, Julia Child's kitchen – even the 45-carat, famously cursed Hope Diamond lights up a room here. The Smithsonian is actually a collection of 19 free museums, many lined up in a row on the National Mall, and they'll blow your mind. Pick one of the vast treasure chambers, say the National Air and Space Museum, walk in and, holy cow: there's the Wright Brothers' first plane a stone's throw from Amelia Earhart's natty red flyer. Enter the bronze-tiered African American History and Culture Museum, and there's Emmett Till's casket with a solemn procession of visitors lined up to pay their respects. The American History Museum is so school-group clamorous you're almost too distracted to notice you're standing in front of Abe Lincoln's top hat or a piece of Plymouth Rock. A giant squid (at the Natural History Museum); Andy Warhol paintings (American Art Museum); the world's rarest stamp (Postal Museum) – the Smithsonian's 155 million artefacts eye-pop at every turn.

Travel

International
DC has two airports: Dulles International is larger and further flung with global connections. Smaller Reagan Washington National Airport is just 4.5 miles (7.2km) south of downtown Washington. Both have public transport into the city.

Regional
Amtrak trains link Boston, New York and Philadelphia to DC's Union Station multiple times daily. Once in DC, the Metro subway network is the main way to get around. It runs near all the major sights. Fares are from US$2 to US$6 depending on distance travelled; a day pass is also available. Capital Bikeshare is another popular way to zip around.

Stay

Shoestring
Hostelling International – Washington DC The large, well-run hostel attracts an international crowd downtown with amenities including game-filled lounge rooms, free neighbourhood tours and free breakfast. *(Dorms from US$33; www.hiwashingtondc.org)*

Midrange
Hotel Hive Not far from the National Mall, it buzzes with hip travellers drawn to the tiny but cleverly designed rooms and the rooftop bar. *(Rooms from US$99; www.hotelhive.com)*

Flush
Hay-Adams Hotel Set in an elegant old building where 'nothing is overlooked but the White House', the Hay offers the city's best rooms of the old-school luxury variety. *(Rooms from US$400; www.hayadams.com)*

Eat

Shoestring
Woodward Takeout Food Jump in line with all of the office workers to order a gourmet lunch sandwich, pizza slice, salted chocolate croissant or the daily doughnut. *(Sandwiches from US$6; www.woodwardtable.com)*

Midrange
Old Ebbitt Grill This legendary restaurant occupies prime real estate near the White House. Political players and tourists pack into the wood-panelled interior, where thick burgers and jumbo lump-crab cakes reign supreme. *(Mains from US$18; www.ebbitt.com)*

Flush
Equinox It sources meat, fish and vegetables from nearby farms in the Shenandoah Valley and Chesapeake Bay. Dishes are seasonal and up to 50% plant-based. *(Mains from US$31; www.equinoxrestaurant.com)*

Timing

Peak season is late March to June. July and August are less busy, but hot. From September to November, business travellers keep rates high. Winter (off-season) has fickle weather.

Start early in summer. You'll avoid the crowds and, more importantly, you'll avoid the heat.

The free Smithsonian Folklife Festival is held in late June and early July, with music, dance, crafts, storytelling and food from around the world.

Some of the 60,000 items in the National Air and Space Museum's collection.

Jospeh Henry, first Secretary of the Smithsonian Institution, stands at the entrance to its 'Castle'.

Cherry blossoms along Washington DC's National Mall.

Representatives of Native American peoples consulted on the design of the National Museum of the American Indian.

Best value itineraries

3 days
Stay in DC for the duration, as there are loads of sights. Start at the National Mall, home to the mother lode of Smithsonian museums and the iconic Washington Monument, Vietnam Veterans Memorial and Lincoln Memorial. The next day, tour Capitol Hill, visit the National Archives and saunter by the White House. At night go to U Street or Shaw for eats and drinks. On day three, stroll around historic Georgetown or head to Dupont Circle to gape at the mansions along Embassy Row. In the evening, catch a show at the Kennedy Center.

9 days
After immersing in the US capital, take the train (about 3½ hours) to New York City and spend three days exploring the mighty metropolis. Start with the famed sights in Lower Manhattan and around the harbour. People-watch in the West and East Villages and museum-hop down the Upper East Side. Have a ramble in Central Park or detour to Brooklyn. Next, catch the train (about 4½ hours) to Boston for two days of visiting historic sights, dining in the North End and pub-hopping in Cambridge. Add on a final day in Cape Cod, with its idyllic dunes and pretty shores.

© Sean Pavone / Getty Images

© Paul Franklin / Getty Images

1

© Tony Shi Photography / Getty Images

CANADA/USA

Niagara Falls

In terms of sheer volume, there's nothing like it –
more than 2830 tonnes of water plummet over the
brink every second.

OK, so it's crowded and has carnival-tacky environs.
But when those great muscular bands of water arc
over the precipice like liquid glass, roaring into the
void below, Niagara Falls impresses big time. Great
plumes of icy mist rise like an ethereal veil as the
water crashes over the edge and hits the river below.
Rainbows pop up and pierce the haze. But you don't
just stand back and admire this view from afar.
Instead you sail right towards it in a little boat, getting
sprayed, soaked and deafened by the thundering
water. You *feel* Niagara's mighty breath.

The falls are comprised of three separate cascades
that drop on different sides of the United States-
Canada border: Bridal Veil Falls and American Falls
let loose in New York State, while Horseshoe Falls
descends in Ontario. Horseshoe has the grandest and
most powerful flow – and the one that attracts all
the daredevils who go over the falls in a barrel (like
63-year-old Annie Taylor, who started the trend in
1901 and lived to tell the tale).

Travel

International
Toronto Pearson Airport on the Canadian side and Buffalo Niagara International Airport on the US side are the main hubs. Buses run from each airport to the falls; it takes about 1½ hours from Toronto, and one hour from Buffalo. Amtrak trains arrive daily from Buffalo, Toronto and New York City.

Regional
It's easy and economical to get around on public transport once you're in Niagara. WEGO buses cover all the sights and accommodation on the Canadian side, which is the larger, more amenity-laden zone, whereas the Niagara Scenic Trolley loops around the American-side attractions.

Stay

Shoestring
Hostelling International Niagara Falls The homely, multicoloured building sleeps about 90 people. Well-maintained facilities include a sizeable kitchen, pool table and cool basement lounge. *(Dorms from C$29/US$22, rooms from C$84/US$64; www.hostellingniagara.com)*

Midrange
Niagara Parkway Court Elegant rooms in a variety of styles, free breakfast and transport to the falls from its pleasant spot just outside of town make this motel a great choice. *(Rooms from C$109/US$82)*

Flush
Giacomo A luxe property located on the falls' American side, Giacomo occupies part of a gorgeous art deco office tower. Its spacious and ornately decorated rooms offer a rare bit of style. *(Rooms from US$247; www.thegiacomo.com)*

Eat

Shoestring
Flying Saucer If you're looking for a great diner steeped in a kitschy, galactic vibe, it's right here. Don't miss the C$1.99 early-bird breakfasts, which are served from 6am to 10am with a beverage purchase. *(Mains from C$8/US$6; www.flyingsaucerrestaurant.com)*

Midrange
Taps on Queen Brewhouse & Grill It offers a mix of dishes, from shepherd's pie to ancient-grains curry (quinoa, couscous, adzuki beans and veggies), plus tasty beers brewed in-house. *(Mains from C$13/US$9.85; www.tapsbeer.ca)*

Flush
AG The seasonal menu features dishes such as fennel pollen pickerel, roasted venison loin and crispy skinned trout, all sourced locally. Ace service, decor and presentation add to the fineness. *(Mains from C$18/US$14; www.agcuisine.com)*

Timing

July and August are the warmest and busiest months. June and September are great times when the weather is still good and the crowds are thinner.

Many places shut down from November into early April, when temperatures plummet.

To cross the border from the US side to Canada or vice versa, bring your passport and arrange visas in advance. There's a small fee to cross the Rainbow Bridge.

Niagara Falls seen from the American side, with the scattered high-rises of Niagara in the distance.

With a 50m-drop, Niagara has the world's highest flow rate and gushes with a thundering roar.

Ponchos required to see Horseshoe Falls up close.

A cinnamon and sugar pastry fix at Beaver Tails in Ottawa.

Best value itineraries

3–4 days
When you finish bowing down before the power and grace of Niagara Falls, trundle up the road for 16 miles (26km) to Niagara-on-the-Lake, a quaint 19th-century town of tree-lined streets and impeccably restored houses. En route you'll see signposts for the many wineries that speckle the landscape, so stop and sip as needed. Make your final destination Toronto, 80 miles (130km) to the northwest. Take a rocket ride up the CN Tower, browse St Lawrence Market, visit the Hockey Hall of Fame, chow in Chinatown or Little Korea: Canada's multicultural megacity can easily fill a few days.

7–10 days
Do the Niagara-to-Toronto route, then begin your eastward haul. The misty, mansion-covered Thousand Islands dot the St Lawrence River; Victorian Gananoque makes a good break for a day in their midst. Continue to Ottawa, Canada's capital, for a couple of days to get your culture fix at the national museums. Save room for your next stop, Montréal, where the French exuberance seduces via Euro-cool clubs and foodie-beloved cafes. Finish in Québec City – the charismatic Old Town, walled and dramatically poised on a bluff, impresses big time. The journey is about 685 miles (1100km) in total; most of it is reachable by train.

© Igor Sh / Shutterstock

© ZisaPhoto / 500px

South America

Caribbean Sea

NORTH PACIFIC OCEAN

SOUTH PACIFIC OCEAN

⭐ Tikal

GUATEMALA HONDURAS

EL SALVADOR

NICARAGUA

COSTA RICA PANAMA

VENEZUELA

Angel Falls ⭐

COLOMBIA

Caño Cristales ⭐

ECUADOR

Amazon Rainforest ⭐

Galapagos Islands ⭐

PERU

Machu Picchu ⭐

BOLIVIA

Salar de Uyuni ⭐

PARAGUAY

Easter Island (Chile)
⭐ Moai

ARGENTINA

CHILE

Marble Caves ⭐

GUYANA
SURINAME
French Guiana
(FRANCE)

NORTH ATLANTIC OCEAN

BRAZIL

⭐Iguazú Falls

URUGUAY

SOUTH ATLANTIC OCEAN

Scotia Sea

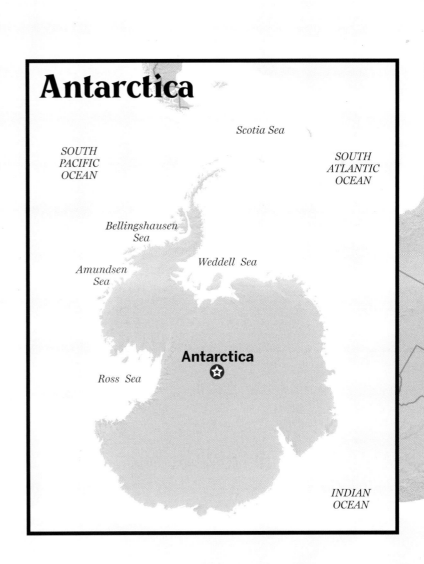

Antarctica

Scotia Sea

*SOUTH
PACIFIC
OCEAN*

*SOUTH
ATLANTIC
OCEAN*

*Bellingshausen
Sea*

Weddell Sea

*Amundsen
Sea*

Antarctica
⭐

Ross Sea

*INDIAN
OCEAN*

PERU/BRAZIL

Amazon Rainforest

Fanning out across nine South American countries and covering roughly 40% of the continent, the Amazon Rainforest is the largest patch of green on planet Earth.

To enter into its midst is to disconnect from the modern world entirely. The tannin-rich rivers become your roads, the monkeys your companions and the cacophonous birdsong your morning alarm. Those who venture into the heart of the Amazon learn quickly how to get comfortable being uncomfortable. Bugs are part of the scenery, weather is erratic and the thick air has a tangible presence as it coats your exposed skin. But all of this is what makes the Amazon incomparable.

Three national parks along its Andean edge each claim to be the most biodiverse protected area in the world. No one knows for sure which one is, but suffice to say that nature here knows no bounds. From the blue poison dart frogs to the pink river dolphins, orange-winged parrots and scarlet macaws, the Amazon is a kaleidoscope of surprises. Whether you approach it from Bolivia's Parque Nacional Madidi, French Guiana's Parc Amazonien de Guyane, or the innumerable pockets in between, the experience of giving yourself over to the whims of the world's largest rainforest leaves few visitors unchanged.

© Jonne Seijdel / 500px

Travel

International
The most common tourist hubs in the Amazon Basin include Manaus (Brazil), Leticia (Colombia), Iquitos (Peru), Puerto Maldonado (Peru) and Rurrenabaque (Bolivia). All have airports, though Manaus is the only one to receive international flights from outside South America. For the rest, transfer in Bogotá, Lima and La Paz respectively.

Regional
Most visit the Amazon on a guided tour that begins in one of these regional hubs. Transport is often by boat as there are few roads through the region's spectacular national parks. Travellers with more cash may consider a multiday river cruise; those with less can hop aboard no-frills cargo ships.

Stay

Shoestring
Amazon Antonio's Lodge This splendid lodge on the banks of Brazil's Rio Urubu is surrounded by a pristine tract of riverine forest rich in wildlife and tall trees. There's a hammock dorm and wooden chalets. *(Room and board from R$330/US$89; www.antonio-jungletours.com)*

Midrange
Boulevard 251 The best place to stay in Iquitos, for the location, high above the riverbanks, and the chic environs. *(Apartments from S157/US$47; www.iquitosapartments.com)*

Flush
Chalalán Ecolodge Successful community-based ecotourism project with simple, elegant huts surrounding an idyllic lake and tours through the rainforest to view native wildlife. *(All-inclusive packages per day US$145; www.chalalan.com)*

Eat

Shoestring
Belén Mercado At this Iquitos market look out for specialities including meaty Amazon worms, *ishpa* (simmered sabalo fish intestines and fat) and *sikisapa* (fried leafcutter ants; abdomens are tastiest). *(Set menu from S5/US$1.50)*

Midrange
Burgos's Restaurante This standout Puerto Maldonado restaurant calls itself an exponent of Novo Amazonica cuisine, but what's really on offer are dependable Peruvian Amazon staples cooked to perfection, rather than with particular innovation. *(Mains from S19/US$5.70)*

Flush
Amazônico Peixaria Regional However you get your *tambaqui* (perhaps the tastiest of all Amazonian fish) prepared at this Manaus staple – stewed, grilled, ribs – the execution is great. *(Mains from R$36/US$9.70; www.amazonico.com.br)*

Timing

In much of the Amazon Basin, the dry season runs roughly from June to December, when river levels drop and there are better opportunities for wildlife watching.

The wet season typically runs from January to April, but it doesn't rain every day. It's often easier to travel by river than land at this time of year.

When the rains subside in May, courtship season begins for many Amazonian birds.

Geography in action as the Napo River winds through Amazonian rainforest in Ecuador.

Boats are the best way to explore the Amazon, here on Ecuador's Limoncocha Lagoon.

The jaguar: South America's mammalian prime predator and an unlikely sight on your Amazonian travels.

Best value itineraries

7 days
Fly directly to Puerto Maldonado in Peru or brave the 10-hour bus ride from Cuzco, gateway to Machu Picchu. From here, you can kick back for a week in a thatch-roofed bungalow with a view, either along the Río Madre de Dios, near lovely Lago Sandoval, or along the Río Tambopata, where a national reserve protects one of Peru's largest clay licks. Alternatively, take an overland tour from Cuzco to the Manu area, with remote tracts of virgin forest holding diverse animals from kinkajous to caimans; it's one of the most biodiverse areas on the planet.

14 days
Start in Manaus (Brazil), the largest city in the Amazon, by visiting the opera house, market, indigenous museums and nature parks. Next, head up to the Rio Urubu, where you can base in ecofriendly lodges and take in some great wildlife-watching opportunities. Afterwards, go west of Manaus to the small town of Novo Airão, the jumping-off point to the Reserva Extrativista Baixo Rio Branco-Jauaperi, a remote and pristine rainforest reserve. Outside of Tefé, visit the Mamirauá Reserve where you can see dolphins, sloths, macaws, various monkey species (including the rare uakari) and other wildlife. From there, continue by river to Tabatinga, and into Leticia in Colombia for stays at jungle lodges along the Rio Javari.

BOLIVIA

Salar de Uyuni

Covering more than 12,000 sq km of southwestern Bolivia, the Salar de Uyuni is so much more than just the world's largest salt flat.

It's the ethereal afterglow of a long-gone lake and a white oasis carved into the heart of the burnt-orange Altiplano, which rivals Tibet as the planet's most extensive high plateau. Wandering through its pearly white realms at the oxygen-thinning altitude of 3653m is like setting foot on the moon. Your breath quickens, your heart thumps. You get a quick preview of what it'll be like to exert yourself when you're 80.

Few places on earth have the power to be so demonstrably disorientating as this blinding white expanse, which is home to 70% of the world's known lithium reserves. When a thin layer of reflective water covers the *salar*'s cracked surface it's as if you're standing atop a dreamland of candyfloss clouds. When it's dry, you feel the overwhelming solitude of unfathomable emptiness. When you lay your head to rest on a salt bed in a hotel made entirely of the white stuff, you can't help but feel a profound connection to the parched earth.

❷

Travel

International
The quickest way to reach the city of Uyuni is by air via Bolivia's de facto capital of La Paz, which receives international flights from most major South American hubs. Amaszonas and Boliviana de Aviación both operate connections between La Paz and Uyuni twice daily (one hour). You can also travel this route by bus (nine hours).

Regional
Theoretically you can visit Salar de Uyuni independently, but it's extremely challenging due to unreliable transport and the remoteness of the area. It's best to take an organised tour from Uyuni, which probably works out cheaper than doing it alone anyway. Tours cost B$800 (US$116) to B$1200 (US$174) for three days at a standard agency, and B$1200 (US$174) to B$1500 (US$217) at a high-end operation. The price includes a driver (who also serves as your guide, mechanic and cook), two nights' accommodation, three meals a day and transport. There are cheaper tours, but they don't include English-speaking guides.

Stay

Shoestring
Maya Hostal de Sal Run by a local Aymará family in Coquesa, this is a nice, traditional choice. The beds are built on salt blocks, the doors and windows of cactus wood, and the dining room has salt tables. *(Rooms per person B$50/US$7.25)*

Flush
Hotel Palacio de Sal Right on the edge of the *salar*, near Colchani, is this luxurious salt complex, the first such hotel in the region. There is a good onsite restaurant and magnificent salt-flat views. *(Rooms from B$1050/US$152; www.palaciodesal.com.bo)*

Eat

Shoestring
Wiphala Pub This Uyuni pub has a traditional atmosphere and welcoming feel with its wooden tables, earthy vibe and board games. It serves tasty Bolivian dishes, specialising in llama meat and quinoa, and has quinoa beer. *(Mains from B$35/US$5)*

Midrange
Tika In Uyuni, Tika's chic, modern dining room is an appealing setting in which to sample contemporary takes on traditional Bolivian dishes, such as *charque lipeño* (sun-dried llama meat with potatoes, cheese and corn). *(Mains from B$40/US$5.80, www.tikarestaurante.com.bo)*

Timing

From the end of December to the end of March, the salt flat floods and many tour agencies shut down, which means that you can only visit the edges of the salt flat at this time.

In winter months (June to August), heavy snow along the border with Chile can make the popular onward journey to San Pedro de Atacama difficult.

Land meets sky and reality meets reflection in the strange world of Salar de Uyuni.

Polygon patterns are formed in the salt when surface water evaporates.

A railway linking Bolivia and Chile once ran through Uyuni; the trains' cargo of gold and silver has long gone, but the locomotives remain.

Best value itineraries

1 day
Most people visit the Salar de Uyuni on organised tours from the city of Uyuni. Quick day trips typically depart around 10am, stopping first at Cementerio de Trenes (a train 'cemetery') and the Colchani salt extraction areas (where you can buy souvenirs), before heading on to Playa Blanca Salt Hotel and Isla Incahuasi, a cactus-covered outcrop within the *salar*. At this point the day-trippers turn back and the hardcore travellers continue on to enjoy the dramatic rainbow-coloured sunset before heading to their hotel.

3 days
Follow the one-day itinerary, spending the first night in a salt hotel near the village of Chuvica (on the eastern edge of the salt flat), before entering the remote and beautiful region of Los Lípez on the second day. Many tour groups spend the second night in the dormitory accommodation at Laguna Colorada, or a little further on in the village of Huayajara, for the coldest night on the trip. On day three, you wake at dawn to visit the large geyser field dubbed Sol de Mañana. If you're not heading to San Pedro de Atacama in Chile, the final afternoon drive back to Uyuni has a few potential worthwhile stops in Valles de Rocas and San Cristóbal.

COLOMBIA

Caño Cristales

Sandwiched between the Andes and the Amazon are the tropical plains of central Colombia, home to millions of cattle, seasonally flooded grasslands and the world's most flamboyant river: Caño Cristales.

Alternatively called 'The River of Five Colours' or 'The Liquid Rainbow', Caño Cristales' nicknames give you an idea of what to expect on a visit to this remote marvel within Parque Nacional Natural Sierra de la Macarena. The unusual colours are thanks to an endemic alga that blankets the riverbed each year from about July to November, imbuing the river's once crystal-clear waters with the kind of magic realism characteristic of Colombian novelist Gabriel García Márquez.

A visit to Caño Cristales means sweaty hikes though rocky canyons, followed by shoulder massages under tumbling waterfalls. It also means boat trips down the Río Guayabero in search of wildlife and breathing in the herbaceous air on hikes to hilltop overlooks. Back in the tourist hub of La Macarena, nights are filled with the jovial folk music of *joropo* bands. This part of Colombia has only recently opened up to tourism after years under FARC (Revolutionary Armed Forces of Colombia) control, so small-scale community tourism remains the name of the game.

Travel

International
Most tours include transportation to La Macarena Airport by charter or scheduled flight from Bogotá, Medellín or Villavicencio, though it's perfectly possible to book your own transportation and arrange your tour to begin at the airport. Easy Fly offers direct flights from Bogotá three times a week in high season (July to November). Alternatively, get yourself to Villavicencio (a three-hour bus ride from Bogotá) and then take one of the daily flights to La Macarena from there.

Regional
You cannot visit Caño Cristales on your own – you are obligated to go into the national park with an official local guide, even if you do make it to La Macarena under your own steam. Most tours include air transportation to La Macarena, hotels, meals and guide services. You'll sleep in La Macarena and spend your days inside the national park.

Stay

Shoestring
Hotel Antony's You're right in the heart of town at this simple but clean place where some of the rooms even have natural light – quite a rarity in La Macarena! *(Rooms from COP$40,000/US$13)*

Midrange
Hotel Punto Verde This is the best hotel in La Macarena, with a large pool, gorgeous tropical garden and good cafe to boot. From June to November, travel with Ecoturismo Sierra de La Macarena to get a room here. *(Rooms from COP$100,000/US$31)*

Flush
Hotel La Fuente One of the most comfortable places in town, La Fuente has bright and airy rooms surrounding a garden with a pool, bar and restaurant. It also has friendly staff and pleasing design touches. *(Rooms from COP$120,000/US$38; www.hotellafuentejn.com)*

Eat

Midrange
El Caporal This is by far the smartest place in La Macarena, with a busy bar, central fireplace, large stage (for live music performances) and meat-heavy menu, though vegetarians are well catered for too. *(Mains from COP$12,000/US$3.80)*

Timing

The river is most colourful between the months of July and November when an eruption of algae forms an underwater blanket of bright red.

Though remote, Caño Cristales is no secret – Colombians swarm to it on long weekends (called *puentes*) when the maximum daily visitor count of 180 isn't always enforced. These holiday weekends are best avoided. Come midweek if you're able to.

Algae causes the red colour of Caño Cristales but that sounds less romantic than the Liquid Rainbow.

Visit in the rainy season to see the river at its best.

There's plenty more to explore in La Macarena National and Ecological Reserve Park, including mountains, savannah and many species of animal.

Best value itineraries

3 days
Catch an early morning flight from Bogotá to La Macarena, where you'll receive a mandatory 30-minute brief from the tourism bureau about the strict rules for all visitors. After you settle into your hotel and change into hiking gear, it's time to cross to the far side of Río Guayabero and enter Parque Nacional Natural Sierra de La Macarena. One of Colombia's best-protected national parks, it contains the fabulous rivers, streams and waterfalls collectively known as Caño Cristales. Spend the afternoon hiking to the El Mirador lookout before returning the following morning to swim and relax in the famed natural pools. Back in La Macarena that evening listen to a traditional *joropo* band. Get up before dawn on the final morning for a sunrise hike through the stony canyon of Los Pilones before your afternoon flight back to Bogotá.

5 days
With a few extra days you can explore the full spectrum of waterfalls and swimming holes, including Piscina del Turista, Piscina de Carol Cristal, Cascada del Aguila, Cascada de Piedra Negra and Caño la Virgen. Spend your fourth day bouncing between these prismatic pools and tumbling cascades, and your final morning kayaking down the Río Guayabero in search of flora and fauna.

© Juergen Ritterbach / Getty Iamges

© David Basulto / 500px

BRAZIL/ARGENTINA

Iguazú Falls

More than 275 cascades parade across the border from southern Brazil into northern Argentina to form Iguazú Falls, the world's largest waterfall system.

Nothing can quite prepare you for your first vision of it. Surveying the scene from the safety of a boardwalk, you find yourself utterly surrounded by curtains of water tumbling over leafy-green hills into a steamy abyss below. Flocks of great dusky swifts dart, improbably, in and out of the falls, while toucans flaunt their oversized beaks in the adjacent hills. Just when the tropical heat threatens to scorch your sweat-damp skin, a cloud of mist rises over the boardwalk to the rescue. Meanwhile, the thunderous roar of pounding water is so electric you can feel it rattling your bones.

Three times wider than its North American cousin Niagara – and in the middle of a jungle with jaguars, monkeys and toothy caimans – Iguazú is so awe-inspiring that even former First Lady of the United States Eleanor Roosevelt couldn't help but mourn 'poor Niagara' at the sight of it. Try to trace one small patch of the river as it makes its way through the cataracts and you, too, will be similarly awed by the power of water in shaping planet earth.

Travel

International
Puerto Iguazú in Argentina and Foz do Iguaçu in Brazil have airports, and you can take a taxi from either to accommodation on the far side of the border. The airport in Foz is slightly busier. Most overseas visitors will pass through Buenos Aires, São Paulo or Rio de Janeiro on the way.

Regional
Puerto Iguazú has good bus connections to Buenos Aires and other parts of Argentina. Similarly, Foz is well connected to São Paulo and Rio. These journeys will take the better part of a day. To get to the falls themselves there are regular local buses from Puerto Iguazú (30 minutes) and Foz (20 minutes).

Stay

Shoestring
Tetris Container Hostel Brazil's coolest hostel, located in Foz, is crafted from 15 shipping containers – even the pool is a water-filled shipping container! – and makes full use of other industrial byproducts as well, such as sinks made from oil drums. *(Dorms from R$50/US$13; www.tetrishostel.com.br)*

Midrange
Jasy Hotel These 10, two-level peaceful rooms in Puerto Iguazú, which have great designs for family sleeping, climb a hill like a forest staircase and are all equipped with a balcony. *(Rooms from US$95; www.jasyhotel.com)*

Flush
Belmond Hotel das Cataratas You'll find spectacular views from the Sheraton on the Argentine side, but nowhere on either side of the falls is as delightful, delicious and deluxe as this 193-room luxury hotel by the falls on the Brazilian side. *(Rooms from R$1079/US$290; www.belmond.com)*

Eat

Shoestring
Albayan Doceria Arabe If you want to immerse yourself in Foz de Iguaçu's Middle Eastern culture, this divine sweet shop across from the Omar Ibn Al-Khattab mosque is the place to go. *(Sweets per kilogramme from R$40/US$11)*

Midrange
Bocamora A romantic location overlooking two rivers and three nations is reason enough to come to this place. It specialises in grilled meats and river fish. *(Mains from AR$145/US$3.90; www.facebook.com/bocamoragrillwine)*

Flush
De La Fonte This exquisite hotel restaurant is strong on presentation, whether a plate of homemade pasta or inventive molecular-gastronomy creations. *(Degustation menu AR$1250/US$34; www.boutiquehoteldelafonte.com)*

Timing

Iguazú Falls is great any time of the year. However, it's generally more hot and crowded from December to March.

No matter when you go, it really is worth arriving at either park by 9am – the gangways are narrow, and getting stuck in a conga line of tour groups in searing heat and humidity takes the edge off the experience.

1750 cubic metres of water flows over the falls every second, cascading down 60-80m.

Salto Arrechea, one of numerous waterfalls worth seeking out in Parque Nacional Iguazú.

There can be more than 200 separate drops in the entire area of Iguazú falls, depending on the time of year.

Best value itineraries

3 days
Kick off your morning in Brazil's Parque Nacional do Iguaçu, whose panoramic views offer the grandest first impressions of the majestic falls. In the afternoon head to Parque das Aves, a 12-acre (5ha) park located 300m from the entrance to the falls, with 800-plus bird species, including red ibis, bare-throated bellbird and flamingos galore. The following day, pop over to the Argentine side for a more intimate, close-up experience hiking the short rainforest trails of Parque Nacional Iguazú, including Circuito Inferior, Circuito Superior and Garganta del Diablo. Return again the next day to explore Isla San Martín, where another trail gives the closest look at several falls, including Salto San Martín, a huge, furious cauldron of water. Cap off the adventure by getting completely soaked on an action-packed boat trip under a pounding cascade.

7–10 days
With more time, you can visit the world's second-largest hydroelectric power station, Itaipu Binacional, hike the 5.5 mile (9km) Trilha do Poço Preto trail, or visit some indigenous Guarani communities. Spend your final days heading south though Argentina's Misiones Province to visit the evocative ruins of Jesuit Missions, like San Ignacio Miní. Finish the trip in Parque Esteros del Iberá, an amazing wetlands preserve full of capybaras, caimans and birds.

© Matt Munro / Lonely Planet

❶

© DC_Colombia / Getty Iamges

Galápagos Islands

There are few places left in the world that are as tranquil as the Galápagos Islands, where the wildlife just gives a collective shrug of the shoulders at the sight of humans.

These 21 volcanic isles, which spill across either side of the equator, 1000km off the coast of Ecuador, are home to some of the highest levels of endemism on the planet, with some 97% of the reptiles and land mammals found nowhere else on earth. Rather than running away in fear, these unique creatures are at the most vaguely perturbed by all the flashing cameras and their owners, many of whom are lured here by the tales of 19th-century English naturalist Charles Darwin. The chance to follow in his footsteps, and to meet the animals that triggered his theory of evolution, is bucket-list gold for animal lovers.

Many envision the Galápagos as a tropical paradise of perky palms and piña coladas, but its allure is much more dramatic. Boating around the archipelago on a small expedition cruise, you call at islands with stark, lava-scared landscapes, bizarre red-sand beaches and barren volcanic craters, all while keeping an eye out for lethargic marine iguanas, giant geriatric tortoises and feathered blue-footed boobies. Even if the animals seem indifferent to your presence on the islands, you most certainly won't be.

2

Travel

International
To get to the Galápagos Islands you'll first need to arrive in mainland Ecuador. Quito and Guayaquil are the two hubs with onward connections. Both receive flights from across the Americas, as well as a few European cities.

Regional
The way in and out of the Galápagos is by air unless you're on a pre-arranged cruise. The three airlines flying to the islands are Tame, Avianca and LATAM. Flights from mainland Ecuador arrive at two airports: Isla Baltra, just north of Santa Cruz, and Isla San Cristóbal. It is possible to fly into one and out of the other.

Stay

Shoestring
Casa de Laura Hostal This friendly, family-owned hideaway is one of the best-value places on Isla San Cristóbal. It's located in an adobe building with a nicely landscaped courtyard and hammocks in the cactus garden out front. *(Rooms per person US$20)*

Midrange
Casa Blanca Not only does this whitewashed adobe building have charmingly decorated rooms, but it sits directly across from the pier in Puerto Baquerizo Moreno, which means that rooms with sea-facing balconies have great views. *(Rooms from US$70; www.casablancagalapagos.com)*

Flush
Iguana Crossing Boutique Hotel Isabela's most upscale hotel has attractive rooms with lovely wooden decks overlooking either the lagoon or the ocean. Think glossy design-magazine furnishings and tastes throughout. *(Rooms from US$278; www.iguanacrossing.com.ec)*

Eat

Shoestring
Cuencan Taste Join afternoon crowds in Puerto Baquerizo Moreno for baked magnificence: chocolate or cinnamon bread, empanadas, pastries and tarts. *(Snacks from US$0.50)*

Midrange
Conchalagua Hands down the best place for a meal on Floreana, tiny Conchalagua has delicious pizzas, sandwiches and burgers. The charming owner has loads of great stories about growing up on the island. *(Mains from US$15)*

Flush
Coco Surf This sidewalk cafe in Puerto Villamil serves up some of the tastiest seafood dishes in the Galápagos. You'll hardly notice the high price points once the live band starts jamming to jazzy island tunes. *(Mains from US$15)*

Timing

From January to May the islands are warm and sunny with occasional downpours. The water is relatively calm and the winds slacken.

June to December is the cool and dry season when the seas tend to be choppier due to the Humboldt Current. Sea mammals and land birds are typically at their most active at this time of year.

Beaches on volcanic Bartolomé Island in the Galápagos archipelago.

A male frigatebird on Genovesa Island puts on a show for passing females.

Marine iguanas on Española Island, once derided by Charles Darwin as 'hideous-looking' lizards, are actually vulnerable herbivores.

Best value itineraries

5 days
Fly into San Cristóbal and get briefed on island nature and history at the Interpretation Center. Board your expedition cruise and voyage south on day two to Isla Española. Spend the morning on the white coral sands of Gardner Bay, a breeding site for turtles and sea lions. Snorkel in the bay, then hike Punta Suárez in search of blue-footed boobies. Day three is all about Isla Floreana. Begin in Post Office Bay, home to an old mailbox for American and British whalers, then visit the lagoon at Cormorant Point to search for flamingos. It's off to Isla Santiago and Sullivan Bay on day four to view a lunar landscape of cooled black lava. Spend the final morning in Black Turtle Cove, on Isla Santa Cruz, before zipping over to Isla Baltra to catch a flight out.

8 days
Stick around on Isla Santa Cruz for a few more nights, using Puerto Ayora as a base for terrestrial explorations. Start with a trip to the Charles Darwin Research Station, then head to Las Grietas for nice swimming and snorkelling in a water-filled crevice. The next day, sign up for a morning dive, and then walk the boardwalk path at Laguna de las Ninfas. End the trip with a bang at the El Chato Tortoise Reserve, observing giant tortoises in the wild.

CHILE

Moai, Easter Island

Marooned in the middle of the Pacific Ocean like castaways standing watch over their windswept isle, the *moai* of Easter Island are mystery personified.

What gave an isolated civilisation the gall to carve out 887 stony-faced statues? How did they drag 288 of them from an interior quarry to ceremonial *ahu* platforms on faraway coasts? And why had all of them been toppled by the start of the 19th century? The Chilean territory of Easter Island, known locally as Rapa Nui, lures inquisitive travellers into its enigmatic orbit, but sends most home with more questions than answers.

Easter Island is so secluded that when you stare off into the endless ocean you'd swear you see the curvature of earth. Though it may share a Polynesian heritage with Tahiti and Hawaii, any sense of a tropical idyll was long ago stripped away by an advanced culture that outgrew its resources. Today, it's a barren volcanic outcrop where the smell of freshly cut grass mixes with the salty slap of the cobalt sea. There's a dollop of sand, plentiful sun and rolling waves, but you don't fly into the world's most remote airport for that. You come to amble though an open-air archaeology museum, gaze into the eyes of a 10m-tall *moai* and ponder the stories he could tell.

© Walter Weinberg / 500px

© Walter Weinberg / Lonely Planet

Travel

International
To reach Easter Island you'll need to transfer in Santiago. The city's Arturo Merino Benítez International Airport receives flights from the US, UK, Australia, New Zealand and mainland Europe. Due to the frequency of onward connections, most people spend at least one night in the Chilean capital.

Regional
The only airline serving Easter Island is LATAM. Flights to and from Santiago are daily and last about five hours. There are also once-weekly flights to/from Pape'ete in French Polynesia. A less common way to arrive is by cruise ship. About five or six anchor at Hanga Roa (the island's main town) each year, mostly in the summer months.

Stay

Shoestring
Tipanie Moana If only all camping grounds in the world could be this clean, with spotless bathrooms, spacious shared kitchens and racks on which to dry your clothes. (*Campsite with tent CH$7000/US$10; www.camping-tipaniemoana.cl*)

Midrange
Cabañas Christophe The best-value option in Hanga Roa, this charming venue seduces those seeking character and comfort, with four handsomely designed bungalows that blend hardwoods and volcanic stones. (*Doubles from CH$60,000/US$87; www.cabanaschristophe.com*)

Flush
Explora Rapa Nui This luxury resort blends into a forested patch of volcano-singed countryside. Rooms, all overlooking the Pacific, are abundant in indigenous materials (local rauli wood, volcanic stone) that instil a sense of place. (*Three-night all-inclusive package for two US$4450; www.explora.com*)

Eat

Shoestring
Tía Berta Surrender to some melt-in-your-mouth seafood empanadas prepared mamma-style in this no-frills den. (*Empanadas from CH$3000/US$4.40*)

Midrange
Haka Honu Fish dishes, steaks, homemade pasta, burgers and salads round out the menu at this well-regarded eatery blessed with ocean views. The grilled fish with papaya chutney is particularly tasty. (*Mains from CH$11,000/US$16*)

Flush
Te Moai Sunset Make this chic restaurant with superb ceviche your go-to spot in the late afternoon when the *moai* of Tahai are silhouetted against the setting sun just below your table. (*Mains from CH$12,000/US$17*)

Timing

Peak season is between January and March, when you can expect high prices and scarce hotels, particularly around February's Tapati Rapa Nui festival.

Chillier weather between July and September makes the winter months less suitable for sun and sand time at the beach.

The shoulder seasons offer a temperate climate and moderate crowds, and are ideal for hiking and horse riding.

The extinct volcano Rano Kau lies on the southwest headland of Easter Island.

The crater of the Rano Raraku volcano was used as a quarry for the giant stone figures; half of the island's *moai* remain here.

The annual festival of Tapati Rapa Nui is a celebration of Polynesian culture.

Best value itineraries

4 days
Start the day by visiting the Museo Antropológico Sebastián Englert for some historical background. Next, hike up to the crater lake of Rano Kau. It resembles a giant witch's cauldron and is a wild greenhouse of endemic biodiversity. Perched 300m above, on the edge of the crater wall, is Orongo Ceremonial Village, which was the focus of an island-wide 'birdman cult' linked to the god Makemake in the 18th and 19th centuries. On day two take a full-day tour to marvel at the *moai* of Rano Raraku and Ahu Tongariki. On your return to Hanga Roa head straight to an atmosphere-laden bar on Av Policarpo Toro for the night vibe. Day three is all about Hanga Roa. Hit the *mercado* (market) to put a dent in the wallet and amble down Av Te Pito o Te Henua to enjoy the sunset by the *moai* of Ahu Tahai. Attend a traditional dance show later in the evening. Day four should see you lazing the day away at Anakena beach.

7 days
Follow the four-day agenda, then make the most of the island's outdoor adventures. Book a horse-riding excursion along the wild north coast, spend a day diving off Motu Nui, scramble up and down Maunga Terevaka, and explore Península Poike.

Antarctica

To visit Antarctica is to meditate on the elemental forces – snow, ice, water and rock – that shape earth's final frontier.

The first thing you notice when you arrive is just how white everything is. Some say white is the absence of colour, but when you're cruising past a giant sheet of ice, when the clouds and the snowy hills merge into one, when all you can see in the distance is a cliff face that looks for all the world like a stack of white pancakes, you'll beg to differ. Antarctica is a study in white: how it reflects light, fills spaces and forms its own all-white rainbow. White may symbolise purity, but in Antarctica it often means chaos.

The next thing you notice about the Great White South is that everything is unimaginably extreme, from the snot-freezing midday temperatures to the vast numbers of tuxedo-clad Adélie penguins huddled together on icy promontories. Even arriving is hard earned, be it by a treacherous sea voyage across Drake Passage or a hairy landing on not-so-solid ground. Once you've made it, your days are framed not by the time and schedules, but the whims of the weather. How white is it outside today?

2

Travel

International

Unless you're planning your own expedition, you'll visit Antarctica as part of a group tour, almost certainly on a ship. This has the advantage of combining your transportation, meals and accommodation, and also means that no infrastructure has to be built ashore in Antarctica's delicate environment. Ushuaia, Argentina, is the most common departure point, but ships also leave from Punta Arenas, Chile. There are less frequent departures from Invercargill, New Zealand, and Hobart, Australia, to the Ross Sea side.

Regional

It's also possible to do a day-long flyover from Melbourne, fly to the interior from Cape Town or do a so-called fly-cruise from Punta Arenas, which allows you to avoid the lengthy (and often uncomfortable) crossing of Drake Passage. The International Association of Antarctica Tour Operators (iaato. org), which promotes environmentally responsible travel to the continent, is a great place to get informed about the various travel options.

Stay & Eat

Shoestring

Bark Europa The three-masted tall ship *Europa* sets sail with a professional crew of 14 in addition to 48 'voyage crew members'. Trips include one from Ushuaia to Cape Town. *(www.barkeuropa.com)*

Midrange

Quark Expeditions Sails 108- to 486-passenger ships, including a carbon-neutral cruise on *Ocean Diamond*. Snowshoeing is free, while camping, kayaking, skiing and climbing are offered for a fee. *(www.quarkexpeditions.com)*

Midrange

Antarctica XXI Flies from Punta Arenas over Drake Passage to Frei Station on King George Island (1½ hours), where you transfer to a 68-passenger or 100-passenger boat for several days of cruising in the Antarctic Peninsula. *(https:// antarctica21.com)*

Flush

Aurora Expeditions *Polar Pioneer* carries 54 passengers and is equipped with Zodiacs for shore landings. Activities include scuba diving, polar snorkelling, kayaking, mountaineering, photography workshops and camping. Fly-sail expeditions are available. *(www.auroraexpeditions.com.au)*

Timing

Most cruises depart for Antarctica between November and March. In November, the ice breaks up and penguins court. December and January are peak tourism months, with up to 20 hours of sunlight each day and the warmest weather the continent will see. It's also when penguins hatch eggs and feed chicks. Penguin chicks are fledging by February and March, which is also prime time for whale watching.

A summer sunset illuminates the icy peaks of Antarctica.

King penguins are a common sight on the sub-Antarctic islands to the north of the mainland.

Captain Scott wrote that 'hut' was a misleading name for his Shore Party's base on Cape Evans, saying it was more like a house: 'the finest that has ever been erected in the polar regions.'

Best value itineraries

2 weeks

The Antarctic Peninsula is an excellent introduction to Antarctica, and is the most popular trip to the Ice. Depart from Ushuaia and spend two to three days crossing Drake Passage. Make your first landing at one of the South Shetland Islands, such as Deception Island – an active volcano with a hidden 'amphitheatre', which is home to the largest chinstrap penguin rookery in the peninsula region – or Livingston Island, with its penguins and wallowing elephant seals. Next, steam down to the peninsula and take Zodiac trips in aptly named Paradise Harbor or along the rumbling glaciers above Neko Harbor. Then head to the museum at Port Lockroy. Homeward bound, keep an eye out for Cape Horn off port side.

3 weeks

After leaving the peninsula, head east to the South Orkney Islands, home of early sealers, whalers and bases. Next, cruise past the lonely, wave-thrashed Shag Rocks while looking for their eponymous birdlife. Your first South Georgia landing is likely to be at Grytviken, home to an abandoned whaling station, museum and Ernest Shackleton's grave. Other South Georgia highlights include St Andrews Bay and Salisbury Plain, where you can watch the antics of king penguins by the thousands. On the way back to Ushuaia, call in at the Falkland Islands.

①

© Philip Lee Harvey / Lonely Planet

PERU

Machu Picchu

Astonishing ancient ruins are one thing, but when you place them amid a backdrop of forested mountains spiking up from deep Andean valleys, you set the stage for an epic adventure.

The so-called Lost City of the Incas, Machu Picchu was never discovered by Spanish conquerors and lay abandoned for centuries until American explorer Hiram Bingham arrived on the scene in 1911. Part of the enduring appeal is reaching this hilltop citadel along the route its ancient inhabitants once used. The four-day Inca Trail takes you through dense cloud forests, over three oxygen-thin Andean passes, past several minor Incan ruins and into remote Quechua communities of potato farmers and llama drovers.

Upon arrival at Machu Picchu, you'll find a grand complex of ceremonial plazas and ornate temples shrouded in mist and blanketed in lush vegetation. Terraces (some of which are being cultivated again) spill down steep cliffs overlooking a U-shaped curve in the Río Urubamba. Nearby, crowds fight for the chance to climb Wayna Picchu, the looming mountain at the back of the ruins, for the ultimate condor's-eye view of this awe-inspiring city. We may never know with certainty what the Inca did at Machu Picchu, so your imagination can run amok as you stare down at the masterpiece of a once-great civilisation.

Travel

International
To reach Machu Picchu, you first need to catch a plane to Cuzco's Alejandro Velasco Astete International Airport. For travellers arriving from outside South America, this typically means a transfer in Lima, which receives numerous daily flights from North America and Europe. LATAM is the largest carrier that operates in Peru and it offers the most international connections.

Regional
From Cuzco, the only way for non-hikers to reach the service town of Aguas Calientes (and access Machu Picchu) is via train (three hours). Peru Rail operates the flagship service, with many daily departures from Estación Poroy, 20 minutes outside Cuzco. Inca Rail has three daily departures from the Sacred Valley town of Ollantaytambo, which you can reach via a cheap *combi* (minivan). From Aguas Calientes, frequent buses for Machu Picchu (25 minutes) depart from a ticket office along the main road from 5.30am to 3.30pm. Otherwise, it's a steep walk of 5 miles (8km).

Stay

Shoestring
Mamá Simona Your best bet for hostel digs in Aguas Calientes is this stylish spot featuring mixed and female dorms with raw wood furnishings, lockers, attached bathrooms and TVs. *(Dorm beds from S46/US$14; www.mamasimona.com)*

Flush
Sanctuary Lodge Machu Picchu Run by Belmond, this exclusive hotel has one feature no other can match: location (it's the only place right at Machu Picchu). Attention is impeccable and rooms are exceedingly comfortable. *(Rooms from US$1600; www.sanctuarylodgehotel.com)*

Eat

Shoestring
Mapacho Rabidly friendly, this street-side cafe in Aguas Calientes is popular with the backpacking set (perhaps it's all the craft beer on offer). Try the *lomo saltado* (beef stir-fried with onions, tomatoes, potatoes and chilli). *(Mains from S28/US$8.35; www.mapacho.pe)*

Midrange
Indio Feliz Hospitality is the strong suit of French cook Patrik at this multi-award-winning restaurant, but the food does not disappoint. The set menu (S78/US$23) is extremely good value for a decadent dinner. *(Mains from S34/US$10; www.indiofeliz.com)*

Timing

High season is late May until early September, with June to August being the busiest months.

A visit midweek during the rainy season guarantees you more room to breathe, especially during February, when the Inca Trail is closed. Avoiding the crowds has become harder than ever, especially since visitors are largely expected to walk a set route through the ruins, instead of spontaneously wandering.

Above the clouds: construction started on the site in the 15th century.

Traditionally clothed Quechua people.

Admire the impressive Incan stonemasonry at Machu Picchu.

A demonstration of Incan weaving.

Best value itineraries

4 days
The most famous hike in South America, the four-day Inca Trail is the ultimate way to approach Machu Picchu. Although the total distance is only about 25 miles (40km), the ancient trail laid by the Incas from the Sacred Valley to the hilltop citadel winds its way up and down and around the mountains, snaking over three Andean passes en route. The views of snowy mountain peaks, distant rivers and ranges, and cloud forests flush with orchids are stupendous – and walking from one cliff-hugging pre-Columbian ruin to the next is a mystical and unforgettable experience.

7 days
Spend three extra days acclimatising for the trek in the city of Cuzco. Kick things off at Mercado San Pedro, then get cultured in some of the city's many museums. Museo Quijote and the Museo Histórico Regional are highly recommended for fine art; Museo de Arte Popular for folksy art; and the Museo Inka for pre-conquest Peruvian artefacts. The following day, see the most imposing relics left by the Incas and the Spanish conquistadors, respectively, at Qorikancha and La Catedral. On the last day, walk through artsy San Blas up to the impressive fortress of Sacsaywamán and check out the nightly music and dance show at the Centro Qosqo de Arte Nativo.

Marble Caves

Imagine if the bold brush strokes of Van Gogh's *The Starry Night* were crystallised into solid marble and placed in a fairy-tale cave next to a turquoise lake.

Now picture yourself kayaking into that cave in the early morning hours, contorting your body around arching columns to gaze in awe at the cavern walls. As the low sun enters the caves, the water forms a perfect mirror. You look down at the reflection, then arch back to follow the striations as they bend their way towards the roof above. To enter these marble caves is to experience the sensation you might have if you could travel into the bowels of a gemstone.

This marvellous site was formed over thousands of years by waves crashing against calcium carbonate. It claims a privileged spot along the cliff-lined shores of Chile's Lago General Carrera, where freezing glacier-fed waters bear a deceptive Caribbean hue. Reaching the lake means travelling several hours down the bumpy contours of the Carretera Austral (Southern Highway). It's the only artery connecting the isolated communities of Northern Patagonia to the wider world and, like the caves themselves, provides the kind of astonishing imagery fit for the canvas of an artistic visionary.

Travel

International
The regional capital of Coyhaique is the closest city to the Marble Caves with an airport. Both LATAM and Sky Airline offer a few daily flights connecting it to the Chilean capital of Santiago. From Coyhaique, it's another five hours down the Carretera Austral to Puerto Río Tranquilo, the base for trips out to the Marble Caves.

Regional
A few daily buses between Coyhaique and Cochrane will drop passengers off in Puerto Río Tranquilo. Car rental in Coyhaique is expensive and availability is limited in summer. However, it's a popular option as public transport along the Carretera Austral is infrequent.

Stay

$ Shoestring
Camping Pudu Near Puerto Río Tranquilo, this beach-side campground offers hot showers, laundry service, tourist info and even a sauna. *(Campsites per person CH$8000/US$12)*

$$ Midrange
Explora Sur Right on the water, these smart, modern rooms with central heating are a comfortable and toasty choice. A shared balcony overlooks the lake. The lodging also offers boat trips to the Marble Caves directly from its private dock. *(Rooms from CH$45,000/US$66; www.explorasur.cl)*

$$$ Flush
El Puesto This smart 10-room hotel pampers with woollen slippers, hand-woven throws and rockers. There's even a swing set for kids. English-speaking owners Francisco and Tamara also run reputable kayaking tours to the Marble Caves. *(Rooms from US$168; www.elpuesto.cl)*

Eat

$ Shoestring
Cerveceria Rio Tranquilo A welcoming pub that makes beer on site, which is served with large plates of *chorrillana*: a bomb of fries with meat or fried onions and peppers topped with a few fried eggs. *(Craft beers from CH$3000/US$4.40)*

$$ Midrange
Donde Kike The small cafe in front of the gas station does decent Chilean classics – from soups to meat or fish with rice and potatoes – with the limited ingredients that arrive in the region. *(Meals from CH$6000/US$8.75)*

$$$ Flush
Mate y Truco This cheerful cafe redeems the dining scene with pizza, homemade gnocchi and steak with morel-mushroom sauce. It's a two-woman show, so chill with a local microbrew or espresso while you wait. *(Mains from CH$8000/US$12)*

Timing

●
Patagonia heats up after a long winter in November and stays busy with tourists till March. Crowds peak in January and February when the weather's warm and the days are long. You'll find the best bus connections on the Carretera Austral at this time, as well as Festival Costumbrista, which honours the region's pioneer culture in small towns near the Marble Caves.

●
Public transportation tapers off in the winter when some hotels close.

The 'Marble Chapels' in General Carrera Lake take on a blue hue from the waters below.

Running the Futaleufú River in Patagonia, which is fed by glacial waters, is for experts only.

Beginners can safely take a rented kayak into the Marble Chapels after some tuition.

Best value itineraries

3 days
Ranking among the world's ultimate road trips, the Carretera Austral (Southern Highway) runs 770 miles (1240km) alongside ancient forests, glaciers, pioneer farmsteads, turquoise rivers and the crashing Pacific. Pick up the trail in Coyhaique, Patagonia's de facto capital of craft beer. From here, wind your way south to Parque Nacional Cerro Castillo, a sprawling 1800 sq km park with fine hiking in southern beech forest and open high-alpine terrain. Zigzag through a desolate, volcano-scarred landscape over to Puerto Río Tranquilo and the Marble Caves. Head out in a kayak to explore this wonder in the calm morning hours, then spend the afternoon driving into the Valle Exploradores for memorable views of the Northern Patagonian Ice Field.

10 days
With more time you can begin your journey further north in Puerto Montt at the start of the Carretera Austral. Catch a car ferry over to Parque Nacional Pumalín to enjoy verdant rainforest hikes and a climb to the steaming crater of Volcán Chaitén. Then ramble down the Carretera Austral to Futaleufú for stunning rural vistas and heart-pumping white water. Check out the hot-spring options near Puyuhuapi or camp under the hanging glacier at Parque Nacional Queulat. Coyhaique is the next major hub, from which you can follow the three-day itinerary.

VENEZUELA

Angel Falls

Angel Falls isn't one to brag, but at a height of 979m, and with an uninterrupted plunge of 807m, it is kind of a big deal.

Reaching earth's highest waterfall involves at least one modern plane and one rudimentary canoe. There is no road connecting it to the wider world, which is just as well as it keeps crowds at bay. When you finally set your eyes on the falls, after canoeing in from the remote indigenous village of Canaima, you find a sky-scraping river that has carved a ribbon-thin path through a Jurassic wilderness. Twice the height of the Empire State Building – and 15 times that of Niagara Falls – it dominates the landscape and is audaciously tall, demanding your utmost attention.

The fact that Angel Falls barrels over a heart-shaped tepui (sandstone-capped mesa) into a place known as Devil's Canyon only ups the intrigue. No visit to Venezuela's star attraction is complete without a night in a hammock at the base of the falls, watching as the tumbling torrent takes on an amber glow at sunset. An invigorating early morning shower in one of the lower cascades prepares you for further adventures into the sharply hewn valleys and virgin rainforests of the greater Parque Nacional Canaima.

© Vadim Petrakov / Shutterstock

© robertharding / Alamy Stock Photo

Travel

International

The waterfall is in a distant, lush wilderness. The village of Canaima, about 31 miles (50km) northwest, is the major gateway to the falls. Canaima doesn't have a road link to the rest of the country either, but is accessed by numerous small planes from Ciudad Bolívar and Puerto Ordaz. Most international visitors will first touch down in Caracas.

Regional

Almost everyone arrives in Canaima on an all-inclusive tour, as it's not really worth the hassle or negligible savings to try to arrange it independently. Multi-day packages typically include flights, transfers, food, accommodation and the trip to Angel Falls. Simply turning up in Canaima without a tour booked is unwise.

Stay

Shoestring

Posada Wey Tepuy The cheapest bed in town, this simple place also provides some of the lowest-priced meals for guests. It's opposite the old school in the south part of Canaima. *(Rooms per person from US$8)*

Midrange

Posada Morichal This attractively set out *posada* (guesthouse), moments from Canaima's landing strip, is nestled in well-tended gardens. It has nine comfortable and clean rooms with traditional-style wooden fittings, rattan ceilings, hot water and pleasant patios. *(Rooms from US$55)*

Flush

Tepuy Lodge This comfortable place on the lagoon shore is both small and intimate, while also being professionally run. The 10 rooms are in thatched huts and share wonderful gardens. *(Room and board per person US$70)*

Eat

Shoestring

Mentanai This little burger and sandwich grill inside Campamento Churúm, in the heart of Canaima's indigenous community, has a pool table and a bar serving beer and Cuba Libres. *(Mains from US$2)*

Shoestring

Bar Morichal This is as raucous as Canaima's nightlife gets: a pleasant bar with a spectacular view of the waterfalls on the lagoon where locals and tourists alike gather at sundown to drink cold beers and cocktails. *(Beers from US$1)*

Timing

The amount of water going over Angel Falls depends on the season. In the dry months (January to May), it can be pretty faint – just a thin ribbon of water fading into mist before it reaches the bottom. Boat access is impossible in the driest times. In the rainy season, particularly in the wettest months (August and September), the waterfall is a spectacular cascade of plummeting water, but rain and clouds can often obscure the view.

With a plunge of almost a kilometre, Angel Falls will wow any visitor.

The forested cliffs of Parque Nacional Canaima are full of other waterfalls and wonders to view, and it's an adventure to explore.

St Thomas Cathedral in Ciudad Bolívar, the state capital.

Best value itineraries

3 days

Start the trip with a flight to Canaima, where you can enjoy the Laguna de Canaima, a broad blue expanse framed by a palm-tree beach, a dramatic series of seven picture-postcard waterfalls and a backdrop of anvil-like tepui mountains. The next day, set off for the short boat trip over to Angel Falls. Be sure to hike behind some of the cascades to experience the hammering curtains of water, and don't miss walking up to the viewpoint, which is truly spectacular. Do as most visitors do and stay overnight in a hammock at one of the camps near the base of the falls. The trip upriver, the surrounding area and the experience of staying at the camp are as memorable as the waterfall itself. Return to Canaima the following day to catch a flight out.

10 days

If you have more time you can start your trip in the colonial city of Ciudad Bolívar and explore the historical district along the mighty Río Orinoco. From there, fly to Canaima, take the boat tour to Angel Falls and spend the night in the jungle. Then get some sand in your shoes as you sunbathe and snorkel in the islands of Los Roques or along the virgin beaches of the Península de Paria.

①

© Richard Waters / 500px

Tikal

With towering steep-sided temples, broad causeways and grand plazas, there's nothing run-of-the-mill about the ruins of Tikal.

Tikal was once one of the most powerful kingdoms of the Maya civilisation, reaching its apogee between 200 and 900 AD. Ambling past its many temples, which rise more than 40m above the Guatemalan rainforest, you can imagine what it was like when this city was populated by dynastic rulers, fierce warriors and thousands of tireless builders. Tread lightly and you'll hear the faint patter of its modern residents (agoutis, coatis and spider monkeys) rustling beneath the trees.

The sunrise hike to Templo IV – the second-highest pre-Columbian building in the western hemisphere – is the stuff of travellers' legends. A steep wooden staircase leads to the top, where you have the perfect vantage point to watch the tangerine sun cast a spotlight on faraway temple tops peeking above the canopy. In these early morning hours, when the air has the rich, dewy smell of damp soil, the guttural roar of howler monkeys echoes through the forest. By afternoon, when the sun has baked everything (skin included) dry, you can find royal flycatchers, keel-billed toucans and emerald toucanets feeding in the foliage. At Tikal, the 21st-century flora and fauna is as impressive as the ancient man-made marvels.

Travel

International
The closest cities to Tikal with sizeable airports are Belize City and Guatemala City. Both are easily accessed from most major North American hubs, though the latter is the only one that receives flights from Europe and South America.

Regional
Flores lies about 35 miles (60km) southwest of Tikal and is the main tourism node of Guatemala's Petén Department. Flores has the only functioning civil airport in the country outside of Guatemala City, from which it receives two daily connections. There are also daily flights over from Belize City, though the journey is less than five hours by bus. Several daily buses connect Flores with Tikal.

Stay

Shoestring
Jaguar Inn The inn of choice for young independent travellers has duplex and quad bungalows with thatched roofs and hammocks on the porches, plus tents on a platform for rent. *(Tents from Q115/US$15; www.jaguartikal.com)*

Midrange
Jungle Lodge Nearest of the hotels to the site entrance, this was originally built to house archaeologists working at Tikal. Self-contained bungalows, plus a bank of cheaper units, are well spaced throughout rambling, jungle grounds. *(Rooms from Q360/US$47; www.junglelodgetikal.com)*

Flush
Tikal Inn Built in the 1960s, this resort-style lodging offers standard rooms and thatched bungalows alongside the pool and lawn, with porches out front. All are simple, spacious and comfy. *(Rooms from Q500/US$65; www.tikalinn.com)*

Eat

Shoestring
Restaurante El Mirador Refreshingly not aimed at foreign travellers, this traditional eatery along Flores' Parque Central does toothsome home cookin' with such hearty options as *caldo de res* (beef stew). *(Set menu Q25/US$3.25)*

Midrange
Comedor Tikal This is one of a series of little open-air *comedores* (basic cafeterias) along the right-hand side of the access road to Tikal. Pasta and hamburgers are among the offerings. *(Mains from Q50/US$6.50)*

Flush
Antojitos Mexicanos Every evening in Flores these characters fire up the grill and char steak, chicken and pork ribs of exceptional quality. The speciality is *puyazo* (sirloin) swathed with garlic sauce. *(Grilled meats from Q60/US$7.80)*

Timing

The ruins here can be slick from rain and organic material, especially during the wet season (June to October).

Seeing the sunrise from Templo IV at the west end of the main site is possible from about October to March, but to enter the park before or after visiting hours you must purchase an additional ticket for Q100 (US$13), as this is not covered in the normal park entry.

Sunrise over the rainforest reveals the tops of Tikal's towers.

Temple V, once the highest building in the Mayan world, sits at the centre of the site and dates from 700 AD.

A Mayan shaman performs traditional rites.

Best value itineraries

3 days
Start in the regional tourist hub of Flores, a quaint small town on an island in the Lago de Petén Itzá. Spend your first day exploring the colourful homes of its cobbled streets, then catch the first morning bus over to Tikal. Spend the entire day summoning your inner Indiana Jones as you stroll down the broad causeways. Though many plazas have been cleared of vines, and temples uncovered and partially restored, as you walk from one building to another you'll still pass beneath a dense canopy of rainforest. Stay overnight at Tikal itself before returning to Flores to catch a flight or bus out.

10 days
While in the Flores/Tikal area, make time to take in further impressive Mayan sites such as Yaxhá and Uaxactún. Then head southwest to the relaxed riverside town of Sayaxché, which is at the centre of another group of intriguing Mayan sites: Ceibal, Aguateca and Dos Pilas. The road south from Sayaxché is paved all the way to Chisec and Cobán, jumping-off points for a whole series of pristine natural wonders, such as jungle-ringed Laguna Lachuá, the Grutas de Lanquín cave system and the turquoise lagoons and waterfalls of Semuc Champey. Finally, make your way back to Guatemala City for your flight home.

Mediterranean Sea

SYRIA

LEBANON

**Temple Mount &
Dead Sea**

Petra

ISRAEL
& THE
PALESTINIAN
TERRITORIES

JORDAN

IRAQ

Caspian
Sea

UZBEKISTAN

Door to Hell

TURKMENISTAN

KAZAKHSTAN

KYRGYZSTAN

TAJIKISTAN

**Naqsh-e
Jahan Square**

IRAN

AFGHANISTAN

KUWAIT

The
Gulf

SAUDI ARABIA

BAHRAIN

QATAR

UNITED
ARAB
EMIRATES

Burj Khalifa

Golden Temple

PAKISTAN

**Punakha Dzong &
Taktshang Goemba**

NEPAL

Taj Mahal

**Mt
Everest**

Red Sea

OMAN

**Ghats of
Varanasi**

INDIA

BANGLADESH

YEMEN

Gulf of Aden

Arabian Sea

**Temples
of Hampi**

Bay of Bengal

SRI
LANKA

MALDIVES

INDIAN OCEAN

Asia & Middle East

THAILAND

Grand Palace

The full, 43-syllable name for Bangkok describes the Grand Palace as akin to the 'heavenly abode where the reincarnated god reigns', so expect something special from Thailand's most important palace.

The residence of the kings of Siam since 1782, this humble crib covers more than 100 buildings, crowned by a veritable garden of golden stupas and Khmer-style *prangs* (temple towers). On sunny days the palace gleams like a jewel box, adorned with a riot of bling. It can be hard to move for all the gold trim, mirrors and mosaics (bring shades or be blinded).

If the palace looks a little like a monastery, that's no accident; the kings of Thailand were revered as reincarnations of Hindu gods. As you wander the gilded cloisters, you'll jostle for space with pilgrims laden with lotus blooms, incense sticks and other offerings, filling the air with perfume. At the heart of the palace compound is the most sacred *wát* (temple) of them all, Wat Phra Kaew, the eternal resting place of the revered Emerald Buddha. This miniature carving of the seated Buddha bounced from one Southeast Asian nation to another before coming to rest in Bangkok, a reminder that in Asia powerful things sometimes come in small packages.

Travel

International

Bangkok is one of Asia's busiest hubs, with hundreds of flights landing daily from Asia, Australia, Europe and the Gulf. Gleaming Suvarnabhumi International Airport is the main focus for long-haul arrivals, while ageing Don Mueang International Airport hosts the budget carriers. To cut costs, consider flying to another regional hub and connecting with one of Asia's many low-cost airlines. Alternatively, vans and buses buzz across to Thailand's neighbours, and international trains run south to Kuala Lumpur and Singapore.

Regional

With Bangkok's notorious traffic jams, getting around is easiest on the elevated BTS Skytrain or the underground Metro. Travel by road is slow, but Bangkok's taxis are inexpensive and blissfully air-conditioned. Considering the traffic and fumes, the city's famous *túk-túks* are more atmospheric than practical. By far the most pleasurable way to get around is by boat; longtail river taxis buzz along Bangkok's *klorng* (canals), and ferries zip along the larger canals and the Chao Phraya River.

Stay

Shoestring

Chern This sleek hostel serves up minimalist-style, ice-white interiors and wide-open spaces for travellers who want a boutique vibe on a backpacker budget. *(Dorms from 400B/ US$12, rooms from 1400B/US$43; www.chernbangkok.com)*

Flush

Mandarin Oriental Every Asian capital has its grand dame hotel, and in Bangkok an old-world elegance spills from the Mandarin Oriental's Garden and Author's Wings. *(Rooms from 14,000B/US$425; www.mandarinoriental.com)*

Eat

Shoestring

Err Street-food vendors, assemble! South of the Grand Palace, Err serves up a delicious sampling platter of Bangkok street treats, as well as microbrewery beers to wash it down. *(Mains from 65B/US$1.98; www.errbkk.com)*

Flush

Namh Aussie wunderkind David Thompson's flagship modern Thai eatery is Michelin-starred and regularly fêted as one of the best restaurants in the world. *(Mains from 310B/US$9.40; www.comohotels.com)*

Timing

November to March is arguably the best time of the year to visit as the weather is relatively cool and dry, although it also means crowds and inflated rates.

Early morning is the best time to evade the crowds at the Grand Palace, but the afternoon offers the best light, as the sinking sun saturates the colours of the murals and mosaics. After the palace gates close, head to the riverbank and ride the tiny ferry to Wat Arun to watch sunset pick out the stupas and *prangs* in burnished gold.

The Grand Palace features lawns, gardens and courtyards among the buildings.

Wat Phra Kaew, also known as the Temple of the Emerald Buddha, is at the heart of the palace complex; its ground was consecrated in 1782.

The classic architecture of Wat Arun, Temple of the Dawn.

A giant statue at Wat Arun.

Best value itineraries

3–4 days

If you've only a few days, it pays to stay local. Set aside the whole of days one and two to explore the iconic Grand Palace and pay your respects at Wat Pho and other landmark *wát* (monasteries) scattered around Ratanakosin island. As dusk falls, ride the wind-cooled riverboats of the Chao Phraya Express to reach towering Wat Arun and Chinatown, with its flickering neon, gleaming shopfronts and fabulous food. Devote day three to a Thai cooking course, then spend day four cruising the malls and markets of Sukhumvit and Siam Square for tasteful knick-knacks to haul home.

7–10 days

A week or more gives you time to really explore. Whatever happens, you want to be in Bangkok at the weekend for the mercantile chaos of Chatuchak Weekend Market. Spend several days on Ratanakosin, but dig into the hidden corners and the bustling lanes along the Chao Phraya River, and cross the city by riverboat to the Thai-timbered Jim Thomson House. Devote a day to exploring Ko Kret, the potter's island in the far north of the city, then take the train to Ayuthya, to roam the ruins of Thailand's former capital. Save the last day for a mobile feast in Bangkok's street-food markets.

UNITED ARAB EMIRATES

Burj Khalifa

If the world's tallest building seems a little brash and ostentatious, that comes with the territory. Ever since Dubai began its stratospheric rise in the 1960s, the emirate has been reaching for the skies, literally in the case of the Burj Khalifa.

Gazing on this astonishing piece of engineering, towering like a lightning rod over Dubai's skyscraper-studded skyline, you almost wonder if the Burj's architects have gone too far, challenging heaven itself, like the builders of the mythical Tower of Babel. In fact, the Burj's gargantuan proportions are hard to gauge at street level. To really appreciate the full stature of this 828m behemoth, you need to look from some distance away, or ride the elevator to the viewing decks on the 124th and 148th floors. Only then will the centuries-old Islamic principles of the tower's construction – a futuristic nod to the spiral minaret of the Great Mosque at Samarra – become apparent.

To secure a spot on either deck, you'll need to book online well ahead of time, but the minutes counting down to sunset can normally be relied on to deliver that Saturn-V-on-take-off view you were hoping for. There's no better place to contemplate Dubai's meteoric expansion from desert outpost to billionaire city state.

1

2

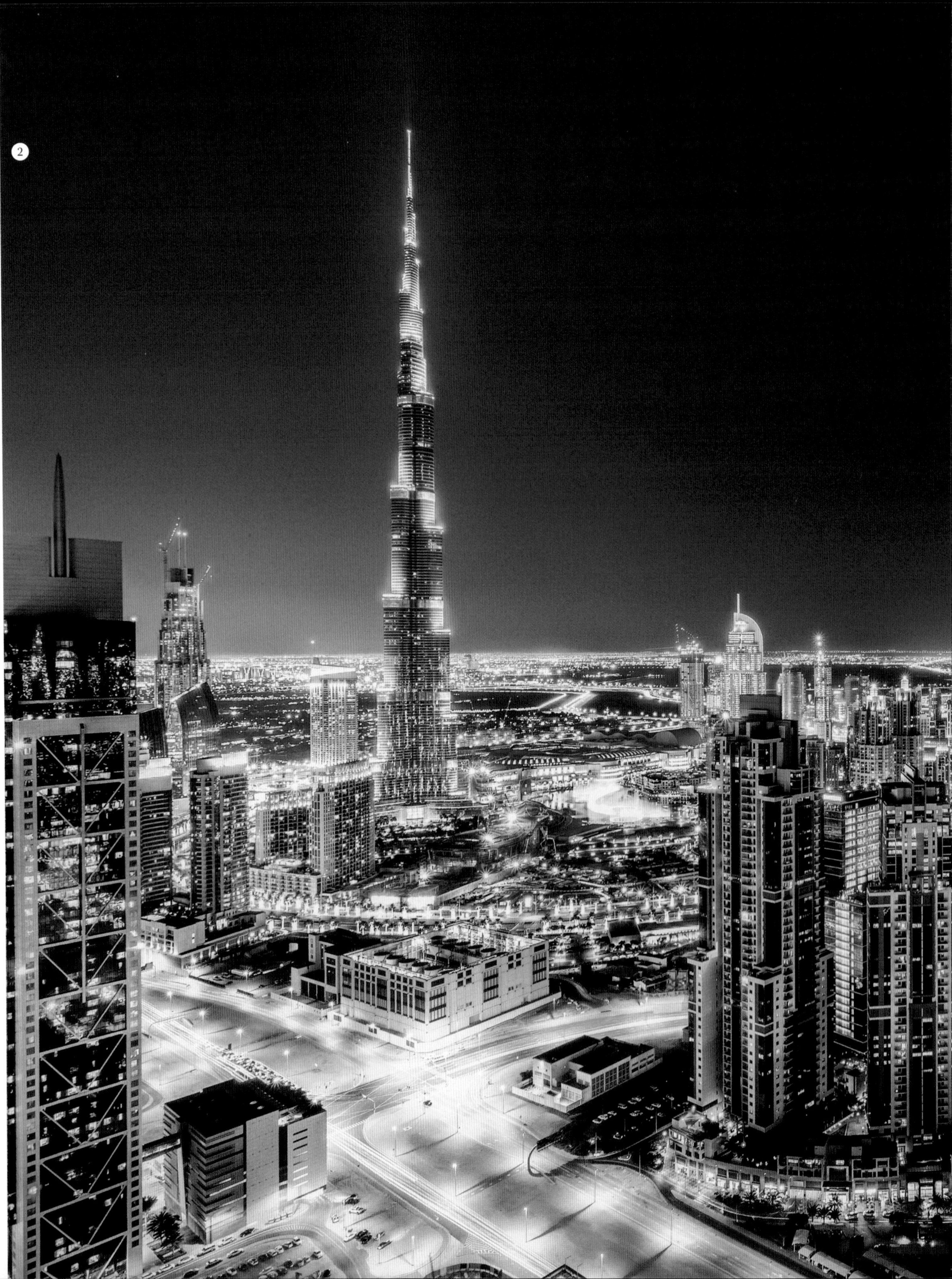

Travel

International
Dubai International Airport is the Middle East's busiest hub, and the busiest passenger airport in the world. Flights land day and night from almost everywhere in the world, half of them operated by Dubai's well-regarded state carrier, Emirates. With excellent connections to Europe and the Americas in one direction, and to Africa, Asia and Australia in the other, it's easy to slot in a visit to Dubai on the way to somewhere else.

Regional
Having reached the gleaming international terminal at Dubai, the only real hassle you have to deal with en route to the city is the heat when you step out into the street. The air-conditioned metro will buy you some time before you have to face the thermometer, with regular services from 5.30am to midnight or later (from 10am on Friday). At other times there's a 24-hour bus service, or taxis, charging reasonably pocket-friendly rates.

Stay

$ Shoestring
Ibis Mall of the Emirates Cheap beds are hard to find in Dubai, but this sparkling clean chain hotel has a prime location – near the cathedral to shopping that is the Mall of the Emirates. *(Rooms from Dhs320/US$87; www.ibis.com)*

$$$ Flush
Grosvenor House One of the pioneers from the days before skyscraper hotels really took off in Dubai, Grosvenor House still offers some of the best rooms, restaurants and watering holes in the city. *(Rooms from Dhs1000/US$272; www.grosvenorhouse-dubai.com)*

Eat

$ Shoestring
Ravi It's cash only at this legendary Jumeirah Pakistani grill and curry house, frequented by everyone from city cabbies to Dubai high-fliers. *(Mains from Dhs8/US$2.20)*

$$$ Flush
Pierchic Set atop a historic wooden pier in Jumeirah with front-row views of the Burj Al Arab and serving some of the best seafood in the city. *(Mains from Dhs125/US$34)*

Timing

Dubai has a classic Arabian desert climate, with incendiary summers and a hot but manageable winter. From November to March, temperatures hover just above 30°C, prime time for the theme parks, beaches and desert trips. However, the theme parks in particular can be mobbed. Prices dip from June to September, but the mercury climbs above 40°C, driving everyone indoors to the air-conditioning.

Above the clouds: Burj Khalifa's design was actually inspired by a desert flower, the spider lily, not science fiction.

It features 26,000 glass panels that reflect the lights of the city below.

The view over downtown Dubai from the tower.

Best value itineraries

4 days
Four days is the perfect length for a Dubai stopover. Book a place on the viewing decks at the Burj Khalifa well ahead of a visit, and make time to view the tower from other vantage points – the Madinat Jumeirah marketplace and Jumeirah Beach are top spots for photos. A day of mall shopping is almost mandatory and there's enough in the Dubai Mall to fill a day or more. For a reminder of what Dubai grew from, wander the Al Fahidi Historic District or cruise on Dubai Creek, then spend the last day in the desert on a camel safari or dune-bashing 4WD trip.

7–10 days
With a week or more, there'll be time to relax by the beach, as well as tour the sights. After the obligatory visit to the Burj, malls and Al Fahidi Historic District, set aside a day or two on the sand. Swish resorts such as the Jumeirah Beach charge steep rates for day passes, but the sand is just as sparkly along Kite Beach, Jumeirah Public Beach or JBR Beach in Jumeirah. Continue the sand theme on a self-drive trip to the dunes, then experience thrills of a different kind at a Dubai theme park – IMG Worlds of Adventure and Wild Wadi top the rankings.

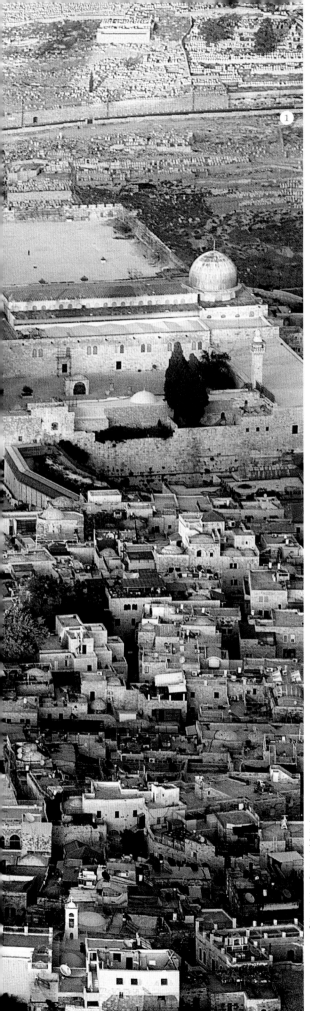

© Yann Arthus-Bertrand / Getty Images

ISRAEL & THE PALESTINIAN TERRITORIES

Temple Mount

Located in Jerusalem's Old City, this ancient site is steeped in history so profound that it has been a cornerstone in Judaism and Islam since their inceptions. That fact also makes it one of the most divisive pieces of land on the planet.

Inside feels like a world away from the cacophony and congestion of the Old City's alleys, and it sets the tone for both religious reverence and silent reflection. Walk on its open plaza among the cypress trees and contemplate its early beginnings that lie beneath. The Talmud states that Har HaBāyit (Temple Mount) is the site where God gathered earth to form Adam, and the Bible tells of David erecting an altar here, on which Solomon built Judaism's First Temple. That sacred temple and its successor were both destroyed, by the Babylonians and Romans respectively.

The Islamic heart of Al Haram Ash Sharif (The Noble Sanctuary), as it's known to Muslims, is more front and centre. The Dome of the Rock, which has a gold-plated top that dominates the skyline, has been one of Islam's most important shrines since 691 AD. The rock slab it protects speaks to the site's tangled history: to Jews, it was used by Abraham to prepare his son for sacrifice; to Muslims, it is the place from where the Prophet Muhammad ascended to heaven.

It's a place of conflict, but wonder too.

Travel

International
Most travellers reach Jerusalem by bus or train from Tel Aviv, or by bus or *sherut* (shared taxi) from Ben Gurion Airport, which is 32 miles (52km) northwest of Jerusalem. It's also possible, though time-consuming, to travel overland from Jordan across the Allenby (King Hussein) Bridge.

Regional
There are four major entry points from which to walk into Jerusalem's Old City: Jaffa Gate, Damascus Gate, Dung Gate and Lions' Gate. The light rail stops at City Hall (from where it's a short walk to Jaffa Gate or New Gate) and Damascus Gate. Bus 1 and 3 from the Central Bus Station arrive near Dung Gate and the Western Wall.

Stay

$

Shoestring
Abraham Hostel This lively downtown option has the traveller covered – 24-hour reception, nearby public transport, laundry, shared kitchen and a sweet bar and lounge. *(Dorm beds from 85NIS/US$23.50; abrahamhostels.com)*

$$

Midrange
Hashimi Hotel An oasis in the Old City, this hotel in a 400-year-old building has light-flooded, floral-patterned rooms (ask for a corner room with a view). *(Rooms from US$75; www.thehashimihotel.com)*

$$$

Flush
Christ Church Guesthouse This wonderful destination can offer period atmosphere, multilingual staff, a prime Old City location and a garden setting. *(Rooms from 430NIS/US$120; www.cmj-israel.org/christ-church-guest-house)*

Eat

$

Shoestring
Abu Shukri So popular, it has spawned many imitators. Enjoy rich, smooth hummus – topped with chickpeas, tahina, *fuul* (stewed fava beans) or pine nuts – with crunchy veg, pita bread and falafel. *(Hummus 20NIS/US$5.50)*

$$

Midrange
Abu Kamel In a cave-like corner of the Muslim Quarter by Mouristan Market you'll find specials such as *makloubeh* (roast vegetables, spices, rice and meat) or *quzi* (peas, carrots, rice and meat). *(Mains from 35NIS/US$9.70)*

$$$

Flush
Machneyuda Is it New York comfort food, Italian fine dining or haute cuisine? This superb restaurant owned by three of Israel's most acclaimed chefs has won plenty of local acclaim for its playful menu. *(Mains from 86NIS/US$23.84; www.machneyuda.co.il)*

Timing

April and May are pleasant and sunny, but be prepared for crowds and hefty hotel rates. Temperatures sizzle in July and August when the calendar is packed with festivals and events. September and October have excellent, mild weather.

Note that you should take religious holidays (and the weekly Shabbat) into consideration: many sites, shops, bars and restaurants will be closed, and accommodation prices can be much higher.

1

An aerial view of Temple Mount, showing Al-Aqsa Mosque (grey dome), one of Islam's holiest sites with Muslims believing Muhammed was transported here from Mecca, and the Dome of the Rock (gold dome).

2

The Dome of the Rock shrine on Temple Mount.

3

The Cotton Merchants' Gate connects Old Jerusalem with Temple Mount.

Best value itineraries

3–4 days
Start at Temple Mount before meandering to the majestic Church of the Holy Sepulchre. Next, wander the souq and alleyways of the Christian and Muslim quarters. Finish the day with the mesmerising sound and light show at the Tower of David. On day two check out the Dead Sea Scrolls at the Israel Museum, then take in the wonder of the Western Wall before exploring the Jewish Quarter. On day three, visit Yad Vashem for its sobering and enlightening exhibitions about the Holocaust. Conclude your tour in the City of David, one of the city's most significant (though controversial) archaeological sites.

7–10 days
Jerusalem is the starting point of so much Middle Eastern history. After experiencing Temple Mount and the city's other wonders, make for the biblical towns of Bethlehem and Jericho by public transport. In Israel's north, timeless Akko and the world-class ruins of Caesarea are worth as much time as you can give them. On your way back, don't miss Tel Aviv, a lively place to let your hair down and discover the hedonistic side of Israeli life. Its antithesis, the Negev desert, is a wilderness area that you simply don't expect to find in this ever-crowded corner of the earth.

© eFesenko / Shutterstock

© Mike Rowbottom / 500px

© john spies / john13 / 500px

Hang Son Doong

Have you ever wanted to step through a doorway into another world? Vietnam's Han Son Doong, the world's largest cave, offers just such an opportunity.

Eroded by millennia of monsoon rains, this massive system of caves and passages is a landscape for giants, the kind of thing Jack might have spied at the top of the beanstalk. In the largest chamber, which has room enough for a fleet of Boeing 747s, stalactites tumble from a ceiling 200m above the corrugated limestone floor. The largest stalagmites are as tall as tower blocks, and eroded furrows formed by vanished rivers overflow with cave pearls crafted by calcite coalescing around grains of sand. Had he ever seen it, Jules Verne would surely have been in raptures. In places, collapsed sections of roof admit celestial shafts of light, illuminating silent pools and cave-floor beaches where visitors set up camp for the night. They also allow bursts of jungle noise to penetrate the subterranean silence.

Getting here is no easy undertaking, but that's part of Hang Son Doong's spell. You'll have to trek for days through virgin rainforest to reach the entrance to the caverns, which drips with jungle foliage like the portal to a lost world.

Travel

International
Hang Son Doong is hidden away in the jungles of Phong Nha-Ke National Park, some 30 miles (50km) inland from Dong Hoi, but the nearest international hub is in Hanoi, 310 miles (500km) to the north, which has good links to major cities in Asia, Europe and the Gulf. Domestic flights buzz between Hanoi and Dong Hoi, or you can make the journey on the coastal train line, travelling on by car to Phong Nha-Ke.

Regional
Reaching Hang Son Doong isn't as simple as getting to Phong Nha-Ke. Access to this natural wonder is tightly restricted and only one operator is permitted to arrange trips: Oxalis (www.oxalis.com.vn), based in the town of Son Trach. Having made your way to Son Trach on the park boundary, it takes four to six days of trekking to visit the cave and return to Song Trach, camping overnight in caverns along the route. The trek costs 69,800,000d/US$2995.

Stay

Shoestring
Easy Tiger A backpacker favourite, this fun hostel has tidy dorms, a pool, a garden and Son Trach's best bar, which is the ideal place to debrief after a trip to Hang Son Doong. *(Dorm beds 160,000d/US$6.87; www.easytigerhostel.com)*

Midrange
Phong Nha Farmstay Enjoy some comfort before you hit the jungle in Son Trach's original traveller hang-out. Rooms have high ceilings and balconies looking out over the paddy fields. *(Rooms from 910,000d/US$39; www.phong-nha-cave.com)*

Eat

Shoestring
D-Arts Zone You'll smell the barbecuing north-Vietnamese sausage before you see this bohemian hang-out, perfect for people-watching on Son Trach's main street. *(Meals from 50,000d/US$2.15)*

Midrange
Bomb Crater Bar A 1.8 mile (3km) bike ride from Son Trach, this aptly named bar has cold beers, a perfect river frontage and, yes, a bomb crater from the Vietnam War. *(Drinks and snacks from 50,000d/US$2.15; www.bombcraterbar.com)*

Timing

Caving is very much a weather-dependent activity. During the monsoon months from November to January, expeditions stay well clear of the caverns, which can fill suddenly with rainwater. The drier months from February to October are a much more pleasant time to be in the jungle.

●

With just one operator offering trips, and only on fixed dates, availability is limited and wise travellers book a year ahead.

A *doline* (or sinkhole) permits light into the Hang Son Doong cave. The light and water encourages plants to grow.

A caver stands on a spiral stalagmite in the cave; the system was first explored by British cavers Howard and Deb Limbert.

The entrance to the cave. Visitor numbers are limited to protect the site from overtourism.

Best value itineraries

4 days
You'll need four full days to get to Hang Son Doong and back to Son Trach, and much of your time will be spent trekking through pristine jungle and hauling yourself into and out of gaping chasms. En route you'll spend nights under canvas on sandy beaches in caves big enough to accommodate battleships. As well as exploring the wonders of Hang Son Doong, trekkers spend a night in Hang En, the third-largest cave on the planet, with its own collection of stalactites, stalagmites and underground beaches.

7–10 days
If you have more time to explore, hang out in Son Trach either side of the trek to Hang Son Doong, sipping cold beers in riverside bars and floating in an inner tube down the Son River. Local homestays can arrange bike trips, hikes and kayaking on the river, as well as trips to a string of smaller caves inside Phong Nha-Ke National Park. Ziplining into the water at Hang Toi probably tops the thrill stakes, while Paradise Cave is a cathedral of illuminated stalactites and stalagmites, reached by zigzagging boardwalks.

© Zarnell Photography / Shutterstock

INDIA

Taj Mahal

Some monuments fail to live up the hype when they are seen in the flesh, but the Taj Mahal more than justifies the superlatives.

Perhaps it's the gleaming marble, which changes tone from white to blue to orange to pink with the shifting light, before revealing itself as an intricate mosaic of semi-precious stones when viewed up close. Perhaps it's the delicate grace of its slender minarets or the astonishing symmetry of its soaring domes. Perhaps it's the tragically romantic story of its construction, by a love-sick sultan, as a mausoleum for a favourite wife lost in childbirth.

As this is the most famous building in the world, you'll have to fight through an army of visitors to get close, but the crowds do little to undermine the atmosphere of the place often described as the greatest monument ever built for love. While observing the intricate, geometrically repeating pierced marble screens, or the delicate *pietra dura* inlay of flowers and Islamic script, you'll be transfixed. Before you leave, make one more stop to fully appreciate the beauty and tragedy of the Taj – the chamber in Agra Fort where Shah Jahan was imprisoned by his zealot son, condemned to gaze out at the final resting place of his beloved Mumtaz Mahal.

Travel

International
Agra's anticipated international airport remains in the planning stage so, for the time being, the nearest hub is Delhi's Indira Gandhi International Airport, served by regular flights from Asia, Europe and the Gulf. Trains will ferry you to Agra from Delhi in a couple of hours. To shave 50 miles (80km) or so from the overland trip, consider a connecting flight to Gwalior, 60 miles (99km) from Agra.

Regional
Agra is on the fast rail line between Delhi and Varanasi, and trains such as the Shatabdi Express and Gatimaan Express will get you there in two hours or less. Travelling by bus will add an extra couple of hours sitting in traffic on the outskirts of Delhi. Having reached Agra, you'll have to navigate the crowded streets to get to the Taj, or haggle hard for a fair fare on an Agra rickshaw.

Stay

Shoestring
Tourists Rest House The friendly owners of this much-loved guesthouse have been helping travellers avoid Agra's pitfalls for generations thanks to their simple, comfortable rooms set around a plant-filled courtyard. *(Rooms from Rs720/ US$8.20; www.dontworrychickencurry.com)*

Flush
Oberoi Amarvilas Agra's top hotel provides the full maharaja experience: Mughal-influenced interior design, Taj views and every imaginable mod-con, plus a stunning pool in a fountain-filled courtyard. *(Rooms from Rs97,750/US$1338; www.oberoihotels.com)*

Eat

Shoestring
Mama Chicken This old-fashioned roadhouse in Agra's Sadar Bazar has an army of cooks churning out veg and non-veg treats from the tandoor. It's standing-room only at lunchtime. *(Mains from Rs40-440/US$0.55-6)*

Flush
Esphahan There are just two sittings at this elegant restaurant at the Oberoi Amarvilas – at 6.30pm and 9.30pm – but a reservation will get you a show-stopping north Indian feast. *(Mains from Rs 1500/US$20; www.oberoihotels.com)*

Timing

You won't regret rising early to be at the Taj when the gates open at dawn. The monument is at its best before the crowds descend, when you'll have an uninterrupted view of its marble majesty. However, morning fog can kill the views from December to January.

Just before closing time is the second-best time to visit, with sunset adding a whole new set of colours to the Taj's palette.

The Taj Mahal viewed through the arches of Mehman Khana.

Dawn is a favourite time to view the marble mausoleum and rewards early risers with beautiful light and fewer people.

The Taj Mahal backs onto the Yamuna River. It's possible to book sunrise or sunset boat trips past the wonder.

© Pete Seaward / Lonely Planet

MALAYSIA

Gunung Mulu National Park

Ask someone to describe a rainforest and they'll paint a picture of Gunung Mulu. Waterfalls thundering into hidden pools. Tropical trees stretching to impossible heights. Creepers falling in green cascades. Brown jungle rivers as wide as highways. In other words, pristine nature, alive with the songs and screeches of yet-to-be-discovered species.

Sprawling for 529 sq km over the karst mountains of northern Sarawak in Malaysian Borneo, Gunung Mulu crams all of this variety into one national park, from razor-sharp limestone pinnacles and bottomless caves to plunging gorges and rainforest rivers, all teeming with weird and wonderful wildlife. On treks through the forest, every ear strains for the barking call of a hornbill and every eye scans the foliage for the flicker of leaves that might reveal a leaping Bornean tarsier or a gangly gibbon. Isolation brings inconvenience – the most practical way into the park is by air, through the tiny airstrip at Mulu – but also splendid preservation. This is the untouched rainforest that greeted early explorers, accessible only to those willing to brave the leeches and step off the track for a dalliance with the unknown.

1

Travel

International
The nearest international airport is Brunei International at Bandar Seri Begawan, but there are no flights or road routes from Brunei to Gunung Mulu, so it makes more sense to fly into either Kuching, which has good connections to Singapore and peninsular Malaysia, or Kota Kinabalu, which receives flights from across Asia. From Kota Kinabalu and Kuching, flights buzz daily to Mulu, the tiny airport at Mulu Gunung.

Regional
Having completed all the plane changes needed to get to Mulu airport, you can walk from the terminal to the park headquarters, but minibuses and SUVs meet incoming flights, offering transfers to the park offices and local accommodation. To get deeper into the park on foot, or to enter caves inside the reserve, you'll need a licensed guide. Longboats can be hired for trips along Gunung Mulu's rivers – make arrangements with your accommodation.

Stay

Shoestring
Mulu Village About 1.8 miles (3km) from the park entrance, this family-run homestay offers bike hire, jungle treks and cooking classes, as well as plenty of other activities inside the reserve. *(Room from RM 50/US$12; www.facebook.com/muluvillage)*

Flush
Mulu Marriott Resort & Spa Melting into its surroundings, this stylish five-star place has wooden rooms around a lovely pool and its own jetty for boat trips. *(Rooms from RM 485/US$116; www.marriott.com)*

Eat

Shoestring
Good Luck Cave'fe Mulu Right outside the park gates, this is the place for a beer and a plate of fried rice at the start or end of a jungle trek. *(Mains from RM 8/US$1.90)*

Midrange
Café Mulu The park cafe is a great place for homestyle breakfasts, cold beers, Indian curries and local treats such as Mulu-style laksa and *umai* (raw-fish salad). *(Mains from RM 12/US$2.85)*

Timing

Peak season for visits to Gunung Mulu is July to September, avoiding the damp monsoon months from October to January and May to June. However, this is also the hottest time of year to trek.

The number of overnight visitors allowed into the park at any one time is limited by the authorities, so always book months ahead for serious caving trips and for treks to the Pinnacles and Gunung Mulu summit.

The karst pinnacles of Gunung Mulu can take a hike of a couple of days to reach but the journey is part of the adventure.

Clearwater Cave in Gunung Mulu National Park is thought to be the eighth longest in the world at 222km (138 miles).

Get your fix of Indiana Jones-style adventure exploring the park.

Best value itineraries

4 days
With four days to play with, you can get deep inside Gunung Mulu by boat and on foot. Book well ahead for the challenging trek to the Pinnacles, a three-day scramble over jungle trails and rocky outcrops, dropping into jungle caves and clambering up narrow gullies. On the last day, day trip out from the park headquarters by boat to show caves such as Wind Cave and Clearwater Cave (no specialist gear required), or consider a proper caving trip into the dark recesses of the vast Sarawak Chamber and Clearwater Connection caverns. Wherever you go, be ready for some challenging jungle hiking in order to reach the cave entrances.

7–10 days
A longer trip provides time to get away from the crowds who just dip into the park for the day. The four-day climb to the summit of Gunung Mulu is a classic Borneo adventure, mixing wildlife encounters, jungle camping and a pre-dawn start to catch sunrise on the mountain top. Or consider leaving Gunung Mulu on foot for the trek to Limbang, following the so-called Headhunter Trail along paths once used by tribal war parties. Before you leave, explore the caves close to the reserve headquarters by boat, on foot, and – if you feel brave enough – with ropes, a hard hat and a caving torch.

© Anders Blomqvist /Getty Images

NEPAL

Mt Everest

What's in a name? The world's highest mountain trades under three different monikers, each bestowed by a different people, reflecting their own particular outlook on the world.

To the Tibetan Buddhists who eye this mighty peak from the north, this is Chomolungma, 'Mother Goddess of the Universe'. To the Sherpa people of Solukhumbu in Nepal, the peak is Sagarmatha, 'Forehead of the Sky'. To unimaginative British colonists, this was first known as Peak B, then Peak XV, then Mt Everest. To the legions of trekkers and climbers who haul themselves up the trails that wind through the Himalaya like silver streams, this is just one hell of a big mountain.

In fact, when approached from the Nepali side, the 8848m summit is almost hidden by neighbouring Nuptse and Lhotse, hence the ritual of arising at dawn and clambering up the black-stone slopes of Kala Pattar for an uninterrupted view. But what a view! Up close, the Himalaya appear hewn by gods, gouged out of rock and ice by hands the size of cities. As you sit afterwards, with a cup of butter tea beside a yak-dung fire, the sense of touching the tallest mountain on earth will linger long after the feeling returns to your toes and fingers.

Travel

International

The most popular approach for trekkers and mountaineers is from Nepal, on foot from the airstrip at Lukla in Solukhumbu, which receives regular daily flights from Kathmandu during the trekking season from October to November and February to April. Kathmandu has air connections to Asia and the Middle East, but lack of competition keeps prices high. Coming from the Tibetan side, Lhasa is the nearest international airport, but flights only come from Kathmandu or other parts of China.

Regional

Flights zip daily from Kathmandu to the town of Lukla in season, but the route relies on good weather. As an alternative, you can trek to Lukla from either Shivalaya or Tumlingtar in about a week. Having reached Lukla, you'll need two weeks more to trek to Everest Base Camp and back via Namche Bazaar. Coming from Lhasa, it takes three days by jeep to reach Tingri, and four days trekking to reach the mountaineers' base camp on the Tibetan side.

Stay

$ Shoestring

Hotel Sherpa A sunny courtyard garden and an on-site cafe and bakery lure trekkers to this veteran trekking lodge in a prime location just outside Lukla's miniature airport. (Rooms from Rs 300/US$2.55)

$$$ Flush

Yeti Mountain Home To add luxury to the trek to Everest Base Camp, stay at the handsome stone lodges run by Yeti Mountain Home, starting with this charmer in Lukla. (Rooms from US$250; www.nepalmountainlodge.com)

Eat

$ Shoestring

Herman Helmer's Bakery Grab a coffee and a bun, and kick back on the sofa or terrace at this European-style bakery in Namche Bazaar, the perfect antidote to altitude fatigue. (Snacks from Rs 200/US$1.70)

$$ Midrange

Café Danphe The liveliest nightspot in Solukhumbu has cold beers, sizzling grills and a pool table much in demand with trekkers in Namche Bazaar. (Mains from Rs 300/US$2.55)

Timing

Nepal has two main trekking seasons, avoiding the wet summer monsoon and the coldest months from December to February. You can trek out of season, of course, but lodges may be closed, flights are less frequent and adverse weather can add to the dangers of crossing high passes. Of the two peak seasons, October to November offers the clearest weather for mountain views, while March to May is quieter, with less competition for beds en route.

1 A group of climbers trekking to Everest Base Camp from the Gokyo Valley in Sagarmatha National Park.

2 Buddhism is an important part of local life in Nepal, with prayer flags fluttering wherever you go.

3 Climbing Everest: the fastest ascent from Southern Base Camp took less than 11 hours for Lhakpa Gelu Sherpa.

Best value itineraries

4 days

On the Nepali trek, most people spend only a night at Gorak Shep, the chilly last stop before Everest Base Camp, before zipping down to a lower elevation. However, properly acclimatised, you can spend several rewarding days among the peaks. Devote one day to the trek to Kala Pattar, for the definitive Everest view, and another to visiting Everest Base Camp itself, the sprawling tent village for mountaineers at the foot of the Khumbu Icefall. With two days spare, consider the climb to the Cho La, the glacier-topped pass linking Solukhumbu to the Gokyo Valley, before heading downhill towards Namche Bazaar.

10–14 days

The standard Everest itinerary takes two weeks to cover the loop between Lukla and Everest Base Camp on the Nepal side, and the only people who spend more than a few days in the immediate vicinity of Everest are medics, scientists and mountaineers. However, coming from Tibet, 10 days is just enough time to trek up to the northern base camp for mountaineers, and climb breathlessly on to the Advanced Base Camp at 6340m. This will serve up a serious taste of the mountaineering experience, with epic views over Everest and the Rongbuk Glacier.

© Vixit / Shutterstock

❶

© Murchundra /Getty Images

IRAN

Naqsh-e Jahan Square

A fantastical expanse of formal fountains and gardens, Esfahan's monumental square is a worthwhile sight in its own right, but the fact that it's surrounded by four historical and architectural treasures makes it a true wonder.

It's late afternoon in Naqsh-e Jahan Square and you're basking in the sun's golden hour. So too are the kaleidoscopic tiles atop the mesmerising dome of Masjed-e Sheikh Lotfollah. To the south, not to be outdone, is the incredible Masjed-e Shah – its huge, blue-tiled dome now a study in contrast, half glowing vibrantly in the light, half subdued in the shifting shadow. The vivid, intricate mosaics framing this mosque's entrance portal, which stands at the end of the expansive square, are radiant and glistening. You also notice that the trees are a richer shade of green and the mountains on the horizon a more vivid red.

The fountains burst into life and local families spill into the square for their evening promenade. The scale of Naqsh-e Jahan – laid out in 1602 under the reign of Shah Abbas the Great – is still hard to comprehend. More than 500m long and 163m wide, it hems in some 83,500 sq metres. On the far side, in the evening's grip, are two more historic treats: the six-storey palace Kakh-e Ali Qapu and the Qeysarieh Portal.

Travel

International
Tehran's Imam Khomeini International Airport welcomes most of Iran's international air traffic. It's small, so delays are possible. Internal flights and some international services branch out to Esfahan, the site of Naqsh-e Jahan. Other airports that could be useful arrival or departure points include Shiraz, Mashhad, Tabriz, Bandar Abbas and Kish.

Regional
Esfahan is accessible from Tehran by daily trains, which take 7½ hours to make the journey. Train tickets must be booked (most easily through a travel agent) well in advance, particularly on weekends or in holiday periods. Numerous buses ply the same route, and take about six hours.

Stay

$

Shoestring
Iran Hotel In an excellent location, this modest hotel with its stylish foyer offers comfy rooms with low beds, Persian rugs and a fridge. *(Rooms from US$26; www.iranhotel.biz)*

$$

Midrange
Isfahan Traditional Hotel Located in the bazaar near the ancient Masjed-e Hakim (Hakim Mosque), this clean and characterful hotel is set around two courtyards in adjoining Safavid- and Qajar-period homes. *(Rooms from US$36)*

$$$

Flush
Abbasi Hotel The Abbasi's main building was once the caravanserai of the Madraseh-ye Chahar Bagh; arranged around a huge garden of ponds and towering cedars, and with a view of the *madraseh*'s dome beyond, this is a special place to stay. *(Rooms from US$150; www.abbasihotel.ir)*

Eat

$

Shoestring
Bastani Traditional Restaurant This atmospheric restaurant set in the shadow of the Masjed-e Shah (Shah Mosque) has an internal courtyard with a fountain, tiled walls and vaulted ceilings with mirror inlay. *(Mains from IR250,000/US$6)*

$

Shoestring
Haj Mahmood Beryani Famous for its *beryani* (lamb shoulder with sheep lungs), which is served with a glass of *dugh* (churned sour milk or yoghurt mixed with water). *(Beryani, IR140,000/US$3.36)*

$$$

Flush
Shahrzad Qajar-style wall paintings, stained-glass windows and black-suited waiters contribute to the Shahrzad's reputation as Esfahan's best reastaurant. Specialities include *chelo fesenjan* (pomegranate and walnut stew). *(Mains from IR500,000/US$12; www.shahrzad-restaurant.com)*

Timing

Mild, clear weather tends to dominate the months of March, April and May, which makes them the ideal time to visit.

Prices are highest and crowds biggest during No Ruz (21 March to 3 April), especially in Esfahan, Shiraz and Yazd.

Summer is hot, while extreme cold, particularly in the northeast and west, grips during winter. Moderate temperatures in late September and October are good for mountain trekking.

Naqsh-e Jahan Square exemplifies the order and symmetry of Islamic design and architecture.

The colour of the tiles here - Persian blue - represents the local stone lapis lazuli.

Construction of the Masjed-e Shah began in 1611; it's one of the wonders of Esfahan.

Masjed-e Sheikh Lotfollah was built during the reign of Shah Abbas I (1571–1629).

Best value itineraries

4–5 days
After a day in Tehran, take a bus to Kashan, where you can explore the bazaar, check out the Qajar-era traditional houses and chill out in the Fin Garden. Stop for a couple of hours to check out the mosque and tomb in Natanz en route to architecturally magnificent Esfahan, and spend two days exploring the blue-tiled mosques of Naqsh-e Jahan Square, the bustling Bazar-e Bozorg, the sublime bridges across the Zayandeh River and the Armenian community at Jolfa.

12–14 days
Spend three days in Tehran seeing the museums and galleries, and taking in the hustle and bustle, then head south for a couple of days to Kashan with its World Heritage-listed Fin Garden. Bus it to Esfahan where you'll need three or four days to soak up the sights of the Safavid-era capital, including the square, and then venture east for a village homestay in Farahzad or Garmeh in the vast Dasht-e Kavir desert – these homestays redefine hospitality. From the desert turn south to the Silk Road trading city of Yazd, stopping in the spectacular Zoroastrian pilgrimage site at Chak Chak en route. You'll need three days in Yazd to wander the maze of lanes, gape at the Masjed-e Jameh (Jameh Mosque) and climb to the Zoroastrian Towers of Silence.

CAMBODIA

Angkor Wat

There are dozens of representations of Mt Meru – the spiritual centre of the universe in Hindu and Buddhist mythology – dotted around Southeast Asia, but all are just warm-up acts for what could well be the greatest temple ever built.

As dawn peels back its veil and the mist parts to reveal the *prangs* (temple spires) of Angkor Wat, it feels like an epiphany: all your travels through Asia were just building up to this point. Angkor was not 'discovered' by European explorers – locals knew about it all along – but visiting it serves up a sense of the buzz that must have greeted the French explorers who pushed back the jungle vines and put the temples on the traveller map. Among the ruins, armies of stone deities wrestle serpents and demons. Fantastical bas relief friezes reveal arcane secrets and legends. And among the tourist crowds, Cambodian pilgrims pay silent respects at a site that has been sacred – first to Hindus, then to Buddhists – since the start of the 12th century. Even better, Angkor Wat is the just the centrepiece of a vast, ghost city of ruined temples emerging from the jungle on all sides.

Travel

International
In the early days, the only way to get to Siem Reap was a long, uncomfortable journey overland, or a round-the-houses boat ride along the Tonle Sap. Today, international flights land straight into Siem Reap International Airport, just a few kilometres from the ruins. There are good connections around Asia, including to Phnom Penh, Hong Kong, Bangkok, Singapore and Kuala Lumpur, where you can pick up long-haul links to Europe, Australia, the Gulf and the Americas.

Regional
There are many ways to reach Angkor from Siem Reap, depending on how much time you have and how well you handle the heat. It's possible to walk to the ruins from town, but the site covers a vast area and most visitors prefer to explore by bike, motorcycle, *remork-moto* (motorcycle rickshaw) or car. Chartering a vehicle for the day is certainly a wise option if you intend to roam out to Banteay Srei and other outlying ruins.

Stay

$

Shoestring
Green Home | Set in a sprawl of rice fields, this homely homestay has spotless rooms and the owners offer cooking classes, village walks and guided birding trips. *(Rooms from US$8; www.thegreenhome.org)*

$$$

Flush
Sala Lodges This unusual boutique hotel looks like a traditional Cambodian village, but the village-style houses, set around a lush green garden are full of stylish features inside. *(Rooms from US$230; www.salalodges.com)*

Eat

$

Shoestring
Marum Enter this charming wooden house to find imaginative and surprising dishes blending familiar and unfamiliar ingredients, such as stir-fried beef with chilli and red ants. *(Mains from US$3.25; www.marum-restaurant.org)*

$$$

Flush
Cuisine Wat Damnak Celebrity chef Joannès Rivière serves inventive and seasonal set menus that showcase the very best of contemporary Cambodian cooking from this traditional wooden home. *(Set menus from US$24; www.cuisinewatdamnak.com)*

Timing

The monsoon washes over Angkor from June to September, bringing heavy rains that can make exploring the ruins a drudge. That said, you'll avoid the crowds who flock here during the dry winter months from November to March. Smart travellers avoid sticky April and May, when the soaring humidity will sap your energy and enthusiasm for clambering over the ruins.

Sunset over Angkor Wat is prime time to absorb the wonder of the site.

Fig, kapok and banyan trees merge with Ta Prohm temple.

The Hindu temple of Banteay Srei (meaning 'Citadel of the Women') in the Angkor region contains some of the world's finest examples of stone carving.

Best value itineraries

3–4 days
Three to four days is really the minimum time you need to explore the ruins at Angkor and fit in some downtime in Siem Reap. In between forays to the temple zone, visit the Angkor National Museum to put the ruins into historical context, fly through the trees on the Angkor Zipline, sign up for a Cambodian cooking course or just enjoy a relaxing massage after all the scrambling up steep temple stairways. After dark most travellers in Siem Reap can be found bar-hopping along Pub St, but set aside one night for the remarkable Phare, the Cambodian Circus, which combines performance art with social commentary.

7–10 days
With a week at Angkor, you can linger over the temples. Angkor Wat is unmissable, but roam to outlying shrines such as Bantaey Srei and Beng Mealea to escape the crowds. For a proper adventure, travel two hours northwest by road to Bantaey Chhmar, a romantic sprawl of Bayon-style ruins spilling from the forest near the Thai border. Closer to Siem Reap, *moto* drivers whisk local pilgrims and the odd traveller up to the plateau of Phnom Kulen, dotted with more Khmer-era ruins. For a break from banyans and Buddhas, take a boat to the stilt village of Kompong Khleang, floating on the Tonle Sap.

© CaoWei / Getty Images

CHINA

Great Wall of China

The tale that the Great Wall of China is the only man-made structure visible from space is sadly a myth, but at ground level the defensive fortifications built by Kheng of Qin and his successors are as humbling today as they must have been to the marauding hordes who found their paths blocked by them.

Whether you take the path most trodden and visit the restored sections near Běijīng, or glimpse the Wall melting into the desert in China's parched northwest, you have only to set foot atop the battlements to realise that this is not just the greatest piece of engineering in Chinese history, it's the most ambitious piece of construction undertaken anywhere, ever.

Paying little heed to tourists, the ghosts of Chinese history swish like arrows over the topography-defying ramparts at Bādálǐng, Mùtiányù and Gùběikou near Běijīng. Vanquished last stands cry out in silence among the wind-eroded buttresses near the desert city of Jiāyùguān. On remote stretches of unrestored wall you might just hear the songs of marching armies and the flapping of pennants floating on the breeze. Going to China and not visiting the Great Wall would be akin to visiting the Caribbean but not going to the beach – in other words, unthinkable.

© Bobby Chen / 500px

1

2

Travel

International
Běijīng is the easiest place to access the Great Wall and also the place where the wall is best preserved (this was, after all, the capital that many parts of the wall were built to defend). Beijing Capital International Airport is served by flights from across the world, but some domestic flights drop into tiny Nányuàn Airport, 8 miles (13km) south of the centre.

Regional
Inexpensive suburban trains take about 80 minutes to reach the section of wall at Bādálǐng from Běijīng North train station. Gŭběikou (Simitai), Huénghuā Chéng, Jiànkòu and Zhuàngdàokŏu can be reached by bus from Dōngzhímén Transport Hub (with a change to a local bus in the suburbs). Buses to Jīnshānlǐng run from the Wàngjīng West subway station and buses to Mùtiányù run from Dōngzhímén Wai bus stand. You may find it easier to arrange a day trip by taxi.

Stay

$ Shoestring
Great Wall Box House Set in a century-old former chessboard factory, this charming courtyard guesthouse is beside a section of the unrestored Great Wall at Gŭběikou. *(Dorms from ¥180/US$26; http://en.greatwallbox.com)*

$$$ Flush
Brickyard Eco Retreat Look beyond the unlikely name; this stylish guesthouse has created beauty from a restored 1960s tile factory and its rooms offer some decent views of the Great Wall at Mùtiányù. *(Rooms from ¥1084/US$156; www.brickyardatmutianyu.com)*

Eat

$ Shoestring
Yan Lan Lou This famous noodle shop brings the tastes of Gānsù and the deserts of the northwest to central Běijīng; locals queue daily for the hand-pulled noodles with mutton. *(Noodles from ¥18/US$2.60)*

$$$ Flush
TRB Hutong It's hard to imagine a more romantic setting than this lavish modern European fine-dining restaurant set in a disused temple north of the Forbidden City. *(Set dinner menus from ¥398-1288/US$57-186; www.trb-cn.com)*

Timing

The best time to see the Great Wall depends on how much cold you can handle. The wild lands around the wall look their most dramatic in the winter, but icy winds make this a bleak time to trek. Spring and autumn offer ideal walking weather, and autumn has the added bonus of vivid red foliage in the forests near Bādálǐng and the Ming Tombs. If you don't like crowds, avoid the restored sections of wall in summer.

The sections of the Great Wall at Jinshanling have been restored so walking the walls is much easier here. The section dates from the Ming Dynasty.

The Jinshanling section has watch towers every 50m to 100m.

Rickshaw drivers can ferry visitors to the most accessible parts of the Great Wall.

Best value itineraries

4 days

Four days is time enough to visit multiple sections of wall and see the contrast between the restored sections and the areas of wall left romantically ravaged by nature. Easily reached by bus or taxi, Mùtiányù is the most enjoyable of the restored sections, with 26 watchtowers linked by towering battlements. It has a chairlift, cable car and toboggan run to keep families entertained. Contrast this slick vision with the untouched 'wild wall' at Jiànkòu, accessible by bus but easier to reach by taxi. Here you can hike in peaceful solitude along crumbling battlements draped along a mountain ridge, overnighting in simple guesthouses in Xīzhàzi village.

7–10 days

With more than a week to explore, remote Jiànkòu offers some of the best wild walking, with potential for camping once you get beyond human habitation. Alternatively, consider the easier hike from unrestored Gŭběikou to the restored, but less explored, section at Jīnshānlǐng. Having seen what the Ming emperors achieved in life, you can visit their tombs at the foot of Tiānshòu Mountain near Bādálǐng. To observe the Great Wall meeting the ocean, take the express D or G train to Shānhǎiguān. Finally, for a break from masonry-related sightseeing, ride the subway to Xiangshan Park, a scattering of pavilions amid forest that burns red with autumn colour.

© Thien Bui / 500px

© AlexeIA / Shutterstock

TURKMENISTAN

Door to Hell

Every now and then, the natural world serves up an experience so surreal that it could only be supernatural, until you discover the science behind the spectacle.

At Darvaza in Turkmenistan's parched Karakum Desert, the very ground is alight. Flickering tongues of flame climb the cliffs like cursed seraphs, struggling to escape from a mouth-like crater that yawns like the gates of Hell. But the explanation is surprisingly down to earth. It's natural methane gas, leaking constantly through the shattered rocks of a collapsed cavern. The effect is both sinister and spectacular – imagine a set from the video game *Doom* brought vividly to life and you'll have some idea what to expect.

It would be pleasing to say that this was an ancient spiritual site, revered by local shamans, but the truth is that the crater was set alight deliberately by Russian oil-exploration workers in the 1970s. It was hoped that the potentially deadly gas would burn off in a matter of weeks, but four decades later and the Door to Hell is still burning. Getting here is a bit of a mission; sensible travellers come on a tour, rather than hiking for hours from the highway and camping overnight in this remote and spooky spot.

Travel

International
Turkmenistan lies off the usual tourist flight routes and Ashgabat International Airport in the capital is the closest the country has to a proper air hub. Lufthansa and Turkmenistan Airlines provide connections to Europe and a handful of minor carriers serve Russia, the Middle East and Urumqi in China. From Ashgabat, you'll have to complete the journey overland to Jerbent, the ramshackle oasis that is the jumping-off point for the crater.

Regional
Due to the remote location in the desert north of Jerbent, most travellers choose to come on a tour arranged in Ashgabat. However, those truly committed to the desert experience can reach Jerbent and the turn off to the crater by road – all public buses between Ashgabat and Konye-Urgench or Dashoguz pass this way. From the unsigned turn off on the highway, it's a two-hour walk through the dunes to reach Darvaza and you'll need to camp.

Stay

Midrange $$
Hotel Aziya True budget hotels are almost non-existent in Ashgabat, but this cost-effective Berzengi hotel has vast rooms with Turkmen rugs and a Chinese restaurant on site. *(Rooms from US$55)*

Flush $$$
President Hotel Perfectly named for a nation which reveres its leader like a deity, Ashgabat's top hotel is lavish and luxurious; even the rooms are decked out with gold trim. *(Rooms from US$180)*

Eat

Shoestring $
Erzurum The Turkish influence is strong in this popular locals' hangout in Ashgabat, serving hearty meals of *pide* (Turkish pizzas) and lamb kebabs. *(Mains from 10M/US$2.85)*

Flush $$$
Sim Sim Ashgabat's top European restaurant is hard to find, but worth seeking out for excellent Italian-inspired cooking and a grown-up wine list – a rarity in Turkmenistan. *(Mains from 30M/US$8.55)*

Timing

Turkmenistan has a desert climate, which can bring cold nights at any time of year and bitter cold in winter. The spring season from April to June and the autumn season from September to November offer warm but not uncomfortable days and clear skies, plus manageable night-time temperatures. The insane heat of peak summer is best avoided, as are the chilly months from December to February.

The part of the Karakum desert around the Darvaza gas crater was declared a nature reserve by Turkmenistan's president, Gurbanguly Berdimuhamedow, in 2013.

After 40 years aflame, the Door to Hell burns on for another night.

A local market trader at Ashgabat.

Best value itineraries

3–4 days
As it takes most of a day to reach Darvaza from Ashgabat by road, you'll need to spend the night at the crater, either camping or sleeping in basic beds in *chaikhanas* (roadhouses) on the highway near Jerbent. This way, you'll also get to experience the crater at dusk and in full darkness, when it's at its most atmospheric. You can continue the journey north to anonymous Dashoguz, connecting on to infinitely more interesting Konye-Urgench, whose unpaved streets are littered with the mausoleums of 12th-century saints and other ancient relics that conjure up the romance of the Silk Road.

7–10 days
If you have more than a week, you can work Darvaza in as part of a longer itinerary through Turkmenistan. Starting in Ashgabat, allow a couple of days to wander the carpet markets, monuments and museums, and ride the cable car for city views, then take a tour to Darvaza, overnighting in this spooky desert location. Continue overland to Konye-Urgench, to wander its Silk Road ruins, then loop back to Dashoguz to pick up a flight to Mary, gateway to the ancient Greek and Persian ruins at Merv. One last flight will zip you back to Ashgabat to close the loop.

INDIA

Golden Temple

The most sacred site in the Sikh religion is more than just a temple; it is the embodiment of a whole philosophy of honour, respect and hospitality.

Centred on a man-made lake, constructed personally by the fourth Sikh guru, the Golden Temple is known to devotees as Sri Harmandir Sahib (the abode of God), and the entire compound crackles with a palpable sense of concentrated devotion and belief. Don't be surprised if the hairs on the back of your neck stand up just a little as you enter.

As at the time of its founding, Sikhism remains a martial order and swords, spears and daggers are prominently on display, but the pilgrims who arrive in a continuous tide have eyes only for the sacred tank, imbued with the power to wash away sin, and the gold-encrusted, jewel-box shrine in the centre of the pool. As a human tide carries you towards the causeway leading to the inner sanctum, which pulses to the chanting of passages from the Guru Granth Sahib, the Sikh holy book, you'll feel less of an observer and more of a participant in something greater, particularly if you join the crowds at the temple *langar* – the volunteer-run kitchen that feeds an estimated 50,000 pilgrims every day.

© Matt Munro / Lonely Planet

Travel

International
Perhaps unsurprisingly considering the huge Sikh diaspora around the world, Amritsar's Sri Guru Ram Dass Jee International Airport is served by growing numbers of direct international flights, most from the Middle East and Central and Southeast Asia. Cost-wise, though, it may be cheaper to come in via Delhi, either on a connecting low-cost flight or on the train (an easy six-hour ride that will introduce you to the joys of Indian rail travel).

Regional
The centre of Amritsar is fairly compact, but the railway line cuts a transect through the historic heart, splitting most of the accommodation from the busy bazaars surrounding the Golden Temple. You'll almost certainly want to take a rickshaw or autorickshaw between the two halves of Amritsar, but once among the bazaars, the best way to explore is on foot, soaking up old Amritsar's magnificent potpourri of sights, smells and sounds.

Stay

Shoestring
Tourist Guesthouse It's the traveller vibe that sells this old stalwart near Amritsar railway station, set around a courtyard garden. *(Dorms from Rs 200/US$2.75, rooms from Rs 600/US$8.25; www.touristguesthouse.com)*

Flush
Ramada Amritsar After the chaos and crowds of downtown Amritsar, retreat to the air-conditioned calm of the city's top hotel, an island of luxury looking over the old city. *(Rooms from Rs 4700/US$64; www.ramadaamritsar.com)*

Eat

Shoestring
Kesar da Dhaba This much-loved Punjabi *dhaba* (roadhouse) in Shastri Market serves satisfying *paratha* plate meals, topped off with sublime lassis and *firni* (ground rice pudding). *(Dishes from Rs 70/US$0.95)*

Flush
Crystal Restaurant With the mirror-lined walls and ornate stucco trim, there's a fin-de-siècle air to this long-established restaurant in Crystal Chowk serving superior Mughlai cooking. *(Mains from Rs 300/US$4.10)*

Timing

The heat and humidity of the plains sits on Amritsar like a pressure cooker – avoid the hot, rainy months from June to September unless you have built in air-conditioning. Temperatures dip agreeably from October to December, and rainfall stays low right through until May.

To experience Amritsar at its most frenetic, visit during Baisakhi in April, the biggest festival in the Sikh calendar, when the streets fill with dancing, feasting and song.

The temple is a *gurdwara*, or place of worship, for Sikhs. It has been nominated as a Unesco World Heritage Site.

One of the more elaborate Sikh turbans that you're likely to see.

The *langar*, or community kitchen, at the Golden Temple serves a daily free meal to around 50,000 people and as many as 100,000 during festivals.

Best value itineraries

3–4 days
Due to the noise and heat, four days is as much as some people can handle in Amritsar, but the Golden Temple warrants repeat visits at different times of day to appreciate the changing mood. Visit at dawn, when the shrine is at its most serene, and at sunset as the sky turns red over the Amrit Sarovar pool. And you'll want to be here at least one lunchtime to visit the Guru-Ka-Langar – the great pilgrims' kitchen behind the Golden Temple. A day in the bazaars is also essential, as is a visit to the Mata Temple and Jallianwalla Bagh, site of the most notorious massacre under British rule.

7–10 days
If you have a week, you can mix days downtown with trips out to the surrounding countryside. Explore the maze of gurdwaras (Sikh temples) around the Golden Temple, then trade the spiritual mood for the theatre of the border-closing ceremony at the India-Pakistan frontier at Attari-Wagah. To better understand Sikh traditions, head to the pilgrimage centre of Anandpur Sahib, where the Khalsa Heritage Complex will introduce you to the rich history of the Sikh brotherhood. An overnight trip to Patiala is another must, to experience the faded grandeur of what was once one of India's most prestigious princely states.

© Hari Mahidhar / Shutterstock

CHINA

Terracotta Army

When emperor Qin Shi Huang went to meet his maker, he didn't go alone. The first ruler of unified China passed into the next life with a personal bodyguard of some 8000 warriors, along with 500 horses, more than 100 chariots and an astonishing armoury, all executed in brick-red terracotta.

To gaze for the first time upon this astonishing funeral procession – perhaps the grandest collection of grave goods that's ever been assembled – is as heart-stopping today as it must have been for the farmers who stumbled upon the warriors while digging a well near the emperor's funeral mound at Mt Li in 1974. As you wander between the excavated pits, these days covered by hangar-like canopies, and note that no two faces are alike, just as your guidebook promised, you'll feel an extra frisson of excitement when you realise that this is just part of a far larger necropolis stretching for almost 100 sq km under the ground beneath your feet. Consider the vanity of a man so sure of his role in the hereafter that he commissioned this vast funeral cortege not to protect his corpse, but to serve him eternally in the manner to which he had become accustomed.

1

Travel

International
The discovery of the Terracotta Army firmly put Xī'ān on the map and Xi'an Xianyang Airport receives flights from almost every corner of China – with particularly good connections to the east coast – as well as international flights from Korea, Japan, Malaysia and Thailand. Coming from Europe, it may be cheaper to fly to Běijīng or Shànghǎi and change to a low-cost domestic airline, or make the transfer to Xī'ān by comfortable overnight Z-class train.

Regional
As one of China's most famous tourist destinations, Xī'ān is well set up for visitors heading to the sights. Tourist buses zip to the Terracotta Army site, and most other sights in town, from right in front of Xī'ān's main train station. Alternatively, the town's public buses and metro reach many of the same locations for penny prices. Once you reach the Terracotta Army site, electric buggies zip from the car park to the excavated pits.

Stay

$

Shoestring
Han Tang Inn The staff at this friendly hostel will help you maximise your time at the sights, and the clean, comfy dorms have en-suite bathrooms. *(Dorms from ¥40/US$5.75, rooms from ¥180/US$26)*

$$$

Flush
Bell Tower Hotel This smart four-star place has a lavish marble lobby and rooms upstairs that are almost as plush, right by Xī'ān's 14th-century Bell Tower. *(Rooms from ¥900/US$130; www.xabth.com)*

Eat

$

Shoestring
Ma Hong Xiaochao Paomoguan The crowds can be extraordinary at this legendary Chinese Muslim restaurant, but the *paomo* (meaty stew with chopped flatbread) is worth queuing for. *(Meals from ¥17/US$2.45)*

$$

Midrange
Jamaica Blue Look beyond the un-Chinese name; this hostel-lobby cafe is a great place to connect with other travellers. Come for global snacks, good coffee and evening beers with live music. *(Dishes from ¥32/US$4.60)*

Timing

The canopy over the Terracotta Army keeps the site open year-round, but the best time to travel to Xī'ān is spring or autumn, when the balmy weather and fresh mountain breezes make for ideal conditions for trawling the tombs and temples, and climbing Huá Shān.

Come in the frosty winter months and the Huá Shān trails are mostly off limits, but the crowds vanish at the Terracotta Army and other Xī'ān sights.

 1
Rows of terracotta warriors are assembled according to their rank and duty.

 2
The city of Xī'ān marks the eastern end of the Silk Road in Shaanxi Province.

 3
The figures were all made by hand and were substitutes for actual human sacrifices, which previous rulers had demanded.

Best value itineraries

3–4 days
There's so much to see in Xī'ān you'll only make a dent in four days. The Terracotta Army warrants at least one day, and you'll need another to visit the Tomb of Emperor Jingdi and other sites north of the centre. It would be easy to fill the next two days exploring the area inside Xī'ān's ancient city walls, including the historic Muslim Quarter, home to the city's Hui Muslim community. As well as touring the temples, tombs and Terracotta Warriors, take time to graze the city's dumpling houses and famous Muslim *paomo* (meat and bread stew) restaurants.

7–10 days
The historic sites can easily fill a week, particularly if you roam beyond the Terracotta Warriors and the walled city to less-visited temples and tombs. As well as actual ancient history, Xī'ān has excellent museums to help make sense of all the relics, displaying everything from ancient Confucian inscriptions to Terracotta soldiers you can get right up close to. Just half an hour from Xī'ān by G-class train, Huá Shān is one of Taoism's five sacred mountains, a garden of knife-edge peaks, climbed by a cable car or perilously narrow hiking trails, including a nerve-jangling via ferrata plank-walk.

JORDAN

Petra

Nobody who has ever seen a picture of the ancient Nabataean city of Petra can forget the spectacle, its buildings cut majestically into the red rocks of a remote desert canyon. Visit the site and you'll have rich memories full of wonder, emotion and fulfilment.

As you sit under a dark sky painted with constellations, the first evidence of light is the flickering of candlelight on the walls of the Siq passageway. Soon, local Bedouin, each cloaked in a traditional *thoab* (long white robe) and red *keffiyeh* (head scarf), start to flow slowly out of the narrow chasm and into the foreground of the Treasury, Petra's most spectacular site. Shadows and light dance on the ancient sandstone facade as the Bedouin, one by one, place their torches on the ground. Soon the entire scene is glowing warmly in their combined radiance – it is a sublime and timeless sight.

Emotions rise as the men take turns singing songs that have been passed down through countless generations. Although this place may have been 'forgotten' by the outside world prior to Jean Louis Burckhardt's visit in the 19th century, it has always been at the core of life here. On nights like this, it's impossible to forget that.

This spectacular city, which includes palaces, temples, tombs, storerooms and stables, was hewn out of the soft sandstone cliffs by craftspeople of the Nabataean kingdom in the 3rd century BC.

②

Travel

International
Amman's Queen Alia International Airport, 22 miles (35km) south of the city, is the main point of entry for visitors into the country. From the capital, Petra is four hours away by bus. Minibuses also reach Petra from Aqaba (two hours) and from Wadi Rum (1½ hours). If driving to or from the Dead Sea, consider travelling along the spectacular and seldom-used road that links Little Petra with Wadi Araba through Namleh. Signs stating that this route is closed are outdated, but flash floods often cause damage to the road, so it's worth checking locally before attempting the drive.

Regional
The nearby town of Wadi Musa is the transport hub for Petra. There are usually plenty of yellow taxis with green plates travelling up and down the main road of Wadi Musa towards the entrance for Petra, especially in the early morning and late afternoon. They congregate outside Petra Visitor Centre.

Stay

Shoestring
Cleopetra Hotel One of the friendliest and most efficiently run budget hotels in Wadi Musa, Cleopetra has bright, fresh rooms. There's a communal sitting area where wi-fi is available. *(Rooms from JD18/US$25)*

Midrange
Petra Guest House Hotel Guests really can't get any closer to the entrance to Petra without sleeping in a tomb – and indeed the hotel's famous Cave Bar is located in one. *(Rooms from JD75/US$106; www.guesthouse-petra.com)*

Eat

Shoestring
Nabataean Tent Restaurant With simple Jordanian dishes and one or two international favourites, this casual restaurant at Petra occupies a lovely spot under jacaranda trees. Its packed lunches are a bargain. *(Lunch buffet JD10/US$14)*

Flush
Basin Restaurant This air-conditioned option at the ancient site serves a wide spread of international dishes, including a healthy selection of salads, fresh falafel and barbecued spicy sausage. *(Lunch buffet JD16/US$22.50)*

Timing

Petra can get mind-bogglingly busy in peak season (March to May and September to November), particularly so after 10am when the tour buses from Aqaba to the south and the Dead Sea resorts to the north begin to offload. For a soul-stirring rush, avoid the crush by arriving pre-sunrise or when the site basks in golden-hour sunlight. To see Petra bathed in candlelight, gather at the Visitor Centre at 8.30pm on Mondays, Wednesdays and Thursdays.

1 The individual buildings at Petra are wonders but its the whole site of all the ruins that will amaze.

2 The pillars of the Treasury, which reflected the prosperity of the Nabataean capital, thanks to its location on several trade routes.

3 Originally built as a tomb, crosses inscribed inside the Monastery suggest that it was used as a church during the Byzantine era.

Best value itineraries

3 days
This 50 mile (80km) stretch of the 400 mile (644km) Jordan Trail, which launched in 2017, runs from the mountaintop village of Dana to Petra. On the first day, hike from Wadi Dana to Wadi Feynan, which will take you through green canyons and the furnace-hot desert of Wadi Araba. Day two will lead you into Wadi Feid, an arid section of steep mountains and exposed ridges, which is the wildest stretch of the trek. Sleep under the stars there before walking the final 14 miles (23km) to Petra. Arriving on foot, it's easy to imagine that you are an early explorer.

9 days
After three days exploring the capital, Amman, take the bus along the Desert Highway to Aqaba to swim, snorkel over pristine coral and soak up the atmosphere in this seaside town's souqs. On day six take the morning bus to magnificent Wadi Rum. Hop astride a camel and head into the dunes for a camping experience with the Bedouin. Rise at dawn to catch the minibus to Petra. With two days in the pink city, you can hike to the High Places, learn to cook Jordanian food at Petra Kitchen, watch the sunset from the Monastery and enjoy an evening in the famous Cave Bar. On your last day, bus back to Amman.

© Justin Foulkes / Lonely Planet

CHINA

Forbidden City

Until surprisingly recently, to even gaze upon the Forbidden City was to bring instant death, unless you were lucky enough to be a member of China's imperial family or part of the small, elite group granted a royal audience.

Fear not, no such penalty applies today, though you'll get a powerful sense of the ruthlessly regimented codes of conduct that governed every aspect of life in the palace before the last emperor, Puyi, abdicated in 1912. It is the face of Mao Zedong, not the emperor, that first greets you as you approach from Tiananmen Square, but beyond the sweeping eaves of the Meridian Gate, the grandeur of imperial China endures. On all sides, roof tiles cascade, pillars soar and courtyards open like chasms. As you penetrate the layers of the compound, tiers of pavilions and stairways like marble mountains divide areas of influence until, at the heart of it all, you find the dwelling of the emperor himself, perhaps the most exclusive private apartment on earth. Whether you fancy living like this yourself is another question, but it's impossible not to be humbled by the ritual and pomp of China's most extravagant palace.

Travel

International
Beijing-Capital International Airport is the world's second-busiest passenger airport, served by an astonishing number of daily flights from almost everywhere in the world, as well as flights onward to almost every major city in China. Plenty of airlines fly here direct from major hubs in Asia, Australia, Europe, the Middle East and North America. Travelling overland, it's possible to reach Běijīng via long train rides from Mongolia, Russia, Vietnam and, strange as it sounds, North Korea.

Regional
Getting around downtown Běijīng is easy thanks to the vast number of stops served by the Běijīng subway and the city's inexpensive public buses, which go almost everywhere. Taxis are easy to find, but can be expensive and drivers rarely speak English – carry the address you wish to travel to written in Mandarin. Rickshaws charge even more and take tourists for a ride in more ways than one; it may be easier to walk for short journeys.

Stay

$

Shoestring
Běijīng Drum Tower International Youth Hostel In place of the usual dorms, this central hostel has beds in lockable capsules in the heart of the *hutongs* (traditional alleyways). *(Dorms from ¥88/US$13, rooms from ¥288/US$42)*

$$$

Flush
Côté Cour Taking the *hutong* experience upmarket, this handsome hotel was once the home of musicians appointed to the imperial court; rooms blend Chinese tradition with modern design sensibilities. *(Rooms from ¥1166/US$168; www.hotelcotecourbj.com)*

Eat

$

Shoestring
Baozi Pu True to its name, this street corner hole-in-the-wall serves delicious *baozi* (steamed pork dumplings) by the basket to a hungry, local crowd. *(Dumplings from ¥5/US$0.70)*

$$$

Flush
Duck de Chine Taste Běijīng's most famous dish the way it was meant to be served at this lantern-lit monument to all things duck. *(Mains ¥78-488/US$11-70)*

Timing

Běijīng is a year-round destination, but the spring months from April to May and the autumn months from September to November promise the best weather – cool nights, pleasantly warm days and limited rainfall. Avoid the rain-drenched months of July and August unless you don't mind wrestling your umbrella through the crowds. Winter brings a crisp beauty to Běijīng's *hutongs,* but the dry, cold air chaps lips and wicks moisture from exposed skin – bring plenty of lip balm and moisturiser.

Tiananmen Gate, entrance to the famous square.

You'll probably need to queue to enter the Hall of Supreme Harmony in the Forbidden City; all good things come to those who wait.

A costumed actor at the Běijīng opera.

Best value itineraries

4 days
Four days will hardly make a dent in Běijīng's long list of sights, but the Forbidden City is the place, or should that be palace, to start. After a day of imperial grandeur, continue the story at the pavilion-strewn Summer Palace and the Temple of Heaven Park, with its geometrically perfect Hall of Prayer for Good Harvests. Another day should be devoted to exploring Běijīng's atmospheric and historic *hutong* lanes. And no trip to Běijīng would be complete without a trip to the Great Wall – see the restored version at Mùtiányù or glimpse the romantic ruin of the 'wild wall' at Jiànkòu.

7–10 days
With more time at your disposal, you can roam beyond the obvious sights, though the Forbidden City, the *hutongs* and the Great Wall will use up half your week without even trying. Swing by the Lama Temple for a reminder of Běijīng's spiritual side and attend a Peking opera or a tumbling-filled acrobatic show to experience the city's rich culture. Visit over a weekend to browse Panjiayuan Market, crammed with hawkers selling everything from Communist belt buckles to traditional wood-carvings, and the odd real treasure among piles of fake antiques. Allow another day for the fascinating 798 Art District, where contemporary artists tackle challenging subjects in a disused electronics factory.

© bendao / Shutterstock

1

© Perfect Lazybones / Shutterstock

2

© Matt Munro / Lonely Planet

VIETNAM

Halong Bay

Some places seem to defy the centuries and Halong Bay is just such a location. Away from the built-up bustle of Halong City, this maze of islands and limestone outcrops could have been plucked straight from a pirate legend or a time-worn map showing the wonders of the East and brought back to Europe by a medieval seafarer.

Old-fashioned junks still cruise between the outcrops, but today these atmospheric sailing boats are laden with tourists rather than opium, silk and spices. Somehow, as eerie mists swirl around the sculpted rocks, it doesn't seem to matter. The mood, particularly at dawn and dusk, is otherworldly.

While many content themselves with the views from deck, more hands-on travellers view the terrain up close, splashing around the islets by kayak, climbing the razor-sharp karst overhangs on finger-shredding holds, or plunging into the coral garden beneath the karsts with scuba tanks and fins. World Heritage–listed Halong is far from undiscovered, however; a flotilla of tourist boats to rival the Armada sets out daily from Halong City. Those seeking silence hopscotch to nearby Cat Ba Island, with its own discrete collection of karst towers at Lan Ha Bay.

Travel

International
Halong City is the gateway to Halong Bay, but the nearest international airport is 100 miles (160km) to the west in Hanoi. Noi Bai International Airport has good connections to Asia and less frequent services to Europe and the Middle East. To reach Halong, you'll need to head into town and take one of the regular buses from Gai Lam Bus Station.

Regional
Buses buzz from Hanoi to Halong City's Bai Chay bus stand in roughly four hours, but transfers are included in the price of most Halong cruises booked in Hanoi. If you'd rather book a cruise on arrival, operators have ticket desks at Halong's Tuan Chau pier, which is 8 miles (13km) southwest of central Halong City. For those travellers heading to Lan Ha Bay, ferries run regularly from Tuan Chau to Gia Luan Pier on Cat Ba Island.

Stay

Shoestring
Light Hotel This sparkling Halong City hotel has rooms with space to breathe and friendly staff who will help you to find the right boat in which to navigate the bay. *(Rooms from 300,000d/US$12.85; www.thelighthalong.vn)*

Midrange
Namcat Island Resort Offshore from Cat Ba, this laid-back resort will put you right among the outcrops with some bungalows over the water and others tucked under limestone cliffs. *(Dorm from US$29, bungalow from US$65; www.catbabay.com)*

Eat

Shoestring
Vien Duong Fresh seafood from the bay is served steaming from the hotpot at this lively Cat Ba hotspot, a favourite hang-out for locals (so you know the food is good). *(Meals from 120,000d/US$5.15)*

Midrange
Quang Anh At this fish-farm-cum-restaurant on Ben Beo Pier, you pick your seafood fresh from the pens and it will be grilled, fried or steamed in double-quick time. *(Meals from 200,000d/US$8.58)*

Timing

December and January is peak season in Halong Bay, and also the peak time for crowds, but the weather is actually better in the quiet shoulder months from March to May and September to November. Expect warm but not sticky days, cooler nights and enough sunshine to show the islands at their best. Summer brings lower prices and fewer tourists, but also the risk of heavy rainstorms and typhoons.

 Tourist junks await their passengers at Halong Bay. Cat Ba Island is a good introduction to the archipelago.

 There are thousands of limestone pinnacles and islands, many with grottoes, to explore in the bay.

 A local guide and his junk.

Best value itineraries

3–4 days
Cruises around Halong Bay run the gamut from unimpressive day-trips to multi-day cruises on restored Vietnamese junks. To get the best out of the bay, you want at least one night on the water, or even two. The most lavish junk cruises will make you feel like a pirate princess, but price is no guarantee of privacy; for less company as you cruise the karst islands, consider heading on to Lan Ha Bay. If you have four days in the bank, you should have time for both Halong Bay and the beaches, historic sites and national park on Cat Ba Island.

7–10 days
With a longer timeline, you can cruise Halong at your leisure, and take several days exploring Cat Ba Island. Kick back on the beaches lining Cat Co Cove, kayak around Lan Ha Bay and delve deep into the jungles of Cat Ba National Park, home to the largest population of golden-headed langur in the world. There'll be time to trip south to Haiphong, home of the historic Du Hang Pagoda, or retreat to one of the quietly idyllic islands in Bai Tu Long National Park, which is only just starting to be explored by travellers to northeast Vietnam.

© Matt Munro / Lonely Planet

JAPAN

Sakura

Cascades of cherry blossom, billowing over ornamental gardens beneath the stepped eaves of towering pagodas. Petals gathering in pastel-coloured snowdrifts beneath Shinto gateways and around the bases of Japanese castles. It's hard to imagine a scene more definitively Japanese (except, perhaps, sword-wielding Samurai defending Tokyo from Kaiju monsters).

Hanami, the tradition of viewing the spring blooming of the *sakura* cherry trees, dates back to at least the 18th century, when revered scholar Mootori Norinaga chose the cloud-like blooms as the perfect embodiment of the principle of *mono no aware* – sensitivity to ephemera as symbols of the impermanence of existence. It's a feeling melding profound pathos and uplifting joy, one which cuts past the bullet trains, Manga mythos and miniaturised technology, and takes you to the heart of what it means to be Japanese.

Cherry orchards bloom right across the archipelago; join the crowds promenading, picnicking, drinking sake, nibbling treats, reading classic poetry and just appreciating the glory of the blooms in Maruyama-koen park in Kyoto, pagoda-crowned Arakurayama Sengen-koen park in Fuji-Yoshida or Tokyo's Yoyogi-koen park and you'll get just a little bit closer to the soul of Japan.

© Richie Chan / Shutterstock

Travel

International
Japan has a surprising number of international airports considering its geographical size, served by daily flights from almost everywhere, so you can pick an airport close to your preferred cherry-blossom-viewing location or zip from hub-to-hub by train and catch views of the countryside in bloom along the way. The twin hubs of Kyoto and Osaka probably offer the best *hanami* opportunities, with easy access to Kyoto's Maruyama-koen park, Kimpusen-ji in Yoshino and other bloom-filled public spaces.

Regional
Having arrived in your chosen international hub, the train is the best choice for zipping across the country, from sedate local services to lightning-speed *shinkansen* (bullet trains). Scenic rail routes such as the Yosan Line in Shikoku, Sagano Scenic Railway in Kyoto and Oigawa Railway steam-train route from Kanaya in Honshu seem tailor-made for *sakura* viewing. Alternatively, you can move around by bus or hire car, but the highways don't offer quite such glorious views.

Stay

Shoestring
Hitsuki Guesthouse A lovingly restored, 400-year-old *oshi-no-ie* (pilgrims' inn) at Fuji-Yoshida, with elegant timber interiors and *tatami* rooms divided by sliding screens. *(Rooms from ¥4000/US$35)*

Flush
Tawaraya Ryokan Kyoto's finest *ryokan* inn is personal and private, with a 300-year history of excellent service and atmospheric rooms with wooden bathtubs and garden views. *(Rooms half-board from ¥49,680/US$437)*

Eat

Shoestring
Sakurai Japanese Tea Experience Within easy striking distance from Tokyo's Yoyogi-koen park, this place offers delicate Japanese teas and, for a higher price, the full formal Japanese tea ceremony. *(Tea and sweets from ¥1400/US$12; www.sakurai-tea.jp)*

Flush
Kikunoi Yards from Kyoto's Maruyama-koen park, this palace to *kaiseki* (Japanese haute cuisine) is Michelin-starred and worth every penny for its imaginative, exquisite cuisine. *(Set meals from ¥10,000/US$88)*

Timing

Hanami is an activity with a very narrow time window. The cherry trees only bloom for a few weeks each spring and the exact timing varies every year. The location also matters, with the trees blooming earlier in the south and later in the north of the country. The blossom usually bursts forth in late March or early April – the Japan National Tourism Board issues an annual calendar at www.jnto.go.jp/sakura/eng/index.php.

Himeji Castle, west of Kyoto, is framed by cherry blossom in spring. The blooms sweep along the island from the warm south to the north.

Kyoto's historic Higashiyama district is even more beautiful when spring arrives.

The blossom inspires *hanami* (flower viewing) festivals, such as here in Kyoto's Maruyama Park.

Best value itineraries

3–4 days
Kyoto's parks and public spaces become a sea of colour during the *sakura* season, with the most dramatic flourishes of blooms in gorgeous Maruyama-koen park. Informal cafes set up tables beneath the blossoms around the famous central weeping cherry tree and a party mood pervades. For a more natural *hanami* experience, devote the next day to a picnic at Togetsukyo Bridge on the edge of the Arashiyama mountains. Walking the Philosopher's Path between Ginkakuji and Nanzenji offers another definitive *sakura* encounter. Leave day four for other Kyoto experiences – the sprawling Chion-in temple, wandering beneath Shinto gateways at Fushimi Inari-Taisha or finding inner peace in the Daitoku-ji zen garden.

7–10 days
Tokyo is a fabulous hub for *hanami* and more than a thousand cherry trees burst into life in Shinjuku-gyoen park for alcohol-free viewings. For more energy and noise, devote another day to the area around uninhibited Ueno-koen, where the parties run till late. Spend another day in and around Yoyogi-koen, one of the most animated spots in the city during the *sakura* season. Take an overnight trip by train to Fuji-Yoshida for iconic dawn and sunset vistas of yet more *sakura*, framed by Mt Fuji and Churei-to Pagoda. Finish off away from the blossom with a few days in Tokyo's museums, markets and temples.

© photographer / Shutterstock

INDIA

Meghalaya Tree Bridges

Meghalaya's root bridges look like props from a *Lord of the Rings* world, conjured up by nature itself and too fantastical to have been created by human hands.

For most of the last century, the tribal states of India's far northeast lay tantalisingly out of reach, thanks to colonial-era bureaucracy, geopolitical paranoia and civil war. Today, the risks and red tape have receded, opening a door to a network of tribal cultures that, until recently, drew everything they needed from the tropical forests.

In the rain-drenched hills around Cherrapunjee, the inventive Khasi people of central Meghalaya went one step further, bending the very trees to their will. Where rivers blocked the trails between villages, the aerial roots of mighty rubber fig trees were woven by hand into living root bridges, creating single-, double- and even triple-decker spans across jungle-cloaked gullies. Hiking the ancient trails that cross the Khasi hills is a window to a vanishing way of life and a reminder, in an age of smartphones and home hubs, that half the world still depends on human ingenuity. The only downside is the hassle of getting here, by 4WD and on foot, from the state capital, Shillong.

Travel

International

Reaching Meghalaya involves several changes of vehicle. The nearest international airport is Netaji Subhas Chandra Bose International Airport in Kolkata, served by flights from across India, Asia and the Middle East. Domestic flights zip from Kolkata to Guwahati, where you can transfer to a helicopter for the short hop to Shillong on the Meghalaya plateau. From here you can arrange bus transfers or a guided tour to the tree bridges. Guwahati and Shillong are also connected by bus and 4WD.

Regional

The most accessible tree bridges are dotted around the Khasi hills near the town of Cherrapunjee, 23 miles (53km) south of Shillong. The journey takes three hours by 4WD, then you'll have to embark on foot into the forest. The best-known bridge is the double-decker span at Umshiang, close to the jungle village of Nongriat, a 6½ mile (10km) walk south from Cherrapunjee, but jungle trails provide access to more living bridges in the area. Agencies in Shillong and Guwahati can arrange guides and transport.

Stay

Shoestring

Rest House Nongriat The only place to stay in tiny Nongriat village is extremely humble, but meals are home-cooked and the Umshiang tree bridge is minutes away. *(Rooms with meals Rs 500/US$6.85)*

Flush

Cherrapunjee Holiday Resort This Khasi-owned resort in Laitkynsew village offers guided treks, home cooking and smart en-suite rooms, some with forest views. *(Rooms from Rs 4650/US$64 half board; www.cherrapunjee.com)*

Eat

Shoestring

Trattoria A legendary lunchtime stop in Shillong serving not pasta but such Khasi delicacies as *ja doh* (spiced rice with pork). *(Mains from Rs 100/US$1.40)*

Midrange

Café Shillong After trekking to Meghalaya's tree bridges, recharge over a steak and cold beer at Shillong's liveliest nightspot, to a soundtrack of rock, jazz and blues. *(Mains from Rs 250/US$3.40)*

Timing

Cherrapunjee was once fêted as the wettest place on earth and the monsoon makes overland travel an ordeal. A better time to visit is autumn, from September to November, when roads are passable but waterfalls are still swollen with monsoon rain.

Autumn is also the season for the fascinating Nongkrem festival in the tribal village of Smit, as well as the Wangala drumming festival in the Garo Hills.

The root bridge brings two sides of Nongriat village together. Standard wooden structures would rot in this humid place.

A visit to Nongriat is also an opportunity to learn about the local Khasi tribal people.

Nohkalikai Falls in Meghalaya is India's tallest plunge waterfall – the area is an incredible (and wet) place to explore.

Best value itineraries

4 days

Starting from Shillong, you'll need at least two days to reach Cherrapunjee, walk to the tree bridges and return to the state capital, with an overnight stop in Cherrapunjee or one of the nearby tribal villages. Before you set off, you'll want to drop into Shillong's Don Bosco Museum of Indigenous Cultures, for an introduction to the tribal history of the northeast. After trekking, a visit to Cherrapunjee's waterfalls is almost mandatory – a viewpoint at the end of the ridge at Cherrapunjee offers stunning views over Nohkalikai Falls, which performs spectacularly during the monsoon. Finish with a day exploring Shillong's fading colonial churches, parks and tea-growers' bungalows.

7–10 days

A week gives time to explore some of Meghalaya's more remote corners. Take your time in Shillong and visit the nearby village of Smit, with its bamboo palace, still occupied by the local tribal *syiem* (king). From Cherrapunjee, combine several tree bridges into a multi-day hike, following ancient tribal walking trails. There are more traces of tribal culture on the road to Cherrapunjee, and at Nartiang, where rounded monoliths hint at vanished animist traditions. Allow a couple of days to visit the Jaintia and Garo Hills west of Shillong, where the Nokrek Biosphere Reserve provides shelter for rare hoolock gibbons, red pandas and elephants.

Dead Sea

Stark natural beauty, captivating ancient history and unparalleled levels of pampering (and floating) make the lowest place on earth somewhere to hit new travel highs.

Few lakes in the world have had the likes of Aristotle, Pliny and Galen writing about them, but the Dead Sea is no ordinary lake. And it's certainly no ordinary swim here either. For starters, you'll be doing it in shoes, a simple precaution to protect your precious digits from the crystalline salt formations on the bottom. But as you gently wade in you won't notice much aside from the water's warmth (that is, unless you've recently shaved or have a small, yet-to-be-fully-healed cut, both of which will make this a very painful and short-lived affair). If you've passed that first flinch test and reached a depth that you can squat in, it's time to gently roll over on to your back – and this is when the magic happens.

The water's remarkable salt concentration of over 30% makes its buoyancy beyond anything you'll have experienced before and it's a truly surreal feeling to be almost fully cradled by it – get your balance right and you can even attempt to read a book while floating atop its surface. You couldn't sink if you tried, though it's not something you would want to attempt, as getting any of this water in your eyes or mouth will sting aplenty.

2

Travel

International
Queen Alia International Airport, located 22 miles (35km) south of Amman, is the key entry point into Jordan. If you're planning on visiting the Dead Sea from Israel, Ben Gurion International Airport, 13½ miles (22km) from Tel Aviv, is the main gateway for international flights. Both airports are served by numerous international airlines.

Regional
From Amman, it takes just under an hour to reach the Dead Sea by car, along Hwy 40 and Hwy 65. Alternatively, you can drive from Madaba via Mt Nebo, which provides a spectacular first glimpse of the salt lake. JETT buses (www.jett.com.jo) also provide daily access from Amman. Some budget hotels in Amman and most hotels in Madaba organise day trips. On the Israel side, a visit by car is the most convenient (via Rte 1, Rte 31 or Rte 25). It's possible, though a little bit fiddly, to reach the Dead Sea by public transport from Tel Aviv and Jerusalem.

Stay

Shoestring
Shkedi's Camplodge A wonderful place to linger, this desert retreat in Neot HaKikar (Israel) is especially enchanting at night, when guests hang out around the campfire or in the chill-out tent. On hot days you can mist yourself while relaxing on a hammock. *(Dorms from 100NIS/US$27, rooms from 350NIS/US$95; www.shkedig.com)*

Flush
Mövenpick Resort & Spa A pleasantly green haven in Jordan with two-storey apartments. Guest rooms enjoy sea or garden views in private, while secluded seating areas around a superb infinity pool add to the ambience. *(Rooms from JD180/ US$254; www.moevenpick-hotels.com)*

Eat

Shoestring
Dead Sea Spa Hotel The non-guest access fee (JD25) to this Jordanian resort includes a free snack and drink. The buffet lunch is JD20 extra. *(Food from JD25/US$35; www.dssh.jo)*

Flush
Al Saraya This notable restaurant is within the Mövenpick Resort & Spa. The buffet cost includes day access to the pools and beach. *(Buffet JD50/US$70)*

Timing

March, April and May are the perfect months to visit, as they have warm days and cool nights. As such, it's a popular period, with costs climbing and reservations needed. Prices drop in the heat of summer (June to August), but the air temperatures can be stifling. The shoulder season of September to February can bring rain (and even snow) into the desert, which could curtail activities such as camping.

The high salt content of the Dead Sea results in a greater density than is normal for water, meaning that anybody should float.

Salt formations on the shore. Experiences at the Dead Sea range from modern spas to hiking in the Judean Desert.

A must-have Dead Sea mud pack is rich in magnesium, sodium, potassium and calcium.

Best value itineraries

4 days
Hire a car in Amman and head to the Roman ruins of Jerash. On day two, amble down to the Jordan Valley via Ajloun and the Islamic Ajloun Castle. Pause where John allegedly baptised Jesus at Bethany-Beyond-the-Jordan, before flopping, floating and luxuriating with fluffy towels at the lowest place on earth. On day three, drive to nearby Mukawir, where Salome reputedly danced for John's head on a platter. Skirt the plateau ridge to the friendly mosaic town of Madaba and on day four visit Mt Nebo or the dolmens of Wadi Jadid. From Madaba, it's an hour back to Amman.

7 days
Ride south by bus from Jerusalem to Be'er Sheva – its revitalised old city is the site of Biblical wells. From here follow the call of the Negev desert along Rte 40, with a possible 4WD detour. The next day visit the ancient ruins of Avdat, squeezing in a short hike. Now move to Sde Boker for its fantastic desert setting, before halting to gaze at Mitzpe Ramon, Israel's 'grand canyon'. Next is the vastly different Eilat, a popular Red Sea resort. A few hours on a bus north from here is the Dead Sea. After bobbing and baking, head back to Jerusalem via Masada.

© Zurijeta / Shutterstock

BHUTAN

Taktshang Goemba

With a creation story this extravagant, it's little wonder that Taktshang Goemba (Tiger's Nest) became such an essential stop for travellers making the once-in-a-lifetime trip to Bhutan.

According to ancient Bhutanese legend, this revered monastery was founded personally by Padmasambhava, the Indian master who brought Buddhism to Tibet. Adding to the drama, the great lama is said to have travelled to this lofty eyrie on a flying tiger, meditating on the nature of the universe in a hidden cavern before emerging in eight sacred forms, sanctifying Taktshang for all eternity.

As you climb through the forest beside ribbons of flickering prayer flags and first glimpse the monastery clinging to the rock face, it wouldn't stretch the imagination to believe the legend that Taktshang is held in place by the hair of angels. In fact, not all is as it appears at Taktshang – although it seems impossibly ancient, the monastery has been repeatedly reconstructed following fires and other disasters, most recently in 1998. Nevertheless, from the spectacular setting to the magnificent murals and meditative mood, Taktshang delivers everything you could hope for from a Buddhist monastery: stunning scenery, sublime serenity and more than just a sprinkling of the supernatural.

Travel

International

There is only one air route into Bhutan, via the kingdom's international airport at Paro, but this puts you on the doorstep of Taktshang and the other sights in the Upper Paro Valley. Druk Air and Bhutan Airlines are the only carriers permitted to fly into Paro's dramatically located airport, so you'll change planes en route – Delhi, Mumbai, Kathmandu, Bangkok and Singapore are all easy places to connect.

Regional

Due to Bhutan's unique tourism model, all your food, accommodation, entry and guide fees, and transport will be included as part of the mandatory daily fee – currently US$250 per person per day (US$200 a day from December to February and June to August). The most popular itineraries combine Paro and Taktshang with visits to the capital, Thimphu, and the famous monastery at Punakha, dropping in at viewpoints, monasteries and sacred sights between the three valleys.

Stay

Shoestring

Gangtey Palace The daily fee includes accommodation, so seek out a package that includes lodging at this 19th-century palace with its valley views and mural-filled tower. *(Rooms from Nu 3696/US$51; www.gangteypalace.com)*

$$$

Flush

Uma Paro If you're going for a full luxury package, there's no substitute for this elegant hotel, which blends traditional architecture with top-end service and facilities. *(Rooms from US$696; www.comohotels.com/en/umaparo)*

Eat

Shoestring

Champaca Café After tramping up trails and monastery steps, recharge with strong South Indian coffee and tasty sandwiches in this bright and inviting Paro cafe. *(Light meals and snacks from Nu 50/US$0.70)*

$$$

Flush

Tou Zaiga Restaurant Chefs in training hone their skills at the house restaurant of the Bondey Institute of Hotel Tourism; this may well be the best meal you have in Bhutan. *(Set meals Nu 500/US$6.95; www.bihtbhutan.org)*

Timing

Bhutan is touched by the monsoon, which brings rain that washes away roads, and clouds that obscure the mountain views. The best weather for sightseeing and travelling in Bhutan is in autumn, from October to November, or in spring, from February to April. The chilly months of deep winter are best avoided, as passes may be blocked by snow.

Late March or April is the time to catch outrageously colourful masked dances around the Paro Valley.

1

Bhutan's National Museum in Paro.

2

Taktshang Goemba was first built in the 1600s but has since been rebuilt several times; as Buddhists point out, buildings are temporal but ideas can live forever. As you climb to the monastery you'll pass prayer flags and *tsa-tsas* – reliquaries containing ashes of the dead – squeezed into rock crevices.

3

Monks use prayer wheels to purify the mind.

© robert salthouse / Alamy Stock Photo

INDIA

Ghats of Varanasi

India is awash with sacred cities, but in Varanasi, said to be the second-oldest continually inhabited city on earth, it is a sacred river washing over the city that makes the location so spiritually significant.

The Ganges, the most revered of India's seven holy rivers, achieves wish-fulfilling status at Varanasi, and those who die in sight of the sacred waters are said to be liberated from the cycle of birth and rebirth and ushered into a state of *moksha*, or unification with the divine. Accordingly, the banks of the river are lined with ceremonial ghats – centuries-old stone stairways dropping down to the water's edge – where pilgrims come to pray, meditate and enter the world beyond in the funeral fires that burn day and night at Manikarnika and Harishchandra.

With all of life unashamedly on display, the sense of spiritual energy in Varanasi is palpable and the colours are irresistible, as legions of pilgrims gather on the riverbank to consult with holy men, receive blessings, light sacred lamps and bathe in the sacred waters. Viewed from a bobbing riverboat on the Ganges, the ghats, with their iridescent palette, and backdrop of temples and towers, present what is simply one of the most striking vistas on the planet.

© Adrian Pope / Getty Images

❷

Travel

International
Varanasi's miniature Lal Bahadur Shashtri Airport is currently only served by a handful of international flights from Bangkok, Colombo and the Gulf. It's easier to connect via Delhi or Bengaluru on an Indian low-cost carrier. Air India offers an interesting route via Agra, so you can tag on a trip to the Taj Mahal. Alternatively, you can fly into Delhi and take an overnight train for a gripping introduction to Indian rail travel.

Regional
The streets of the old city are closed to traffic from 9am to 9pm, so rickshaws and autorickshaws drop visitors at Godaulia Crossing, a short walk from Dashashwamedh Ghat, the most popular ghat for pilgrim bathers. The ghats run for miles to the north and south of Dashashwamedh. Rickshaws and taxis can drop you along the strip, but the best vantage point for viewing the ghats is a rented riverboat and operators stalk all the main ghats offering trips.

Stay

Shoestring
Brown Bread Bakery Guesthouse Just back from Pandey Ghat, this spotless guesthouse has a much-loved on-site bakery and a good reputation for organising boat trips. *(Rooms from Rs 250/US$3.40; www.brownbreadbakery.com)*

Flush
Brijrama Palace Set in a meticulously restored riverfront palace from 1812, this graceful heritage hotel is decked out with chandeliers, Asian rugs and other vintage finery. *(Rooms from Rs 21,850/US$300; www.brijrama.in)*

Eat

Midrange
Open Hand This shoes-off cafe-cum-gift shop near Assi Ghat serves real espresso alongside breakfast platters featuring pancakes, omelettes and muesli. There's also a range of salads and sandwiches. *(Mains from Rs 160/US$2.30)*

Flush
Darbangha The Brijrama Palace Hotel's house restaurant takes the humble *thali* (several dishes meal) upmarket, turning a roadhouse standard into a fine-dining feast. *(Thalis from Rs 1750/US$24)*

Timing

The prime time to visit Varanasi is the dry, warm winter from November to February, but the crowds can be overwhelming. October and March offer a quieter experience, at least in terms of having to share the sights with other tourists. The rain-drenched monsoon from June to September swamps the streets, but also ushers in some of the biggest festivals.

Bathing at ghats on the Ganges in Varanasi.

Hindus believe that a dip in this holy river purifies the soul, although its waters are far from pristine.

A contemplative *sadhu* (holy man) at an ashram at Varanasi.

Best value itineraries

4 days
Four days will give you time to get under the skin of the ghats. Devote a couple of days to exploring the whole run from Assi Ghat to Raj Ghat on foot and by boat. You'll want to spend at least one evening on Dashashwamedh Ghat for the fire-filled spectacle of the nightly *ganga aarti* ceremony. You'll also want to roam inland through the lanes of the old city to the Vishwanath Temple, a gold-encased beauty dedicated to Lord Shiva as Lord of the Universe. Use your last day to explore Sarnath on the city outskirts, where Buddha gave his first sermons after achieving enlightenment.

7–10 days
With more time to spare, you can roam further afield. Take your time at the ghats and Sarnath, and visit the fascinating Benaras Hindu University with its miniature-painting-filled museum. For a change of scene, it's just three hours by train to Prayagraj (Allahabad), where the Hindu god Brahma came down to earth, sanctifying the confluence of three sacred rivers – the Ganges, the Yamuna and the mystical Saraswati. After visiting the *sangam* (confluence) and Prayagraj's fort and tombs, ride the rails north to Ayodhya, birthplace of the Hindu god Rama, before looping back to Varanasi.

INDIA

Temples of Hampi

Hordes of monkeys surge over the fallen masonry of the ancient kingdom of Vijayanagar, but that's only appropriate – this was, after all, the birthplace of Hanuman, the Hindu monkey god.

Set amid a fantasy landscape of eroded granite outcrops, the remains of more than 1500 temples and pavilions sprawl across the floodplain, giving way at the southern fringes to relics from the Muslim sultanate that replaced Vijayanagar when it collapsed in the 16th century.

For travellers who have a love of history, exploring and rock climbing, this could be the perfect playground. From the towering *gopurams* (tower-gateways) of the Sri Virupaksha Mandir to the iconic stone chariot in the landmark Vittala Temple, there is hardly an inch of rock in Hampi that doesn't bear the mark of a stonemason's chisel. It's easy to lose days wandering through the stony landscape, discovering hidden carvings and forgotten shrines, and scrambling over the boulders and outcrops, before riding back to town in a reed-basket coracle for a cooling *lassi* in the shade of a mango tree. The only disturbance to the peace comes from the government, which periodically cracks down on human habitation within the historic area, including in the traveller hub at Hampi Bazaar.

Travel

International
Hampi is midway between Bengaluru and Goa, and getting here will involve a mix of air, rail and road travel. Bengaluru's Kempegowda International Airport is the easier option, with good connections to Asia, Europe and the Middle East, plus domestic flights from most major hubs in India. Goa's Dabolim Airport is also well served by domestic flights, plus a few year-round connections from the Middle East and seasonal tourist flights from Europe.

Regional
Reaching Hampi from either Bengaluru or Goa will involve a train ride to the sleepy town of Hosapete (Hospet). The route from Goa is slightly shorter at seven hours, but you'll first have to make it to the railway station at Madgaon Junction near Margao. It takes nine hours to reach Hosapete from Bengaluru, but trains are more frequent. From the bus station in Hosapete, local buses zip out to Hampi in half an hour, leaving throughout the day.

Stay

Shoestring
Manash Guesthouse There are just two rooms at this pocket-sized guesthouse, but charming owners and a calm courtyard setting in the old bazaar will make you feel at home. *(Rooms from Rs 1200/US$16)*

Flush
Hampi's Boulders Just north of Virupappur Gaddi, this serene eco-retreat has cottages scattered around lovely gardens, with a natural waterhole for swimming and guided walks included in the price. *(Rooms with full board from Rs 6500/US$89; www.hampisboulders.com)*

Eat

Shoestring
Laughing Buddha Cheap eats come with expansive views of the river and ruins at this laid-back backpacker hangout located on the north shore of the Tungabhadra River. *(Mains from Rs 80/US$1.10)*

Flush
Mango Tree Relocated to the bazaar from its old location in the mango orchards, this traveller favourite serves delicious thalis and richly flavoured vegetarian curries. *(Mains from Rs 140/US$1.90)*

Timing

The dry winter is the prime time to visit Hampi, but daytime temperatures rarely dip below 25°C year-round and the heat can soar uncomfortably in May. The monsoon sweeps in from June to September, bringing rain showers but also greenery to Hampi's parched boulder fields. November and December are the best months for climbing, with dry skies and pleasantly warm days. In mid-winter temperatures drop at night and you'll need long sleeves after dark.

Virupaksha Temple is one of the first you reach on entering Hampi.

The further you venture into the site of the ancient village, the more wonders are revealed, such as this 16th-century stone chariot.

There's a village with food and accommodation at the entrance of Hampi.

Best value itineraries

4 days
You'll have no problem filling four days at Hampi. Just the section of ruins around Hampi Bazaar takes a day to explore and the Islamic ruins to the south warrant another day of exploration. Add on a third day to roam to the villages of Virupapur Gaddi and Anegundi on the north side of the Tungabhadra River, and climb up to outlying temples such as the Hanuman temple on Anjanadri Hill, birthplace of the Hindu monkey god. Spend the last day relaxing under the shade of a mango tree near the river or rock climbing on Hampi's sculpted granite outcrops.

7–10 days
With more time to spare, you can rove beyond Hampi's captivating ruins, though three or four days would be the minimum you need to get a feel for this fascinating and expansive historic site. Continue the temple tour at Badami, north of Hampi, where temples and carving-filled caverns rise around a lakeside village in a natural basin. Stay a day or two at Badami and you can tack on nearby Pattadakal and Aihole, with their magnificent 7th-century shrines. Swap Hinduism for Islam in the mosques and mausoleums of Vijapura (Bijapur), then take the bus back to Hosapete to close the circle.

© Huw Jones / Getty Images

①

© Pierre Ogeron / Getty Images

②

© Steven Duncan / 500px

JAPAN

Himeji Castle

For Europeans, a castle should be a solid mass of stone, guarded by battlements, a moat and portcullis. The Japanese castle is something altogether more elegant: a fluorescence of wooden tiers, stacked like Jenga blocks and topped by tiled pagoda roofs, defying invaders to pit their strength against such graceful, deadly beauty.

Wandering the chambers of the gleaming white fortress that rises over the town of Himeji like an egret's nest, you'll be struck not just by its delicate lines, but by its defences. Constructed in 1580, Himeji-jo was equipped with the latest siege deterrents of its time: towering walls, concentric moats, a profusion of loopholes for archers, and portals for dropping rocks and boiling oil on to attackers trying to scale the walls.

Though Himeji-jo never faced a prolonged onslaught, it's all too easy to imagine the sudden spray of red against the ice-white walls from hand-to-hand combat in its maze of inner passageways. Battle your way to the upper floors, however, and the whole green sprawl of Himeji opens up before you like a three-dimensional map, giving just a hint of the power held by its feudal rulers in the medieval period.

Travel

International

Himeji lacks an airport, but Kansai International Airport is just 78 miles (126km) away in Osaka Bay, and direct flights serve a string of airports in Asia, Europe, the Middle East and North America. Express trains zip from the airport to Shin-Osaka, where you can pick up the *shinkansen* (bullet train) to Himeji. Alternatively, it doesn't take much longer to reach Himeji by *shinkansen* from Kyoto, also served by international flights from almost everywhere.

Regional

By Japanese standards, Himeji is green and quiet, a gentle sprawl of parks and neighbourhoods that spills back from the coast and melts into the countryside. City buses connect most corners of the city to the area around Himeji train station, which is just a 15-minute walk from Himeji-jo castle – as you walk you'll see the rooftops looming at the end of Otemae-dori. Alternatively, the Sightseeing Loop Bus zips up the castle, passing the museum and gardens.

Stay

$

Shoestring

Himeji 588 Hostel The spotless tatami rooms at this homely hostel make it the perfect city base for exploring historic Himeji by rented bike. *(Dorms from ¥2700/US$24; https://himeji588.com/eng)*

$$$

Flush

Hotel Nikko Himeji It's not the stylish rooms that sell Himeji's top hotel so much as the restaurants and the superb views of the castle from the bar. *(Rooms from ¥13,000/US$114; www.hotelnikkohimeji.co.jp)*

Eat

$

Shoestring

Nadagiku Kappa-tei Run by a local sake brewery, this workman-like eatery serves tasty *oden* (hotpots) that go down very well with the house sake. *(Mains from ¥210/US$1.85)*

$$

Midrange

Fukutei Cool stucco and marble set the scene at this civilised restaurant, serving seafood-rich set menus, with sashimi, tempura and nibbles on the side. *(Set meals from ¥1350/US$12)*

Timing

Kansai is blessed by the seasons. From late March to mid-April, *sakura* (cherry blossom) paints the gardens of Himeji and other towns in pastel pinks and tinted whites, while the autumn months from October to December see the landscape burn red as the maple leaves turn for autumn. July and August are hit by high humidity and heat, but this is also festival season in Kansai and life spills out into the streets in the evenings.

The entire site of Himeji-jō is huge, with many buildings and gardens within its walls.

The frame of the castle is constructed from wood. But it was never tested in battle.

Japanese weaponry is on display inside the castle. The fortifications have holes and slots through which to fire rifles and bows.

Best value itineraries

3–4 days

Himeji is flat and self-contained, ideal for exploring on foot or by rented bike or local bus. There's no need to rush, so devote a peaceful day to exploring Himeji-jo and the adjacent Koko-en gardens for a dip into feudal period history. Allow another day for the Hyogo Prefectural Museum of History, with its miniature castle models, and the Himeji City Museum of Art, with works by Magritte, Picasso and Rodin. To make the most of four days, take a day-trip by train to the *onsen* (hot spring) town of Kinosaki Onsen and then choose from dozens of traditional Japanese bathhouses and *ryokan* (inns).

7–10 days

If you have more than a week to spare, Himeji can be the fulcrum for a more detailed exploration of Kansai. With fast *shinkansen* services to Osaka, Kyoto and Hiroshima, you can drop into both of Kansai's dual metropolises before roaming west from Himeji to Hiroshima, a city defined more today by its cosmopolitan buzz than by its WWII history. En route, stop at Okayama for another stunning Japanese castle and the Edo-period elegance of the Koraku-en gardens. There'll also be time for a longer stop at Kinosaki Onsen, taking your time to wander from bathhouse to bathhouse.

CHINA

Zhāngyè Dānxiá Geopark

Geography is not something that was meant to be learned from school books, it was made to be experienced in the flesh. Nothing puts you in your place in the universe quite like standing alone, an insignificant dot in the midst of an epic landscape, in terrain that was ancient before the first human ancestors climbed down from the trees.

It took 55 million years of wind and rain to create the formations of Dānxiá – carved from unique, rainbow-coloured sedimentary rock – that rise around the city of Zhāngyè in northwest China. Nature has transformed the landscape into an impressionist painting of reds, whites, oranges, yellows, ochres and browns. Imagine a Van Gogh blown up to a monumental scale, with human beings reduced to the size of ants, scurrying between the brush strokes. Or picture a divine hand the size of a mountain, pouring patterns in the rainbow-coloured sand.

To minimise the damage to this fragile landscape, visitors are ferried to wooden causeways climbing to the best viewing points for photographing and observing the colours, but if you catch the perfect shot from Platform 4 at sunrise or sunset, with just the right saturation and depth of tone, you really won't mind the company.

Travel

International
Zhāngyè's tiny Zhangye Ganzhou Airport receives a handful of flights from Běijīng, Shànghǎi, Chendu, Lánzhōu and Xī'ān, but the nearest international hub is at Lánzhōu, three hours from Zhāngyè by train, which has excellent connections around China and a few longer routes to other Asian hubs. Zhāngyè is well connected by train to the big cities of central China, but this is China's empty quarter, so expect long journey times; buses are even slower.

Regional
There's no public transport to Zhangye Dānxiá Geopark – this is a patch of desert after all, albeit a stunningly pretty one – so the easiest option is a taxi from central Zhāngyè. You can combine a trip to the sands with a stop at the Mǎtí Sì monastery. Once you reach the site, a hop-on-hop-off bus shuttles visitors around the scenic platforms. Consider the atmospheric Silk Road town of Jiāyùguān, two hours west, as an alternative base.

Stay

Shoestring
Xīxià Youth Hostel Antique wood and quirky design features add character at this cheerful hostel and hotel in downtown Zhāngyè; take your pick from simple but pleasant dorms or plusher hotel rooms. *(Dorms from ¥40/US$5.75, rooms from ¥99/US$14)*

Midrange
Shengjing Holiday Hotel Jiāyùguān is a better base if you want creature comforts; this sparkling new midrange hotel has a prime downtown location and clean rooms with modern fittings. *(Rooms from ¥207/US$30)*

Eat

Shoestring
Huayi Snack Square Zhāngyè's best place to eat is this lively pedestrianised market, great for hand-pulled noodles, dried fruit and other local specialities. *(Snacks and dishes from ¥5/US$0.70)*

Midrange
Yuanzhongyuan Restaurant This Sichuan restaurant near Jiāyùguān's bus station serves spicy *gongbao jiding* (chicken with peanuts and Sichuan pepper) that will warm you up in winter. *(Dishes from ¥15/US$2.15)*

Timing

Zhāngyè lies in the narrow valley that was once the only passage to the Middle Kingdom and temperatures rarely rise above 20°C in this arid desert region.

Summer and autumn offer the best viewing conditions for sunrise and sunset at Zhāngyè Dānxiá Geopark, as temperatures rise to pleasant levels and occasional rainfall moistens the dry desert air. In winter, desert winds push temperatures far below freezing.

Wind, rain and time have sculpted the sandstone of Zhāngyè Dānxiá (landform) into colourful waves.

Fort Jiāyùguān, a Silk Road stop, marked the beginning of the back of beyond for imperial Chinese and it retains a distinctive culture (with camels).

Morning exercises in Zhāngyè's main square.

Best value itineraries

3–4 days
Laid-back Zhāngyè has a historical legacy that belies its sleepy atmosphere. After visiting the Dānxiá formations, devote a couple of days to exploring the town, which Marco Polo called home for a year in 1274. Dàfó Si, also known as the Giant Buddha Temple, was allegedly the birthplace of another iconic figure – Kublai Khan – and it contains a 35m-long wooden reclining Buddha, one of Asia's largest. About 40 miles (65km) north of Zhāngyè, and easily accessible by bus or taxi, Mǎtí Sì (Horse Hoof Monastery) features an astonishing collection of grottoes filled with Buddha images, set in sandstone caves high above the valley floor.

7–10 days
A longer stay will give you time for a couple of trips to get the perfect photos at Zhāngyè Dānxiá Geopark, and time to climb to the higher caves at Mǎtí Sì and hike in the surrounding hills, staying overnight in rustic guesthouses in Mǎtí Xiāng village. For more Silk Road magic, rumble two hours west by train to Jiāyùguān, set in a forbidding lunar landscape at the symbolic end of the Great Wall. Allow several days for Jiāyùguān's tombs, fort and wind-eroded sections of wall, then connect on by train to historic Wǔwēi, for a third dose of Silk Road relics.

BHUTAN

Punakha Dzong

The *dzong* – half-monastery, half-fortress – is Bhutan's signature monument, born of necessity in an age of warring sects of Tibetan Buddhism, and historic Punakha Dzong could well be the kingdom's most beautiful.

Set in an almost impossibly picturesque location, at the confluence of two sacred rivers, and girded by towering, whitewashed walls, Punakha seems impenetrable from the outside, but cross the cantilevered bridge to the main gates and you'll find a calm vision of devotion within. Monks wander the gleaming courtyards, spinning prayer wheels. The chanting of Buddhist sutras rings out from prayer halls, accompanied by the deep bass of Tibetan horns and the metronomic tap of Bhutanese drums. Mountain breezes stir the leaves of the sacred Bodhi tree in the courtyard while the rivers tinkle meditatively by.

Come in spring and you will see the jacaranda trees along the riverbanks burst into lilac bloom, a blaze of purple against the gleaming white walls of the fortress. Come in February and you'll see the monks at their most animated, swirling in embroidered costumes and fearsome masks of divine beings. Even though Punakha is firmly on the travel map, nowhere brings the sacred history of the last Himalayan kingdom so powerfully to life.

Travel

International

Bhutan's only international airport is the miniature terminal at Paro, a four-hour drive west of Punakha. Hemmed in by mountain walls, this is one of the world's most dramatic flight routes and only a handful of pilots are qualified to fly here. Druk Air and Bhutan Airlines are the only carriers permitted to land in Paro, so wherever you come from you'll need to change planes. Delhi, Mumbai, Kathmandu, Bangkok and Singapore are the most convenient places to connect.

Regional

You don't have to worry about the logistics of getting around on a trip to Bhutan. All your food, accommodation, entry and guide fees, and transport is included in the mandatory daily fee – currently US$250 per person per day (US$200 a day from December to February and June to August). Most people include Punakha on a circuit that also takes in Thimphu, Paro itself, and the famed monastery at Taktshang.

Stay

Shoestring

Hotel Lobesa Great for travellers who don't want to pay extra for top-end accommodation, Lobesa offers bright and airy shared spaces, tidy rooms and great valley views. *(Rooms from Nu 2160/US$30)*

Flush

Dhensa Punakha's top overnight stop blends modernity with subtle traditional touches. Rooms have balconies offering sweeping valley views and there's a fire-heated wooden hot tub. *(Rooms from US$324; www.dhensa.com)*

Eat

Shoestring

Phuenzhi Diner The 'Four Friends' is Punakha's favourite lunch spot, with refreshing air-con and delicious Bhutanese dishes such as Bumthang-style pancakes on the menu. *(Set lunch from Nu 400/US$5.55)*

Shoestring

Druk Wangyal Cafe This welcome stop on the Dochu La pass between Thimphu and Punakha serves warming coffee, teas and light meals around a toasty warm *bukhari* (wood stove). *(Set meals from Nu 430/US$6)*

Timing

The best seasons to visit Bhutan are the mild autumn from October to November or the gentle spring from February to April, avoiding the chill of deep winter and the rain and view-masking clouds of the summer monsoon.

Late February or early March is the time to catch fabulous masked dances as part of the Punakha Drubchhen festival, honouring an ancient battle victory, or the Punakha Tsechu, the monastery's biggest annual celebration.

Floods, fires and earthquakes have affected Punakha Dzong but this magnificent marvel has withstood them all.

The annual five-day festival of Domche is held at the dzong and features masked dancers.

In addition to the resident monks, the dzong is still the winter residence of the *dratshang* (official monk body).

Best value itineraries

4 days

With the premium on each day spent in Bhutan, most people spend just a day in Punakha, heading straight for the *dzong*, particularly if the monastery is holding a festival. However, you can easily fill a second day exploring the nearby Mo Chhu Valley, with hikes to *lhakhangs* (Buddhist temples) and memorial *chortens* (stupas). Another day's travel north will take you to Gasa's historic Trashi Thongmoen Dzong and the Gasa Hot Springs, revered for their healing properties. Alternatively, spend a day around Punakha rafting along the Mo Chhu river. You'll need another day to retrace your footsteps back to Paro.

7–10 days

With seven days or more to spare, you'll be able to combine Punakha with time in Paro and Thimphu, and add detours to less-visited parts of Bhutan, though factor in the slow travel time on mountain roads. One option is to continue southeast to Wangdue Phodrang, with its markets, archery ground, and restored *dzong*. Tucked into a side valley to the east, Phobjikha has a full hand of monasteries and temples and visiting blacked-necked cranes from October to March. The Gangte Goemba is the most impressive of the spiritual sites, with a vast pillared prayer hall and sweeping views over the whole valley.

© Jonathan Gregson / Lonely Planet

INDONESIA

Borobudur

Java's cultural capital, Yogyakarta, has ancient history inside the city limits, so it takes something special to lure people out into the surrounding countryside. Looming above the surrounding paddy fields like a man-made mountain, Borobudur rises admirably to the challenge.

A mandala in three dimensions, topped by tiers of perforated stupas, this grey, lava-rock temple mirrors the volcanoes that rise on all sides, but as you climb the levels, your eyes will be drawn not to the view but to the bas reliefs on the walls. Carved in intricate detail are scenes from the life of the Buddha and vivid illustrations of the law of cause and effect (woe betide those who cook fish and turtles alive!).

At the summit, the main dome rises like a petrified lotus bud, surrounded by stupas, some of which have been stripped of their tops, revealing the central Buddha statues, like celestial star pilots in flying saucers. This is ritual geometry on a massive scale, with every measurement and angle transmitting a powerful divine message. In case Borobudur needed any more superlatives, this is the largest Buddhist temple in the world, so have a good breakfast before climbing the steep stone steps to the top tier.

© Sabine Kaufmann / 500px

1

Travel

International
Yogyakarta is the gateway to Borobudur and Yogyakarta Adisucipto International Airport has good connections to the rest of Indonesia, but sees just a few flights from elsewhere – Jakarta, Singapore and Kuala Lumpur are the best places to connect, all with regular services from Europe, Australia, the Middle East and the rest of Asia. Alternatively, you can connect from Jakarta to Yogyakarta by bus or train.

Regional
Having reached Yogyakarta, the easiest route to Borobudur is by public bus, with services every half hour from Jombor bus terminal. However, for an early start to beat the crowds, a taxi chartered for a return day trip may be the easiest option. Buses stop within walking distance of the temple, but you can also be whisked here by *becak* (cycle-rickshaw) or rent a bike or motorbike.

Stay

 $

Shoestring
Rajasa Hotel & Restoran This traditional village home sits 1 mile (1.5km) from the temple, with simple, snug rooms and an above-average restaurant serving Javanese treats. *(Rooms from 250,000Rp/US$17)*

 $$$

Flush
Rumah Boedi Orchids spill from a rainforest in Borobudur's most stylish accommodation; rooms have their own secret gardens and the whole place oozes design cool. *(Rooms from 990,000Rp/US$68; www.rumahboediborobudur.com)*

Eat

 $

Shoestring
Alea Coffee Shop Art gallery cafe by day, restaurant and beer bar by night, Alea in Borobudur village serves tasty Indonesian staples beneath twinkling fairy lights. *(Mains from 10,000Rp/US$0.70)*

 $$$

Flush
Patio Watch Borobudur from the terrace to a soundtrack of traditional Javanese music at this charming upscale restaurant on a hilltop 2½ miles (4km) west of the ruins. *(Mains from 60,000Rp/US$4.10; www.plataranborobudur.com)*

Timing

Borobudur is best viewed at dawn (around 6am) or dusk (come in late afternoon to watch the light turn golden and then red as sunset settles over the temple). These are also the coolest times of day for the climb to the upper tiers. You'll rarely have the place to yourself, but weekdays are quieter than weekends.

Dry season visits from April to October provide better photo opportunities than the wet monsoon months from November to March.

① There are 72 bell-shaped stupas at the top of the Borobudur temple.

② A statue of Buddha at Borobudur at sunset. The site was used as a Buddhist temple until it was abandoned between the 10th and 15th centuries.

③ Travelling through the countryside around Borobudur.

Best value itineraries

4 days
In four days you can string together Borobudur and the sights of Yogyakarta and Prambanan. Start day one in Yogyakarta, exploring the historic palaces of sultans and haggling for Indonesian batik. Take a half-day trip to the Goa Jamblang caves, then devote the afternoon to the museums and the evening to a traditional dance or shadow-puppet show. Spend a day and night in Borobudur so you can see the monument by day and in the magical light of late afternoon, and devote another day to the stunning ruins of the Prambanan temples, just 10½ miles (17km) from central Yogyakarta.

7–10 days
This corner of Java has an amazing concentration of things to do, with short distances between them. Devote a couple of days to the sights, spectacles and flavours of Yogyakarta, then take two days at Borobudur to explore the temple and the surrounding villages. Head over to Prambanan and take in the interesting, outlying temples of the Plaosan group as well as the magnificent structures in the main complex. Allow two more days for the dawn hike to the summit of Gunung Merapi or nearby Gunung Merbabu for views of the fireworks if Merapi is putting on a lava show.

© Philip Lee Harvey / Lonely Planet

Europe

Blue Lagoon ☆ ICELAND

Norwegian Sea

KEY
- ❶ Bay of Kotor
- ❷ Plitvice Lakes
- ❸ Schloss Neuschwanstein
- ❹ Stari Most

Geirangerfjord ☆
NORWAY

Skara Brae ☆   **Trolltunga** ☆

Giant's Causeway ☆

North Sea

IRELAND   UNITED
KINGDOM   DENMARK

*NORTH
ATLANTIC
OCEAN*

**British
Museum** ☆

Stonehenge ☆ ☆ ☆ **Rijksmuseum**
NETHERLANDS

BELGIUM   GERMANY

Mont Saint-Michel ☆   **Louvre** ☆   **Klementinum
Library** ☆

LUXEMBOURG   CZECH
REPUBLIC

FRANCE   LIECHTENSTEIN
SWITZERLAND ↓ ❸

*Bay of
Biscay*   AUSTRIA

CERN ☆   SLOVENIA

Bordeaux ☆   **Matterhorn** ☆   **Grand
Canal** ☆ CROATIA

ANDORRA ↓   ❷

PORTUGAL   SAN MARINO

Sintra ☆   MONACO

SPAIN   **Colosseum &
Sistine Chapel** ☆

**Sagrada
Família** ☆   ITALY

Pompeii ☆

☆ **Alhambra**   *Tyrrhenian
Sea*

Mediterranean Sea

Northern Lights ✪

SWEDEN

Gulf of Bothnia

FINLAND

White Sea

RUSSIA

✪ **Hermitage Museum**

ESTONIA

LATVIA

Baltic Sea

LITHUANIA

Kaliningrad
(RUSSIA)

BELARUS

POLAND

✪ **St. Basil's Cathedral**

Former Aral Sea

UKRAINE

SLOVAKIA

✪ **Szechenyi Baths**

HUNGARY

MOLDOVA

ROMANIA

SERBIA

BOSNIA &
HERCEGOVINA

❹
MONTENEGRO

❶ KOSOVO

NORTHERN
MACEDONIA

ALBANIA

✪ **Meteora**

GREECE

Ionian Sea

Aegean Sea

Acropolis ✪

BULGARIA

Sea of Azov

Black Sea

✪ **Aya Sofya**

Caspian Sea

GEORGIA

✪ **Davit Gareji**

AZERBAIJAN

ARMENIA

Nemrut Dağı ✪

✪ **Cappadocia**

TURKEY

✪ **Ephesus**

© Justin Foulkes / Lonely Planet

NORWAY/ICELAND

Northern Lights

The Inuit thought the dancing rays were the souls of the dead, Scandinavian folklore describes them as the spirits of unmarried women and the Japanese believed that a child conceived under the spectacle would be fortunate in life. Modern science, however, has a different take on the celestial kaleidoscope that we call the aurora borealis, or Northern Lights.

The lights form when solar flares are drawn by the earth's magnetic field towards the North Pole. But you'll form your own interpretation as you watch, spellbound, the ethereal veils of green, white, violet or red light, shimmering and dancing like silent fireworks across the night sky. Although they appear in many forms – pillars, streaks, wisps and haloes of vibrating light – they're most memorable when taking the form of pale curtains wafting on a gentle breeze. Usually, the Arctic aurora appears as a faint green or light rose but, in periods of extreme activity, can change to yellow or crimson.

Three key things are required to see the Northern Lights: dark, clear skies; a far northern location; and a little bit of luck. The northern regions of Norway and Iceland are among the best places on the planet to see them: the town of Tromsø, 250 miles (400km) north of the Arctic Circle, is Norway's best-known base for aurora spotting, while you can take aurora-spotting trips straight from Iceland's capital, Reykjavík.

Travel

International

Tromsø Airport offers direct flights from many Norwegian cities including Bodø, Trondheim and Oslo, with onward international flights from there. Norwegian airlines also serve a few international destinations including London (Gatwick). A growing number of airlines fly to Iceland (including budget carriers) from destinations in Europe and North America. Most fly to Keflavík International Airport, Iceland's main airport, 30 miles (48km) southwest of Reykjavík.

Regional

Many tour companies offer 'Northern Lights tours' (by boat, 4WD or bus) – they are essentially taking you to areas with less light pollution and cloud cover to increase your viewing odds. You can do this yourself, though inexperienced winter drivers should not chase clear skies in remote, snowy areas.

Stay

Shoestring

Reykjavík Downtown Hostel The reviews are so good for this clean, charming, well-run hostel that it regularly lures large groups and the non-backpacker set. *(Dorms from 5700kr/ US$46.60, doubles from 18,400kr/US$151; www.hostel.is)*

Midrange

Smart Hotel Tromsø The Tromsø outpost of this budget mini-chain offers some of the best rates in town and it's a fine base – as long as you don't mind basic facilities and decor. *(Doubles from 725kr/US$86; www.smarthotel.no/en/tromso)*

Flush

Kvosin Downtown The suites at this historic hotel in Reykjavík have espresso machines, kitchenettes and organic toiletries. *(Suites from 43,600kr/US$349; www.kvosinhotel.is)*

Eat

Shoestring

Risø This coffee and lunch bar in Tromsø is always packed. Come for hand-brewed coffee, open-faced sandwiches and delicious cakes. *(Mains from 95kr/US$11; www.risoe-mk.no)*

Midrange

Grandi Mathöll A former Reykjavík fish factory turned pioneering street-food hall. Long trestle tables sit beside stalls selling a diverse range of lamb, fish and veggie delights. *(Mains from 1200kr/US$9.82; www.grandimatholl.is)*

Flush

Fiskfélagið The 'Fish Company' takes Icelandic seafood recipes and spins them through far-flung inspirations. Dine on the terrace or in an intimate-feeling, stone-and-timber room. *(Lunch mains from 2700kr/US$22, dinner mains from 4800kr/US$38; www.fiskfelagid.is)*

Timing

Mid-September to mid-April is the 'official' season for seeing the Northern Lights, but it can be longer given the right conditions.

Peak winter months enjoy the most darkness (an important factor for viewing), but also heavier weather conditions, storms and cloud cover.

To combine the experience with more earthbound festivities, visit Tromsø in late January for the Northern Lights Festival.

The aurora borealis lights up the sky over Reine in the Lofoten islands of northern Norway.

Curtains of light are caused by electrically charged particles from the Sun colliding with gases in the Earth's atmosphere, here over Norway.

The Northern Lights can be best viewed from sunset to dawn during winter months, here in northern Iceland.

Best value itineraries

7 days

For the best aurora opportunities, head to lesser-travelled west Iceland and its landscapes of lava fields, fjords and ice caps. Start in Reykjavík, enjoying the city's museums, cafes and bars while getting acclimatised. Then travel to Borgarnes along the coastal route and learn about the sagas at its excellent Settlement Centre. Next explore the wonderful Snæfellsnes Peninsula and Snæfellsjökull National Park, which offer a multitude of hikes, taking in bird cliffs, volcanic craters, lava tubes and protected native-flower terrain. Best of all, when the clouds clear, the skies are fabulously dark – prime for aurora spotting.

10 days

The mystique of Norway's extreme north has drawn explorers for centuries. Fly straight to aurora-central Tromsø. Spend two days here visiting the Polar Museum, admiring the majestic Arctic Cathedral and aurora spotting after dark. Next head east for the rock carvings of Alta, then Nordkapp: as far north as you can go in Norway without setting out to sea. Then head inland to Karasjok and Kautokeino to the heartland of the Sami people. If time and budget allow, catch a flight from Tromsø to the Svalbard archipelago, one of Europe's last great wildernesses.

Hermitage Museum

It's a question that's vexed generations of scholars: where exactly is the world's greatest museum? London, Paris, Madrid, New York? Well, many would say none of the above: the maestro of museums is in St Petersburg and it goes by the name of the Hermitage.

The enormous collection of more than three million items almost amounts to a comprehensive history of Western European art. Started by Catherine the Great, expanded by Nicholas I and later by the Communist state, this iconic establishment's collection is quite simply mind-boggling, with more Rembrandts than the Louvre and an almost unrivalled collection of early 20th-century art. From imperial porcelain to post-impressionist masterworks, from Egyptian mummies to priceless Fabergé eggs, it's a treasure trove to match any of the world's historical institutions.

Incredibly, however, the main collection is only the beginning. There are 20 times more items contained in the museum's sprawling vaults, not to mention the complex's other sites, including the General Staff Building, Menshikov Palace on Vasilyevsky Island, Imperial Porcelain factory and stunning Winter Palace, a profusion of columns, windows and recesses tinted mint green, white and gold. But for many visitors, it's the dazzling apartments and staterooms of the Romanovs that linger in the memory: a fascinating and poignant glimpse of the centuries-old aristocratic Russia that was swept aside by revolution in 1917.

Travel

International
St Petersburg is well connected to the rest of Europe by plane, train, ferry and bus. The vast majority of travellers arrive in St Petersburg by air at Pulkovo Airport. Train is also a popular way to get here – from Moscow there are pleasantly slow overnight sleeper trains as well as up to eight fast four-hour daytime Sapsan trains.

Regional
St Petersburg's metro is the fastest way to cover long distances (Admiralteyskaya is the stop for the Hermitage). Buses are best for shorter distances in areas without good metro coverage; they can be slow going, but the views are good. Trolleybuses are slower still, but are cheap and plentiful. *Marshrutky* are the private sector's contribution – fast fixed-route minibuses that you can get on or off anywhere along their routes.

Stay

Shoestring
Soul Kitchen Hostel This gorgeous hostel is well located and lots of fun. Choose from chic private rooms or double-width dorm beds, then chill in the lounge with record player and projector. *(Dorms from R1500/US$22, doubles from R5700/US$84; www.soulkitchenhostel.com)*

Midrange
Rachmaninov Antique Hotel The long-established Rachmaninov still feels like a secret. It's pleasantly old world, with hardwood floors and attractive Russian furnishings, particularly in the breakfast salon, which has a grand piano. *(Doubles from R7500/US$111; www.hotelrachmaninov.com)*

Eat

Shoestring
Dekabrist Conveniently located for a post-Hermitage meal, this modern cafe is excellent value. The simple menu includes burgers, grilled salmon, pork schnitzel, falafel and a range of salads and desserts. *(Mains from R320/US$4.75; www.decabrist.net)*

Midrange
Chekhov Superb Russian food served in environs that make you feel as if you're in a traditional 19th-century Russian dacha. Cleverly, the menu is hidden inside classic novels. *(Mains from R550/US$8.15; www.restaurant-chekhov.ru)*

Timing

Outside May to September is the best time to avoid the crowds.

During the first week in January, and the first week or two of May, St Petersburg empties as many residents go on holiday. Museums and other institutions have short hours or are closed during these periods.

The Stars of White Nights Festival, between late May and early July, attracts many visitors – book travel and accommodation in advance.

1
The Winter Palace on St Petersburg's square was designed in the 18th century by Italian architect Francesco Rastrelli.

2
Gold gilding, intricate ceiling decoration and plenty of marble and malachite add to the opulence of the palace interior.

3
The palace was commissioned by Catherine the Great, who clearly liked a little gold.

Best value itineraries

3–4 days
You'll need a whole day for the Hermitage. Decide which parts of the collection you want to see, but the exhibition is so enormous that you'll inevitably discover something unexpected. Spend the rest of the day with a sightseeing cruise on the canals and an evening watching ballet at the Mariinsky Theatre. Over the next few days, climb the dome of St Isaac's Cathedral for superb views of the city, see the dazzling ensemble of Palace Square, the Winter Palace and the General Staff Building, wander along to the Summer Garden and explore the city's beautiful Petrograd side.

7–10 days
Most visitors to Russia have Moscow and St Petersburg high on their wish list. Start in Moscow with the Kremlin, Red Square, the Tretyakov Gallery, a performance at the Bolshoi Theatre and a walk around the revamped Gorky Park. Break your journey between the two big cities at tourist-friendly Veliky Novgorod. It's home to an impressive riverside kremlin, ancient churches and a wonderful open-air museum of wooden architecture. Then arrive in historic St Petersburg and visit the Hermitage and other attractions described above. If you have the time, venture out to grand palaces such as Peterhof and Tsarskoe Selo, easy half-day trips from the city.

1

© Natapong P. / 500px

Cappadocia

As if plucked from a whimsical fairy tale and set down upon the stark Anatolian plains, Cappadocia is a geological oddity of honeycombed hills and towering boulders of otherworldly beauty.

The fantastical topography is matched by the human history here. People have long utilised the region's soft stone, seeking shelter underground and leaving the countryside scattered with fascinating cavern architecture. The fairy-chimney rock formations, fresco-adorned rock-cut churches of Göreme Open-Air Museum and the subterranean refuges of Derinkuyu and Kaymaklı are the most famous sights, while simply bedding down in one of Cappadocia's cave hotels is an experience in 21st-century cave living.

Whether you're wooed here by the hiking potential, the history or the bragging rights of becoming a modern troglodyte for a night, it's the lunarscape panoramas that you'll remember. This region's accordion-ridged valleys, shaded in a palette of dusky orange and cream, are an epiphany of a landscape – the stuff of psychedelic daydreams.

Travel

International
Two airports serve central Cappadocia: Kayseri Airport and Nevşehir Airport. Both have several flights daily from İstanbul and the latter from some destinations in Europe. The main operators are Turkish Airlines and Pegasus Airlines. The nearest train stations are at Niğde and Kayseri. Most buses from İstanbul and other western Turkey destinations travel to Cappadocia overnight.

Regional
Dolmuşes (minibuses) travel through the Cappadocia region between Ürgüp and Avanos via Ortahisar, the Göreme Open-Air Museum, Göreme, Çavuşin, Paşabağı and Zelve, and going in the opposite direction from Avanos. You can hop on and off anywhere you choose along the route.

Stay

$ Shoestring
Dorm Cave Why pay loads to stay in a Cappadocian cave? This hostel in Göreme offers three cave dorms that share bathrooms across the courtyard, and three private rooms upstairs. *(Dorms from €7/US$8; www.travellerscave.com)*

$$ Midrange
Kelebek Hotel Exuding Anatolian inspiration at every turn, the rooms at this Göreme hotel are spread over two gorgeous stone houses, each with a fairy chimney protruding skyward. *(Doubles from €55/US$63; www.kelebekhotel.com)*

$$$ Flush
Hezen Cave Hotel From the foyer's ceiling of recycled telegraph poles to the terrace with 360-degree views, every detail at this design hotel in Ortahisar has been thought through. *(Doubles from €145/US$165; www.hezenhotel.com)*

Eat

$ Shoestring
Keyif Cafe The small menu at this Göreme cafe offers decent salads as well as *gözleme* (savoury pancakes) and Turkish *kebap* classics, and the large selection of local wines is a winner. *(Mezes ₺7/US$1.30)*

$$ Midrange
Saklı Konak Take a taste-bud tour of village food in Uçhisar with owner Rıza. Dishes are cooked in the *tandır* (clay oven); ingredients are sourced from neighbours' gardens. *(Mains from ₺20/US$3.75; www.saklikonakhotel.com)*

$$$ Flush
Ziggy Cafe Named after host Selim's dog, this restaurant in Ürgüp has a two-tiered terrace filled with customers feasting on the finest meze in Cappadocia. *(Meze set menus ₺60-65/US$11-12, mains from ₺20/US$3.75; www.ziggycafe.com)*

Timing

In May art, music and yoga descend on the valley moonscapes during the Cappadox Festival.

July is the best time to pull on your hiking boots, especially tackling the Taurus Mountains.

From December to February, join the snow bunnies at Erciyes Dağı (Mt Erciyes) ski resort.

Hot air balloons are a popular way to view Cappadocia; they take off every morning that has suitable conditions.

You can also explore the place on horseback.

The volcanic outcrop of Uçhisar Castle is riddled with tunnels; arrive early to avoid the tour groups.

Best value itineraries

3 days
Three days is a good amount of time to explore Cappadocia. Base yourself in a cave hotel and visit the Göreme Open-Air Museum's rock-cut frescoed churches and the Byzantine underground cities at Kaymaklı and Derinkuyu. Take a hot-air balloon trip over the fantastical landscape or do some horse riding through the valleys. Take in the panoramic views from Uçhisar Castle, one of Cappadocia's most prominent landmarks, and make time for a hike through the Güllüdere (Rose) Valley, seeking out hidden churches among pigeon-house–riddled cliffs and the thin rock spires known as 'fairy chimneys'.

10 days
It's easy to extend a Cappadocia adventure to 10 days or more. After three days exploring the region, it's on into Anatolia. Stop in Eğirdir and tour the turquoise-domed Mevlâna Museum, containing the tomb of the Mevlâna (whirling dervish) order's 13th-century founder. Lakeside Eğirdir is a good base for hiking the Taurus Mountains (Toros Dağları). Don't miss the stunning ruins of Sagalassos, a Greco-Roman city at 1500m in the Taurus Mountains. Detour to lakeside İznik, where the town's Ottoman tile-making heritage is impressively displayed. The final leg of the journey is a ferry across the Sea of Marmara to İstanbul.

© Roy Conchie / Alamy Stock Photo

ITALY

Pompeii

The ghostly ruins of ancient Pompeii (*Pompei* in Italian) are a remarkably well-preserved slice of ancient life, where it's possible to walk down Roman streets, snoop around millennia-old houses, temples, shops, cafes and amphitheatres, and even step inside a Roman brothel.

Much of the site's value lies in the fact that the town wasn't simply blown away by Vesuvius in AD 79, but buried under a layer of *lapilli* (burning fragments of pumice stone). The result is one of the world's most engrossing archaeological experiences, which can teach us much about life two thousand years ago.

The ancient city was once home to about 20,000 inhabitants, but an earthquake in AD 62 meant many residents were actually living elsewhere by the time Vesuvius erupted 17 years later. In all, it's thought 2000 men, women and children perished in the eruption and its aftermath.

Exploring the ruins is like entering a time machine, hurling you back to the age of emperors and Latin chatter. Here time remains permanently paused, and the city's frescoed homes, businesses, theatres and bathhouses are frozen, forever waiting for their occupants to return. Few archaeological sites offer such an intimate connection to the past, and few are as deeply haunting and evocative.

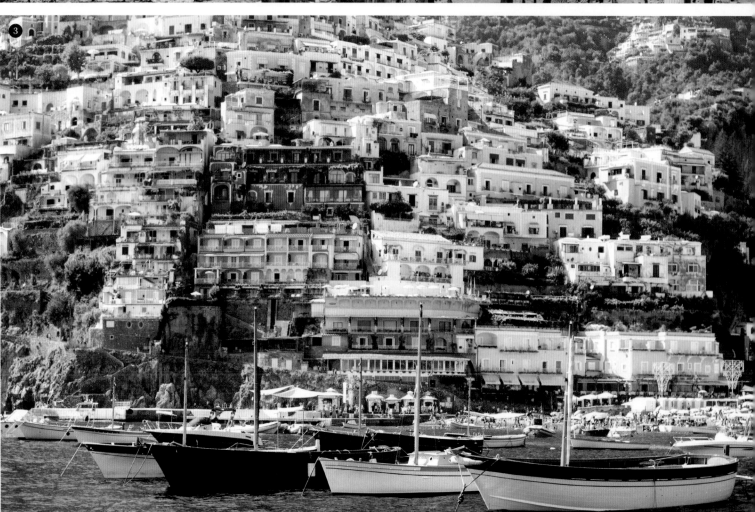

Travel

International
Naples International Airport, which is 15½ miles (25km) northwest of Pompeii, is southern Italy's main airport. It's served by a number of major airlines and low-cost carriers, including easyJet, which operates flights to Naples from London, Paris, Amsterdam, Vienna, Berlin and several other European cities.

Regional
To reach the ruins by train from Naples or Sorrento, alight at Pompei Scavi–Villa dei Misteri station, located beside the main entrance at Porta Marina. If driving from Naples, head southeast on the A3, using the Pompei exit and following the signs to Pompei Scavi. Car parks are clearly marked and vigorously touted. Close to the ruins, Camping Spartacus offers good value, all-day parking.

Stay

Shoestring
Camping Spartacus Opposite the ruins, this satisfactory camping site includes basic, air-conditioned cabins. *(Sites for two adults and car €20/US$23; www.campingspartacus.it)*

Midrange
Case Tolentino This pleasant hotel is run by a team of civic-minded Neapolitans and occupies part of a 16th-century monastery. *(Doubles from €55/US$62; www.casatolentino.it)*

Flush
Hotel San Francesco al Monte Another Neapolitan monastery, where the monks' cells have become elegant rooms and the ancient cloisters house an open-air bar. *(Doubles €162/US$184; www.sanfrancescoalmonte.it)*

Eat

Shoestring
Sofi Street Food Tasty Neapolitan street food like *panino napoletano* (rolls stuffed with cheese and salami) and *involtini* (stuffed pizza wraps). *(Snacks from €1.50/US$1.70, pizza from €3/US$3.40; www.facebook.com/streetfoodpompei)*

Midrange
Melius Not far from the ruins, this gourmet deli celebrates Campanian flavours: *mozzarella di bufala*, Gragnano pasta, smoked Cilento salamis and anchovies from Cetara. *(Cheese and meat platters €12/US$14, meals around €25/US$; www.salumeriamelius.com)*

Flush
President Pompeii's Michelin-starred standout is run by charming owner-chef Paolo Gramaglia, who is well-known for his passion for local produce, history and culinary whimsy. *(Meals from €40/US$45; www.ristorantepresident.it)*

Timing

Summer is high season and queues can be long; buy your ticket online to avoid them.

Visit in the early morning or late afternoon, when the sun's not too hot.

Allow at least three or four hours for the site, longer if you want to go into detail. Wear a hat, sunscreen and comfortable, flat shoes.

Pompeii is frozen in time: the year AD 79. Recent research suggests that the eruption occurred in October that year.

Mt Vesuvius looms in the distance.

The hillside town of Positano is a side-trip from Pompeii.

Frescoes in the Villa dei Misteri in Pompeii.

Ornamental features in the baths of Pompeii.

Best value itineraries

4 days
Base yourself in action-packed Naples for four days, savouring its World Heritage-status pizza and visceral street life. Make time for top-tier antiquities at the Museo Archeologico Nazionale, astounding 18th-century sculptures in the Capella Sansevero and, in season, an evening of opera or ballet at Europe's oldest running theatre, Teatro San Carlo. Take a kayaking tour of the city's coastline, then spend the last day visiting Pompeii by train.

7 days
Campania's coastline is one of the world's most beautiful, inspiring countless artists, romantics and bon vivants. Start with two days in Naples and another in Pompeii. On day four, catch a morning ferry to Capri, giving yourself two days to fall madly in love with this fabled island. Glide into the dazzling Grotta Azzurra (Blue Grotto), ride up to Monte Solaro and lose the hordes on walking trails. On day six, catch a ferry to Sorrento, from where buses and seasonal ferries continue to chic Positano. The historic town of Amalfi makes another easy day trip.

© crystaltmc / Getty Images

© Viacheslav Lopatin / Shutterstock

①

© Jeremy Woodhouse / Getty Images

SPAIN

Alhambra

Set against a backdrop of brooding Sierra Nevada peaks, the Alhambra is Granada's – and Europe's – love letter to Moorish culture.

This fortified palace complex started life as a walled citadel before going on to become the opulent seat of Granada's Nasrid emirs. Their showpiece palaces, the 14th-century Palacios Nazaríes, are among the finest Islamic buildings in Europe and, together with the gorgeous Generalife gardens, form the amazing architectural ensemble known as the Alhambra.

Spanning various stages of construction between the 9th and 14th centuries, the Alhambra (whose name derives from the Arabic *al-qala'a al-hamra*, the Red Castle) is like an *Arabian Nights* fantasy. Wandering its courtyards, patios, staircases and gardens, you'll glimpse masterpiece mosaics, serene pools, tinkling fountains, Islamic statues, glazed tiles and ornamented ceilings. You'll smell the fragrance of citrus trees and flowers of every hue. You'll wander through palatial rooms, peaceful chapels and soaring hallways. You'll get lost in the shady, secret paradise known as the Generalife, the sultans' gorgeous summer estate. And best of all you'll glimpse a knockout view over Granada's jumbled rooftops all the way to the rocky ridge of mountains beyond. Astonishing, amazing, inspiring: the Alhambra surpasses all these adjectives.

Travel

International
Granada Airport is 10½ miles (17km) west of the city, near the A92. Direct flights connect with Madrid, Barcelona, Bilbao, Palma de Mallorca, and, outside Spain, London, Manchester and Milan. It's served by international airlines such as easyJet, Vueling, Iberia and British Airways. Trains and buses arrive from most major Spanish cities.

Regional
Opened in September 2017, Granada's long-awaited metro – in fact more a light rail link, as all but a 1½ mile (3km) stretch of it is overground – runs between Albolote in the north and Armilla in the southwest, serving 26 stations. There is also a useful bus network. Bus C3 runs right to the Alhambra's ticket office from a bus stop just off Plaza Isabel la Católica.

Stay

$ Shoestring
Hostal Arteaga Basic, value-for-money digs in a convenient central location just off Gran Vía de Colón. *(Doubles from €30/US$34; www.hostalarteaga.es)*

$$ Midrange
Carmen de la Alcubilla del Caracol This sought-after small hotel inhabits a whitewashed *carmen* (villa) on the slopes of the Alhambra. Outside, you can bask in the premium views on offer from the spectacular terraced garden. *(Rooms from €100/US$113; www.alcubilladelcaracol.com)*

$$$ Flush
Casa Morisca Hotel Live like a Nasrid emir in this late-15th-century mansion in the historic Albayzín quarter. Some rooms have Alhambra views. *(Doubles from €129/US$146; www.hotelcasamorisca.com)*

Eat

$ Shoestring
Hicuri Art Restaurant Granada's leading street artist, El Niño de las Pinturas, has created a psychedelic backdrop to the delicious vegan food that's served up here. *(Mains from €7.50/US$8.50; www.restaurantehicuriartvegan.com)*

$$ Midrange
Los Diamantes A scruffy old-school joint that is a local institution. Always busy, it's generally standing-room only, but the seafood and tapas are excellent. *(Dishes from €10/US$11; www.barlosdiamantes.com)*

$$$ Flush
La Fábula Restaurante This is the domain of chef Ismael Delgado López, whose artfully composed plates of contemporary Spanish cuisine are guaranteed to impress. *(Mains from €24/US$27; www.restaurantelafabula.com)*

Timing

Late September and October are perfect for sightseeing. The summer tourist hordes have left, but the weather is still warm.

Visit in winter and combine a city break with skiing in the nearby Sierra Nevada mountains.

As one of Spain's most high-profile attractions, the Alhambra can draw up to 6000 daily visitors. Tickets sell out quickly so to avoid disappointment it pays to book ahead, either online or by phone.

The Sierra Nevada mountains of Andalucía lie beyond Granada and the Alhambra.

Water was a significant symbol of luxury for the Moors and the Alhambra has many water gardens.

Several white-awashed villages in Las Alpujarras, such as Trevelez, are easily reached from Granada.

Best value itineraries

4–6 days
Begin in Málaga, which has enough attractions to keep you occupied for one very full day. Allow at least a couple of nights in Granada for the astonishing Alhambra, gilded Capilla Real and medieval Muslim quarter of Albayzín. Rent a car and make for the otherworldly valleys of Las Alpujarras, with their fine mountain scenery and North African–style villages. With more time, you could catch a train to sultry Seville for flamenco and nightlife.

7–10 days
If you have the funds, a longer Andalucían adventure beckons. From Granada, head west for three days along quiet back roads to some of Andalucía's most spectacular villages and towns: Mudéjar Antequera, spectacular Ronda, whitewashed Tarifa, beguiling Vejer de la Frontera, and Arcos de la Frontera, one of Andalucía's most glorious *pueblos blancos* (white villages). With a few days left, leave the car and spend a night in Jerez de la Frontera, allowing time to visit its sherry bodegas.

© Andrew Opila / Shutterstock

ENGLAND

Stonehenge

Welcome to Britain's most iconic archaeological site. This compelling ring of monolithic stones has been attracting a stream of pilgrims, poets and philosophers for the past 5000 years, and is still a haunting echo from Britain's forgotten past and a reminder of those who once walked the ceremonial avenues across Salisbury Plain.

It's also one of Britain's great archaeological mysteries. Despite countless theories about the site's real purpose, from a sacrificial centre to a celestial timepiece, no one knows for sure what drove prehistoric Britons to expend so much time and effort on its construction. Like many stone circles in Britain, the inner horseshoes are aligned to coincide with sunrise at the midsummer solstice, which some claim supports the theory that the site was some kind of astronomical calendar.

An ultramodern makeover at ancient Stonehenge has brought an impressive new visitor centre and the closure of an intrusive road. The result gives a strong sense of historical context, with dignity and mystery returned. Most visitors gaze at the 50-tonne stones from behind the perimeter fence, but with enough planning you can arrange an early-morning or evening tour and gain access to the inner ring itself. In the slanting sunlight, away from the crowds, it's an inescapably mystical, ethereal place.

Travel

International

Travellers from abroad can fly into London, a major destination where five international airports have connections to most of the world, or Bristol Airport, served by flights from more than 100 European cities. Travellers from Europe may also arrive in London via the Eurostar high-speed passenger rail service. The quickest way to Stonehenge is by train to Salisbury, the nearest town. Rail lines run from London Waterloo (1½ hours), Bath (one hour) and Bristol (1¼ hours).

Regional

No public transport goes direct to the site. The Stonehenge Tour (www.thestonehengetour.info) leaves Salisbury's railway station half-hourly from June to August and hourly between September and May. The ticket includes admission to Stonehenge and the Iron Age hill fort at Old Sarum; it stops there on the return leg.

Stay

$

Shoestring

Spire House The small Salisbury B&B has beautifully kept rooms, from quirky and contemporary to heritage chic (four-poster bed, mock oil paints and a mini leather armchair). *(Doubles from £80/US$104)*

$$

Midrange

Chapter House In this 800-year-old boutique beauty in Salisbury, wood panels and wonky stairs sit beside duck-your-head beams, slipper baths and the odd heraldic crest. *(Doubles from £135/US$176; www.thechapterhouseuk.com)*

Eat

$

Shoestring

King's House A cafe made for sightseeing, King's House offers fine views of the soaring spire of neighbouring Salisbury Cathedral from the flower-framed garden. *(Snacks from £4/US$5.20; www.salisburymuseum.org.uk)*

$$$

Flush

Charter 1227 Classic English dishes have a firm foothold here – feast on duck confit, beef fillet or roast lamb. *(Mains £15-20/US$20-26; www.charter1227.co.uk)*

Timing

Major gatherings happen at Stonehenge to mark the summer and winter solstices – plan accordingly.

A pathway frames the ring of massive stones. If you want to actually step inside the circle you need to book one of English Heritage's Stone Circle Access Visits (£38.50/US$50; www.englishheritage.co.uk). Hour-long tours take place in the evening or early morning, but places are limited to 30 people; book at least three months in advance.

The famous stone circle in springtime.

The outer sarsen stones are local sandstone, but the interior bluestones are thought to have been transported 160 miles (257km) from Wales.

The Roman Baths that lend the city of Bath its name date from the first century AD.

Best value itineraries

3–4 days
Catch the train direct from London to Salisbury, where you can spend a day looking around the city and visiting the cathedral before a tour to Stonehenge. It's worth visiting the other archaeological sites nearby too: Stonehenge actually forms part of a huge complex of ancient monuments. North of Stonehenge and running roughly east–west is the Cursus, an elongated embanked oval; the smaller Lesser Cursus is nearby. Two clusters of burial mounds, the Old and New Kings Barrows, sit beside the ceremonial pathway known as the Avenue, which originally linked Stonehenge with the River Avon, 2 miles (3km) away. Another site, Woodhenge, consists of six concentric rings that would once have been marked by wooden posts and may have supported a building.

7–10 days
Starting at the old cathedral city of Winchester, drive west to Stonehenge then head a short distance north to another great stone circle: Avebury. With a diameter of 348m, Avebury is the largest stone circle in the world. It's also one of the oldest, dating from 2500 to 2200 BC. Move west through Somerset to beautiful Bath, where you can wander around the Royal Crescent and Roman Baths. Conclude in the historic university city of Bristol, factoring in the M-Shed Museum, a walk around the harbour and a visit to Brunel's groundbreaking steamship, SS *Great Britain*.

Davit Gareja

Clambering around the echoing chapels, deserted monks' cells and teetering cliffside paths is guaranteed to bring out your inner Indiana Jones.

On Georgia's border with Azerbaijan, the mysterious, ancient complex of Davit Gareja (or Gareji) consists of about 15 monasteries, which have been hacked out by hand into the steep, rocky slopes of Mt Gareja. Sometimes known as 'cave monasteries', they offer an evocative glimpse of the lives of the ascetic monks who lived, worked, studied and prayed in this lunar, almost extraterrestrial, semi-desert landscape. The sprawling complex was founded by St David (Davit), one of the 13 ascetic Syrian fathers who returned from the Middle East to bring Christianity to Georgia in the 6th century.

The 15 monasteries are spread over a remote area, so most visitors usually see only two. The oldest is three-levelled Lavra, where you can visit the caves of Davit and his Kakhetian disciple Lukiane, the 6th-century cave church Peristsvaleba and Davit's tomb. On the hill above it, Udabno is worth seeing for its fabulous frescoes, including striking examples depicting the Last Supper, Christ with his disciples, and a scene of St David and Lukiane surrounded by deer. They're a fascinating window into the world of early Christianity – although you'll need some bravery and dexterity to see some of them.

1

2

Travel

International
Tbilisi International Airport offers direct flights from more than 40 international destinations spread from Paris to Ürümqi (China). *Marshrutky* (minibuses) are the main transport around Georgia and they depart from several terminals around the city. Tbilisi's main train station is the railway hub of Georgia, but the only international trains are currently the sleepers to Baku and Yerevan. Tbilisi is about 1½ hours from the monastery.

Regional
From about mid-April to mid-October, Gareji Line runs a daily return minibus between Tbilisi and Davit Gareja. You get 2½ to three hours at Lavra and Udabno monasteries, plus a stop at Oasis Club on the way back. The ticket allows you to come back any day, so you can stay over at Oasis Club if you wish. There are also day tours from Tbilisi with some hostels and agencies, or you can make your own way by *marshrutka* to Sagarejo and then take a taxi.

Stay

Shoestring
Oasis Club This Polish-run hostel-hotel-restaurant is almost in the middle of nowhere at semi-abandoned Udabno village, 8½ miles (14km) before Lavra monastery. Choose between a 20-bed hostel or cosy wooden hotel rooms. *(Dorms from 25 GEL/US$9, doubles from 100 GEL/US$36; www.facebook.com/oasisclubudabno)*

Flush
Rooms Hotel Tbilisi By far Tbilisi's most stylish hotel. The wood-furnished rooms here are kitted out in contemporary styles, but feature rare throwback details such as transistor radios and iron-footed bathtubs. *(Rooms from US$165; http://roomshotels.com/tbilisi)*

Eat

Shoestring
Oasis Club At the Oasis Club's restaurant-bar, cheerful staff serve up good salads, soups, *khachapuri* (cheese-filled breads) and many other dishes. *(Dishes 5-12 GEL/US$1.80-4.35; www.facebook.com/oasisclubudabno)*

Midrange
Mukhatsakatukha Known to all as 'Mukha', this charming restaurant fashions European-style dishes like pork escalope with mustard-and-cream sauce, or mussels *provençale*. *(Mains 10-20 GEL/US$3.65-7.25)*

Timing

In July and August it can get fearfully hot by the middle of the day, so an early start, getting there by 10am, is ideal.

It takes two to three hours to explore Lavra and Udabno.

The cave monastery complex at Davit Gareja.

Of the 15 monasteries, two have been restored: Lavra and Udabno.

Beautiful frescoes decorate the interior of Udabno monastery.

Georgia is thought to be the birthplace of wine and is home to some ancient varieties of grape.

Best value itineraries

3–4 days
With only a few days to spare, focus on Tbilisi, Georgia's fascinating capital, with its lovely Old Town, still redolent of an ancient Eurasian crossroads. Amble along winding lanes and leafy squares past balconied houses and handsome churches, all overlooked by the 17-centuries-old Narikala Fortress. From Tbilisi, take day trips to Mtskheta and the Davit Gareja cave monastery.

8–10 days
Having thoroughly explored Tbilisi, opt for a couple of nights in the eastern wine-growing region of Kakheti (fitting in your visit to Davit Gareja on the way), then head to the cave city of Vardzia and maybe have a day or two of walking in Borjomi-Kharagauli National Park.

© John Noble / Getty Images

© Andrew Montgomery / Lonely Planet

NORWAY

Geirangerfjord

The fjords are, without a doubt, Norway's most famous (and fabulous) natural feature – and that's saying something in a country as scenery blessed as this. Carved out during the last ice age by long-gone glaciers, there are hundreds of fjords to explore in all – but in terms of sheer size and splendour, none can quite compare to the majestic Geirangerfjord.

Over 9 miles (15km) long, 1 mile (1.5km) wide and a Unesco World Heritage Site since 2005, this vast channel is the best-known of Norway's fjords. Due to its towering cliffs, tumbling waterfalls and shimmering blue-green water, it's a sight that's guaranteed to make a lasting imprint on your memory – although it has to be said, with more than 600,000 visitors every year, you're unlikely to have the place to yourself.

The easiest way to experience it is aboard a boat cruise or on the regular Geiranger–Hellesylt ferry, which chugs up and down the fjord several times a day. Better still, you can paddle out under your own power in a kayak or canoe, which is a sublime way to explore and also enables you to visit the more secluded reaches of the fjord that most cruise ships could never hope to access.

Travel

International
Norway is well linked to other European countries by air. Oslo receives the largest number of flights, but Bergen, Tromsø and Stavanger are also potential options. There are regular bus and rail services to Norway from neighbouring Scandinavian countries, including Sweden and Finland, and car and passenger ferries linking southern Norwegian ports with Denmark, Sweden and Germany.

Regional
The car ferry between Geiranger and Hellesylt sails four to eight times a day between May and early October (1½ hours). From mid-April to mid-October, the Hurtigruten coastal ferry makes a detour from Ålesund to Geiranger on its northbound run. From mid-June to mid-August, sightseeing buses make the spectacular run from Geiranger to Åndalsnes (three hours), known as the 'Golden Route'.

Stay

Shoestring
Geirangerfjorden Feriesenter This lovely campsite has spacious pitches and pretty, well-decorated cabins – many of which have supreme fjord views. *(Lakefront campsite for two adults 255kr/US$31, cabin from 990kr/US$118; www.geirangerfjorden.net)*

Midrange
Hotel Utsikten High on the hill above Geiranger, the family-owned Utsikten, constructed in 1893, has stunning views over town and fjord, although its rooms are on the small side. *(Rooms from 1590kr/US$190, www.classicnorway.no/hotell/hotell-utsikten-geiranger)*

Eat

Shoestring
Geiranger Sjokolade Taste handcrafted chocolate at Bengt Dahlberg's renowned workshop in the basement of an old boathouse near the waterfront. Sample unusual flavours such as truffles or cloudberry. *(Chocolates from 150kr/US$17.50; www.geirangersjokolade.no)*

Midrange
Brasserie Posten Simple salads, burgers, steaks, fish and pizza are elevated well above the norm by a passionate local chef and a stunning fjord-side terrace. *(Lunch mains 140-250kr/US$17-30, dinner mains 195-290kr/US$23-35; www.brasserieposten.no)*

Timing

July and August are the peak months in Geirangerfjord, when the majority of the cruise ships arrive. Avoid them if you can.

Arrive early or late in the day to avoid the worst of the tourist traffic.

For the best (and quietest) views, follow one of the 18 signed walks around the fjord to abandoned farmsteads, waterfalls and vista points. The lengths of the walks range between 1 mile (1.5km) and 3 miles (5km).

Waterfalls, here the Seven Sisters falls, cascade down the steep sides of Geirangerfjord.

Some of the world's most spectacular drives pass by Geirangerfjord, including the National Tourist Route to Trollstigen.

Make a stop at the pretty town of Ålesund.

Best value itineraries

3–4 days
The easiest way to reach Geirangerfjord is from the attractive coastal town of Ålesund, notable for its *jugendstil* (art nouveau) architecture. Daily round-trip cruises run directly to the fjord. Back in Ålesund, you can climb aboard the renowned Rauma Railway, a classic 70 mile (114km) train line which runs all the way to the mountains of central Norway, passing through six tunnels and 32 bridges en route. Stop off for a night in Åndalsnes, then head onwards through Dovrefjell-Sunndalsfjella Nasjonalpark to spot wild reindeer and musk ox before reaching journey's end in Dombås, a popular adventure and winter-sports centre.

7–10 days
This route takes in the sights to the south of Geirangerfjord. It's best done by car, as it includes two of Norway's most scenic roads. Begin in the pretty town of Solvorn on Lustrafjord, then climb up and over the impressive Sognefjellet Road (sometimes called the Snow Road), which runs through Jotunheimen National Park, famous for its many hiking trails. Take a break in Lom and pay a visit to its perfectly sited stave church. Then it's an onward drive to Geirangerfjord, up and over Norway's most spectacular mountain road, the Trollstigen, down to Åndalsnes and then along the coast to quiet, elegant Ålesund.

© Clive Burrow / 500px

© 4Max / Shutterstock

Mont St-Michel

It's one of France's most iconic images: an island abbey crowned by slender spires, stout ramparts and rocky outcrops, rising dramatically from the sea or towering above shimmering sands laid bare by the receding tide.

Despite huge numbers of tourists, the rock-top abbey and its narrow alleys still do a convincing job of transporting visitors back to the Middle Ages. The dramatic play of tides on this abbey-island is both magical and mysterious. Said by Celtic mythology to be a sea tomb to which souls of the dead were sent, Mont St-Michel is rich in legend and history, keenly felt as you make your way across the bridge – or barefoot across rippled sand – to this stunning architectural ensemble. Walk around it alone or, better still, hook up with a guide in nearby Genêts for a dramatic day hike across the bay.

The Mont's main street, the Grande Rue, leads up the slope past staircases and tiny passageways all the way to the crowning attraction: the medieval abbey. Be prepared for lots of steps, some of them spiral – by the time you reach the top, you'll feel that you've really earned the view.

Travel

International
The nearest international airport is in Paris. Alternatively, airports in Brest, Quimper, Rennes, Dinard and Nantes serve the UK and Ireland, as well as other European and domestic destinations. Ferries link nearby St-Malo with the Channel Islands and the English ports of Portsmouth and Poole, while the Brittany town of Roscoff is connected to Plymouth.

Regional
Pontorson is the area's main rail hub and is connected to Mont St-Michel by shuttle bus (€3.20/US$2.30). Direct services to Pontorson run from Bayeux, Caen, Cherbourg and Rennes. Intercity buses stop next to the Mont's parking lot in La Caserne from where shuttles run to the Mont.

Stay

Shoestring
Auberge de Jeunesse Centre Duguesclin This 62-bed hostel in Pontorson has four- to six-bed rooms and kitchen facilities. *(Dorms from €15/US$17; http://auberge.pontorson.fr)*

Midrange
Vent des Grèves A friendly, family-run B&B with five modern rooms, which are furnished simply and enjoy magical views of the Mont. It's located an easily walkable ½ mile (1km) east of the shuttle stop in La Caserne. *(Doubles from €58/US$66; www.ventdesgreves.com)*

Midrange
La Jacotière Built as a farmhouse in 1906, this popular family-run B&B has five comfortable rooms and one studio apartment. It affords some mighty views of Mont St-Michel. *(Doubles from €78/US$89)*

Eat

Shoestring
Crêperie La Sirène This decent *crêperie* is located near the bottom of Grande Rue in Mont St-Michel, up a 15th-century staircase from the souvenir shop. *(Crêpes €4-11/US$4.55-13)*

Midrange
Les Terrasses Poulard Amid cast-iron chandeliers and copper pots, this bright and buzzing eatery serves up bistro classics and *galettes* (buckwheat pancakes). *(Set menus €19-29/US$22-33)*

Timing

The Mont is only totally surrounded by the sea every month or two, when the tidal coefficient is above 100 and high tide is above 14m (check online before you go).

Benedictine monks hold services in the abbey at various times throughout the day.

From Monday to Saturday from mid-July to August there are illuminated *nocturnes* (night-time visits) from 7pm to midnight.

1 A tidal causeway connected Mont St-Michel for centuries until a bridge was opened in 2014.

2 The settlement was so well fortified that it was used as a prison for many years.

3 The handsome port of Honfleur draws artists from around the world.

4 Camembert cheese on a fresh baguette is a Norman treat.

Best value itineraries

3–4 days
Coming by train from Paris, Rouen will be your first stop, with its soaring Gothic cathedral, beautifully restored medieval quarter, excellent museums and vibrant cultural life. From here, you can take a side trip to Les Andelys and Monet's famous garden at Giverny, before continuing on to the highlight of Mont St-Michel.

10 days
If you have an extra week, follow the same route but allow more time for additional side trips. The attractive port of Honfleur and the medieval town of Bayeux with its famous tapestry are must-sees, as are the D-Day beaches – don't miss the affecting American Cemetery above Omaha Beach. Explore Côte d'Albâtre and Le Havre, as well as pretty Trouville and Deauville. You could also lose yourself in pastoral Normandy, famous for its cider and Camembert.

© Gerhard Roethlinger / image library

© Justin Foulkes / Lonely Planet

TURKEY

Aya Sofya

Even in mighty İstanbul, nothing tops the Aya Sofya, or Church of the Divine Wisdom, which was for centuries the greatest church in Christendom. Emperor Justinian had it built in the 6th century as part of his mission to restore the greatness of the Roman Empire. Gazing up at the floating dome, it's hard to believe this fresco-covered marvel didn't single-handedly revive Rome's fortunes.

Consecrated as a church in 537, converted to a mosque by Mehmet the Conqueror in 1453 and declared a museum by Atatürk in 1935, the Aya Sofya surpasses all of Istanbul's monuments with its innovative architectural form, rich history, religious importance and extraordinary beauty.

Aya Sofya's dome is 30m in diameter and 56m in height. It's supported by 40 massive ribs constructed of special hollow bricks and these ribs rest on four huge pillars concealed in the interior walls. As you enter the building and walk into the inner narthex, look up to see a brilliant mosaic of Christ as Pantocrator (Ruler of All) above the Imperial Door. Through this is the building's main space, famous for its dome, huge nave and glittering mosaics depicting biblical scenes and ancient figures, such as Empress Zoe, one of only three Byzantine women to rule the empire. The Byzantine emperors were crowned while seated on a throne placed within the *omphalion*, the section of inlaid marble in the main floor.

© Artur Bogacki / Shutterstock

Travel

International

İstanbul's current main airport, Atatürk International, is 4 miles (23km) west of Sultanahmet (the old city, where Aya Sofya is situated), but from early 2019 flights will be routed to the new, much larger, airport 22 miles (35km) north of the city centre. There is one *otogar* (bus station) in the city from which national and international services arrive and depart. At the time of writing there were no international rail connections, but this situation may change when upgrades to rail lines throughout the country are completed.

Regional

Public transport is cheap and efficient. Purchasing an İstanbulkart (transport card) is highly recommended. Trams run from Bağcılar in the city's west to Kabataş in Beyoğlu, stopping at the Grand Bazaar, Sultanahmet, Eminönü and Karaköy en route, supplemented by a network of metro lines. Ferries travel between the European and Asian shores, along the Bosphorus and Golden Horn, and to the Adalar (Princes' Islands).

Stay

$ Shoestring

Marmara Guesthouse Very few of Sultanahmet's family-run pensions can compete with the Marmara's cleanliness, comfort and thoughtful attention to detail. Its rooms all come equipped with comfortable beds, good bathrooms and double-glazed windows. *(Doubles from €30/US$34; www.marmaraguesthouse.com)*

$$ Midrange

Hotel Ibrahim Pasha Cultural tomes are piled in reception and throughout the 24 rooms of this exemplary design hotel, which also has a terrace bar with knockout views of the nearby Blue Mosque and Hippodrome. *(Rooms from €100/US$114; www.ibrahimpasha.com)*

Eat

$ Shoestring

Birecikli This bustling eatery in nearby Hocapaşa offers an array of liver options, meat *kebaps*, *pides* and *lahmacun* (Arabic-style pizza). *(Pides from ₺16/US$3, kebaps ₺12–33/US$2.25–6.20; www.birecikli.com)*

$$ Midrange

Balıkçı Sabahattin An enduring favourite with diners from near and far who come for the excellent menu of meze and seafood, including fish ranging from red mullet to sole. *(Mezes from ₺10/US$1.90, fish mains from ₺40/US$7.50; www.balikcisabahattin.com)*

Timing

Aya Sofya is closed on Mondays.

Go during lunchtime or late afternoon to beat the crowds.

Buy the Museum Pass İstanbul or hire a private guide to jump the queue for admission.

After exiting, head round the corner to visit the Aya Sofya Tombs and Carpet Museum, both originally part of the Aya Sofya complex.

1 Dozens of windows allow light to illuminate the interior of the Aya Sofya beneath its vast (and weighty) dome.

2 The Aya Sofya sits near the Bosphorus Straits.

3 The ruin of the Library of Census is a highlight of Ephesus, part of the extended itinerary.

Best value itineraries

4 days

Head straight to Aya Sofya Meydanı (Aya Sofya Square) for visits to the Aya Sofya, the Blue Mosque and the Basilica Cistern, then wander through the Hippodrome, where chariot races were held in ancient times. Spend the afternoon in the historic Arasta Bazaar. On day two investigate the lifestyles of the sultans at Topkapı Palace. On the remaining days, explore the streets, cafes and boutiques of Galata, Tophane, Karaköy and Çukurcuma, shop for your life in the city's Bazaar District, visit the most magnificent Ottoman mosque, the Süleymaniye, and end at the amazing Grand Bazaar, with its labyrinthine lanes, hidden caravanserais and endless souvenirs.

10 days

You'll need at least three days in İstanbul to even scrape the surface of its millennia of history. From İstanbul, take a bus to Çanakkale, a lively student town on the Dardanelles. A tour of the Gallipoli Peninsula's poignant WWI battlefields is memorable, as is a visit to the ancient city of Troy, immortalised in Homer's *Iliad*. From Çanakkale, it's a bus to Ayvalık, with its hugely atmospheric old Greek quarter and fish restaurants. Another bus journey reaches Selçuk, a base for visiting glorious Ephesus, the best-preserved classical city in the eastern Mediterranean.

© Mark Read / Lonely Planet

© FreeProd33 / Shutterstock

FRANCE

Bordeaux wine region

The ancient city of Bordeaux is the world's largest urban World Heritage Site – covering half the city, some 18 sq km. But it's better known as the gateway to France's most famous wine region: Bordeaux is surrounded by a sea of green, sun-drenched vineyards that are responsible for producing some of the world's most exquisite (and expensive) vintages.

The mere mention of hallowed names such as Château Margaux, Ausone, Cheval Blanc, Latour and Lafite Rothschild are enough to make oenophiles start to salivate – but there are plenty of smaller growers in and around Bordeaux that are well worthy of your taste buds, too. From celebrated *premiers crus* aged for years to the very first *vin nouveau*, cracked open at festivals after the autumnal harvest, *dégustation* (tasting) is an intrinsic part of life here. There are scores of local wine-growers and châteaux that will gladly welcome you into their cellars for some wine tasting – and if you need to educate your palate, there are excellent guided wine tours and tasting schools on offer as well. Be sure to name a designated driver so you can enjoy them fully.

Travel

International
Aéroport de Bordeaux, or Bordeaux-Mérignac, is 6 miles (10km) west of the city in the suburb of Mérignac, and serves many European and North African destinations. Eurolines connects Bordeaux train station with major European cities.

Regional
Bordeaux is one of France's major rail-transit points, served by the LGV (*ligne à grand vitesse*) that sees high-speed TGV trains to and from Paris cruising between Bordeaux and Tours in the Loire Valley at 320km/h. This puts Bordeaux just six hours from London by Eurostar, with a change of train in Paris. There are also slower regional trains, including to and from Arcachon (one hour) and St-Emilion (35 minutes).

Stay

$ Shoestring
Auberge de Jeunesse Bordeaux's original hostel is housed in a modern building and provides a self-catering kitchen, good wheelchair access and table football to boot. (*Dorms €24.50/US$28; www.auberge-jeunesse-bordeaux.com*)

$$ Midrange
Hôtel La Cour Carrée In an 18th-century house on a side street, this design-led boutique hotel oozes style and peace. (*Doubles €125-250/US$142-285; www.lacourcarree.com*)

$$$ Flush
Grand Hôtel de Bordeaux Bordeaux's flagship hotel squats in a stunning 18th-century neoclassical building opposite the Grand Théâtre in the city centre. (*Doubles from €290/ US$330; https://bordeaux.intercontinental.com*)

Eat

$ Shoestring
Le Magasin General Located on the right bank of the river, this enormous industrial hangar is home to the biggest and best organic restaurant in France. (*Mains €10-20/US$11-23; www.magasingeneral.camp*)

$$ Midrange
Belle Campagne The Beautiful Countryside works with local producers to ensure fresh, seasonal cuisine. Linger downstairs over tasting plates and wine or head upstairs for the Full Monty menu. (*Set-course menu lunch €16-19/US$18-22, dinner €27-32/US$31-37; www.belle-campagne.fr*)

$$$ Flush
La Tupina This bistro is fêted for its southwestern French fare: calf kidneys with fries cooked in goose fat, milk-fed lamb, tripe and goose wings. (*Set-course menu lunch €18/ US$20, dinner €44-52/US$50-59, mains €20-32/US$23-36; www.latupina.com*)

Timing

Bordeaux's many festivals include the river-themed Fête Le Fleuve (every other May); the Bordeaux Wine Festival (June); and the Bordeaux SO Good food festival (November).

Summer is busy in Bordeaux. Reserve your slot for the tourist office's fabulous guided tours a couple of weeks in advance.

Opening hours for some sights, such as Saint-Paul's Grosse Cloche and the bell tower of Basilique St-Michel, are seasonal.

1 Some of the world's most valuable wines are made from the fruit of Bordeaux's vines.

2 The city of Bordeaux is a fantastic place for a weekend and now features a smart museum of wine.

3 A bottle of Château Pétrus from Pomerol is a (very) pricey accompaniment to your dinner.

Best value itineraries

3–4 days
Begin with a bird's-eye view of Bordeaux atop Tour Pey Berland, the fancy belfry of Cathédrale St-André, then delve into the nearby Musée des Beaux-Arts. Visit Basilique St-Seurin, window shop in the boutique-rich Triangle d'Or and walk along the Pavé des Chartrons, lined with townhouses built for wealthy wine merchants in the 18th century. Continue to the Musée du Vin et du Négoce and end on a high with a two-hour visit to Bordeaux's flagship museum, La Cité du Vin. Then spend a day educating your palate with a wine-tasting workshop in town at the prestigious École du Vin de Bordeaux, before joining one of the tourist office's excellent guided *dégustation* tours that explore local Bordeaux vineyards.

7–10 days
Hit Bordeaux's food market, Marché des Capucins, for a breakfast of freshly shucked oysters, fruit and veg, cheese, meat and shoals of seafood. Enjoy a contemplative visit to Basilique St-Michel and an invigorating hike up its bell tower, nicknamed La Flèche, for brilliant city views. With more time, learn about Bordeaux history at the Musée d'Aquitaine, mooch north into Saint-Paul to admire the Grosse Cloche, explore the elegant Place de la Bourse, then cross the river over Pont de Pierre and spend the evening on the Right Bank, sipping locally brewed beer at Magasin Général and watching live jazz at Le Bistrot du Caillou. Beyond Bordeaux, take day trips to visit the honey-stoned wine town of St-Émilion, taste oysters in the Bassin d'Arcachon and see Europe's biggest sand dune, Dune du Pilat.

© Justin Foulkes / Lonely Planet

THE NETHERLANDS

Rijksmuseum

The Netherlands' top treasure house does not disappoint. The crowds huddle around Rembrandt's humongous *Night Watch* and Vermeer's *Kitchen Maid* in the Gallery of Honour, but that just means the remaining rooms are free for browsing.

You could spend days gazing at the beautiful and curious collections tucked into the nooks and crannies. And if you need a break, free sculpture-studded gardens surround the monumental building. Designed by the great Dutch architect Pierre Cuypers, the imposing red-brick museum is one of Amsterdam's landmarks. It reopened to grand fanfare in 2013 after over a decade of renovations costing €375 million.

The prize pieces, of course, are the priceless works by local heroes Rembrandt, Vermeer and Van Gogh. Familiar as these are, seeing them in the flesh is quite a different experience to looking at a reproduction in a book: you'll be impressed by the scale, the texture of the brush strokes, the detail. In total there are some 7500 other masterpieces spread over 1 mile (1.5km) of galleries, so you need to plan your visit. Alongside the Old Master paintings, other must-sees are the wonderful collection of Delftware, some fascinating antique ship models and doll's houses, and the impressive Asian Pavilion.

2

Travel

International

Schiphol is among Europe's busiest airports and has copious air links worldwide. It's the hub of Dutch passenger-carrier KLM. Many international trains arrive at Centraal Station, including the high-speed Thalys from Paris, the Eurostar from Brussels, Rotterdam and London, and German ICE trains from Cologne and Frankfurt. Major bus companies Eurolines and FlixBus both serve the city.

Regional

Of course, bicycles are the locals' main mode of getting around in Amsterdam. Rental companies are all over town; bikes cost about €12/US$14 per day. If you prefer not to pedal, the city's trams are fast, frequent and ubiquitous, operating between 6am and 12.30am. Buses and metros primarily serve the outer districts. Free ferries depart for northern Amsterdam from docks behind Centraal Station.

Stay

Shoestring

Cocomama Formerly a high-end brothel, this boutique hostel's doubles and dorms are decorated stylishly with white walls and designer Delftware or windmill themes. *(Dorms from €42/US$48; www.cocomamahostel.com)*

Midrange

Hotel Fita Family-owned Fita, close to the museum, has 15 rooms and a bountiful breakfast of eggs, pancakes, cheeses and breads. *(Doubles from €159/US$180; www.fita.nl)*

Flush

College Hotel Originally a 19th-century school, now run by hospitality students, this hotel has 40 huge, high-ceilinged rooms; you'd never think they were former classrooms. *(Doubles from €169/US$191; www.thecollegehotel.com)*

Eat

Shoestring

Braai BBQ Bar Once a canal-side *haringhuis* (herring stand), the house speciality here is barbecue ribs and roasted sausages, though there are vegetarian options as well. *(Dishes from €6.50/US$7.35; www.braaiamsterdam.nl)*

Midrange

Ron Gastrobar Ron Blaauw ran his two-Michelin-starred restaurant here before reinventing it as a 'gastrobar' (still Michelin-starred), serving 25 gourmet tapas-style dishes. *(Dishes €15/US$17; www.rongastrobar.nl)*

Flush

Rijks In a beautiful high-ceilinged space, the Rijksmuseum's Michelin-starred restaurant draws on historic Dutch influences. *(Mains €24-32/US$27-36; www.rijksrestaurant.nl)*

Timing

To avoid the biggest crowds, visit the Rijksmuseum Monday to Thursday and before 10am or after 3pm.

Pre-booking tickets online enables fast-track entry.

Many hotels sell surcharge-free tickets to the big museums as a service to guests; be sure to ask your front-desk staff.

The airy atrium of the Rijksmuseum reopened after extensive renovation in 2013.

After checking out the art, take to the city's canals for a relaxing tour.

Viewing *The Night Watch* by Rembrandt at the Rijksmuseum. The painting is being publically restored at the museum so the process is visible to visitors.

Best value itineraries

3–4 days

Begin with the biggies: take a tram to the Museum Quarter to ogle the masterpieces at the Rijksmuseum and Van Gogh Museum. They'll be crowded, so make sure you've pre-booked tickets. Modern-art buffs might want to swap the Stedelijk Museum for one of the others. Devote half a day to the Medieval Centre, including the secret gardens at the Begijnhof, a photo-op on the Dam (the square where the Royal Palace, Nieuwe Kerk and Nationaal Monument huddle) and an evening in the Red Light District. Add another couple of days for cycling in Vondelpark, shopping in the Negen Straatjes (Nine Streets) and exploring the Jordaan, the chummy district embodying the Amsterdam of yore.

7–10 days

If you've more time and cash, you can add in a few of Amsterdam's outlying neighbourhoods, such as foodie de Pijp, edgy Oost and arty Noord, then catch a train around the country's south – including visits to Golden Age Haarlem, Keukenhof Gardens (in season), museum-filled Leiden, the Dutch seat of government, Den Haag, and Vermeer's charming home town of Delft. Finish with a couple of days in cutting-edge Rotterdam.

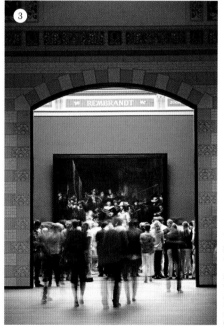

NORTHERN IRELAND

Giant's Causeway

When you first see it you'll understand why the ancients believed the Giant's Causeway was not a natural feature, but the handiwork of mighty, ancient giants.

A bizarre, bewildering, almost extraterrestrial landscape of huge hexagonal stone columns, thrust up from the pounding Atlantic waves, it looks more like a fantasy landscape dreamt up by JRR Tolkien or JK Rowling than a real-life location.

But real it most certainly is and people have come up with a rich tapestry of legends to explain its origins. The most famous story goes that the Irish giant Finn McCool built the causeway so he could cross the sea to fight the Scottish giant Benandonner. All that now remains are its ends – the Giant's Causeway in Ireland and the island of Staffa in Scotland.

In fact, the rocks were formed some 60 million years ago by volcanic activity, but it's the kind of place that seems much more suited to tall tales than dry, dusty science. So as you trek down the rocky coast path, watching the waves crash against the rocks and sea-spray filling the air, let your imagination wander: you're in the land of giants now, and all you need to do is believe...

1

2

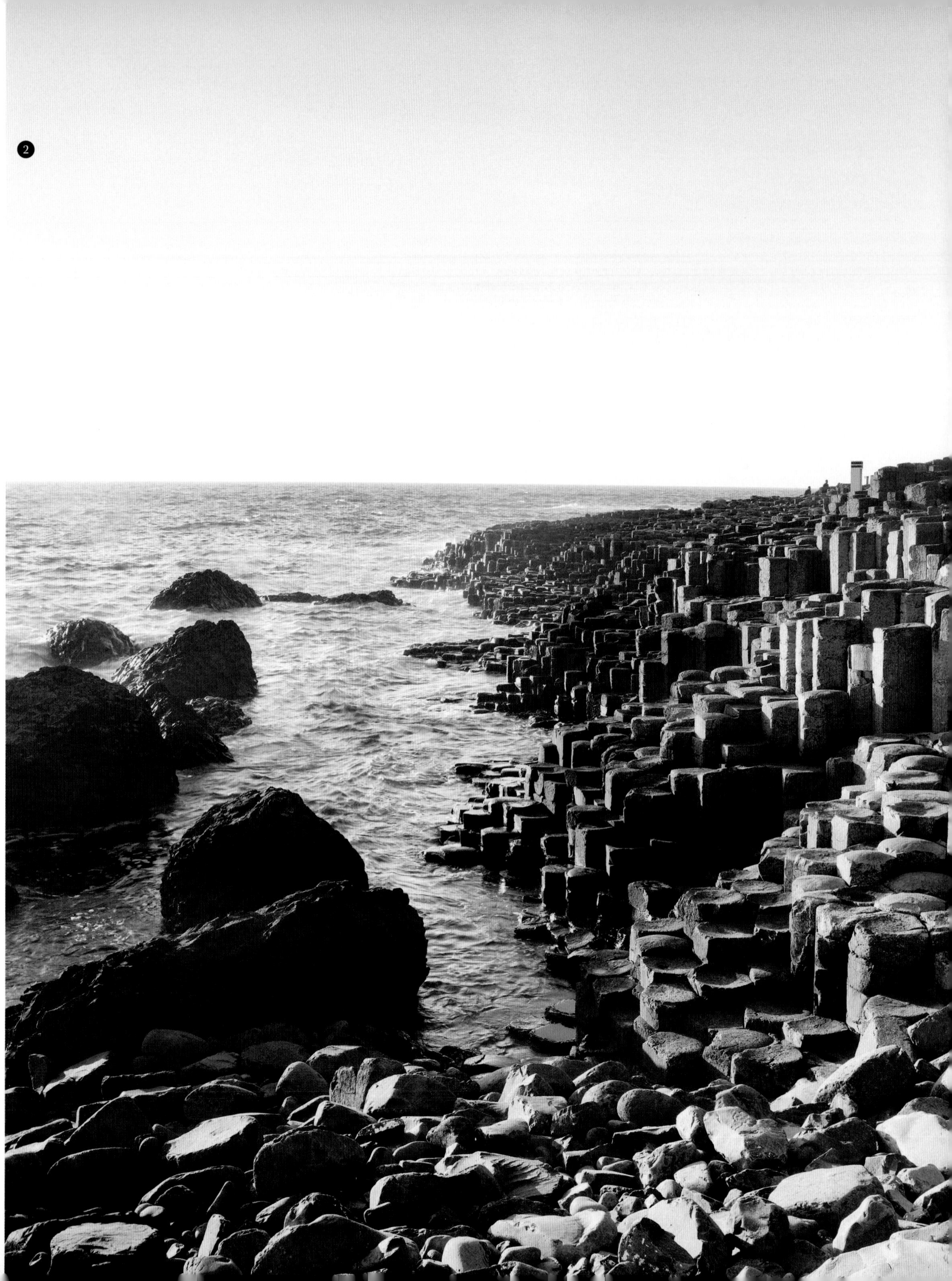

Travel

International

The Giant's Causeway is located in County Antrim. The area's nearest airport is City of Derry Airport, which has direct flights to London Stansted (daily), Liverpool (twice weekly) and Glasgow International (four days a week), plus summer routes to Spain. Flights from other European and international cities arrive in Belfast International Airport or George Best Belfast City Airport. Derry is 40 miles (57km) from the Causeway and Belfast is 60 miles (97km); both routes are covered by train and bus.

Regional

The most enjoyable way to arrive is on the heritage Giant's Causeway & Bushmills Railway from the village of Bushmills (2 miles/3km). Trains run hourly in July and August; weekends only from Easter to June, and September and October. Additional connections are provided by the seasonal bus services Antrim Coaster and Causeway Rambler.

Stay

Shoestring

Bushmills Hostel In the centre of Bushmills, this modern, purpose-built hostel has mostly four- to six-bed dorms, all with attached bathrooms. There's also a kitchen, laundry and bike shed. *(Dorms from £16/US$21; www.hini.org.uk)*

$$ Midrange marker

Midrange

Causeway Hotel Located on the cliffs above the Giant's Causeway, this 28-room National Trust–owned hotel is an ideal base if you want to explore the coast early or late in the day without the crowds. *(Doubles from £130/US$168; www.thecausewayhotel.com)*

Eat

Shoestring

Nook At the turn off to the Causeway, this 18th-century former schoolhouse is now a cosy pub serving open sandwiches, soup, chowder, Irish stew, scampi, fish and chips and the like. *(Mains £9-18/US$12-23)*

Midrange

Bushmills Inn This haven comes with intimate wooden booths and blazing fires, and uses local produce in tasty dishes, such as Atlantic seafood chowder, wild Irish venison and cullen skink (smoked haddock). *(Mains from £12/US$16; www.bushmillsinn.com)*

Timing

The causeway can get overwhelmed by visitors. If you can, visit midweek or out of the high season to see it at its most evocative.

Sunsets in spring and autumn make for great photos.

From the visitor centre it's a 10- to 15-minute walk down to the causeway, but a more interesting approach is to follow the cliff-top path, then descend the Shepherd's Steps. For the less mobile, a minibus shuttles from the visitor centre.

1 Why did the cooling lava of the Causeway form hexagonal columns? The answer requires more space than this caption.

2 The columns extend down to the Irish Sea.

3 White Park Bay on the North Antrim coast is part of the Giant's Causeway World Heritage Site.

Best value itineraries

3–4 days

Begin in big-city Belfast with a visit to the fascinating Titanic Belfast exhibit, where the ill-fated ship was made, and the Thompson Graving Dock, where you descend into the immense dry dock where the liner was fitted out. Head to the appealing resort of Ballycastle and a ferry for Rathlin Island, where you'll see sea stacks and thousands of guillemots, kittiwakes, razorbills and puffins. Take a detour to walk across the Carrick-a-Rede Rope Bridge, which sways some 30m above the waves to an offshore island, then finish up at Northern Ireland's great geological wonder, the Giant's Causeway.

7–10 days

From the causeway, head through Bushmills, with its historic distillery, to Portrush. Soon sea views flood in, then the ragged ruins of Dunluce Castle, the seat of the powerful MacDonnell family, spring into view. Venture on to the 2-mile (3km) Curran Strand, a dune-backed golden ribbon of sand, en route to Downhill Demesne, once the home of the eccentric Bishop of Derry, now a land of follies, mausoleums and a giant, ruined house. Conclude in Derry, Northern Ireland's second city, which surprises with its riverside setting and impressive, 17th-century walls.

FRANCE

Louvre

France is a nation in love with history and when it comes to peering into the past, nowhere can compare to the mighty, monumental, multifaceted Louvre. From ancient art to medieval artefacts, Greek antiquities to Renaissance masterpieces it is, quite simply, one of the world's biggest, richest, finest and most fascinating museums.

The collection is truly vast, encompassing some 380,000 objects and 35,000 artworks. In fact, it's been estimated you'd need about nine months to glance at every artefact on show.

The Louvre's raison d'être is to present Western art from the Middle Ages to about 1848, alongside countless works from ancient civilisations. For many the star attraction is da Vinci's enigmatic *La Joconde*, better known as *Mona Lisa* – although the mysterious *Venus de Milo* statue runs it a close second. But the true joy of the Louvre is wandering around and seeking out the lesser-known treasures – Egyptian sarcophagi, Mesopotamian treasures, Islamic artworks, Byzantine mosaics and so much more besides. Every time you visit you're pretty much guaranteed to discover something new. The richness and sheer size can be overwhelming, but multimedia guides, tours and thematic trails provide a useful introduction. And when it comes to grand entrances, the Louvre surely has to take the prize: its glittering glass pyramid, designed by the Chinese-American architect IM Pei, has become a Parisian icon in its own right.

Travel

International
Most international airlines fly to Aéroport de Charles de Gaulle or the smaller airports at Orly and Beauvais. Six stations handle rail services to the rest of France and Europe. Eurolines connects major European cities to Paris' bus terminal, Gare Routière Internationale de Paris-Galliéni.

Regional
Paris' public-transport system is the Régie Autonome des Transports Parisiens (RATP), an integrated network of underground trains (metros), buses and trams. The same tickets are valid on all services. There is a city-wide bike-hire network called Vélib', and a handy hop-on, hop-off service called Batobus, which stops at nine places along the Seine.

Stay

$

Shoestring
Hôtel du Nord – Le Pari Vélo Near Place de la République, this perennial favourite has 23 rooms decorated with flea-market antiques and free bikes for guests to borrow. *(Rooms from €73/US$83; www.hoteldunord-leparivelo.com)*

$$

Midrange
Hôtel Paris Bastille Boutet A former joinery workshop and chocolate factory, the Boutet nods to its heritage with its timber-panelled hallways, art deco canopy and original mosaic facade. *(Doubles from €199/US$227; www.sofitel.com)*

$$$

Flush
Les Bains Opened in 1885 as a thermal baths, and later a nightclub, this is Paris' most fabulous lifestyle hotel, with 39 rooms of vintage treasures, luxury fabrics and eclectic design. *(Doubles from €392/US$447; www.lesbains-paris.com)*

Eat

$

Shoestring
Fric-Frac The traditional *croque monsieur* (toasted cheese-and-ham sandwich) gets a contemporary makeover at this quayside space. Try the Winnie, with Crottin de Chavignol cheese, dried fruit, chestnut honey, chives and rosemary. *(Sandwiches €11.50-15/US$13-17)*

$$

Midrange
Le CasseNoix The Nutcracker is everything a neighbourhood bistro should be. *Tradition et terroir* dictate the menu, and vintage ceiling fans add to the retro vibe. *(Three-course menu €34/US$39; www.le-cassenoix.fr)*

$$$

Flush
Frenchie Tucked down an alley, this petite bistro with wooden tables and old stone walls serves excellent value, market-driven dishes. *(Five-course dinner menu €74/US$84; www.frenchie-restaurant.com)*

Timing

Louvre queues can be very long, but a Paris Museum Pass (www.paris museumpass.com) facilitates priority. Otherwise, avoid queues outside the pyramid by entering via the underground shopping centre, Carrousel du Louvre.

Buying tickets online (with a small surcharge) and renting a multimedia guide in advance also saves time.

Tickets are valid for the whole day, so you can come and go.

1
Add the Palace of Versailles to your Parisian itinerary; it also contains an extraordinary art collection.

2
The exterior of the Louvre; inside, find paintings and sculpture by Michelangelo, da Vinci, Caravaggio and more.

3
The grand apartments of Napoleon III are in the Louvre's Richelieu wing and worth seeking out.

Best value itineraries

3–4 days
Start with a stroll through the Jardin des Tuileries, stopping to view Monet's enormous *Water Lilies* at the Musée de l'Orangerie. IM Pei's glass pyramid allows you to enter the labyrinthine Louvre. Afterwards, browse the colonnaded arcades of the exquisite Jardin du Palais Royal, visit the beautiful church Église St-Eustache, then head to the late-opening Centre Pompidou for modern art and amazing rooftop views. On subsequent days, climb the mighty Arc de Triomphe for a pinch-yourself panorama, promenade down Paris' most glamorous avenue, the Champs-Élysées, explore the lively Marais and historic Montmartre districts, and climb the Eiffel Tower at sunset.

7–10 days
With more time, you can explore beyond the capital to see châteaux and Champagne. Day one has to be France's grandest castle, Château de Versailles, and its vast gardens. On the second day, feast on France's best-preserved medieval basilica and the dazzling blue stained glass in Chartres, an easy train ride away. Small town Chantilly offers a Renaissance château, formal French gardens and enchanting equestrian performances. On subsequent days, catch the train to the heart of the Champagne region and taste your way around Reims and Épernay. Round things off with visits to Château de Vaux-le-Vicomte and Disneyland Paris.

ITALY

Colosseum

Rome's great gladiatorial arena is the most thrilling of the city's ancient sights. It chills the blood to think that right here, gladiators battled wild animals – and each other – to the death for the amusement of thousands of baying spectators.

Standing in the 50,000-seat Colosseum you can imagine it in its heyday, when it was clad in travertine and covered by a huge canvas awning held aloft by 240 masts. Tiered seating encircles the arena, built over an underground complex (the hypogeum) where animals were caged and stage sets prepared.

Commissioned by the emperor Vespasian in AD 72, the 2000-year-old stadium, also known as the Flavian Amphitheatre, is both an architectural masterpiece and a stark, spine-tingling reminder of the mercilessness of ancient times. To mark its inauguration, Emperor Titus held games that lasted 100 days and nights, during which some 5000 animals were slaughtered. Amazingly, although it was Rome's most fearsome arena, it actually wasn't the biggest (the Circo Massimo could hold up to 250,000 people).

Two thousand years later, it provides a compelling glimpse of the golden age of Rome in all its brutal, bloody majesty.

Travel

International
Rome's main international airport, Leonardo da Vinci, aka Fiumicino, is 18½ miles (30km) west of the city. It's divided into four main terminals. The easiest way to get into town is by train. Rome's main station and principal transport hub is Stazione Termini. It has regular connections to other European countries, all major Italian cities and many smaller towns. Long-distance national and international buses use Autostazione Tiburtina.

Regional
Metro line B has stations at the Colosseum (Colosseo) and Circo Massimo. If taking the metro at Termini, follow signs for Line B 'direzione Laurentina'. Venezia is an important bus hub; many services stop in or near here.

Stay

$

Shoestring
Beehive More boutique chic than backpacker dive, the Beehive is a small and stylish hostel that has a glorious summer garden, storytelling evenings and weekly dinners. *(Dorms from €35/US$40; www.the-beehive.com)*

$$

Midrange
Residenza Maritti Boasting stunning views across the nearby forums and Vittoriano, this hidden gem has rooms spread over several floors. *(Doubles from €170/US$192; www.residenzamaritti.com)*

$$$

Flush
Hotel Campo de' Fiori This rakish four-star really has got the lot – enticing boudoir decor, an enviable location, professional staff and a fabulous panoramic roof terrace. *(Rooms from €280/US$317; www.hotelcampodefiori.com)*

Eat

$

Shoestring
Forno Roscioli A bakery much loved by lunching locals who crowd here for luscious sliced pizza, prize pastries and hunger-sating *supplì* (risotto balls). *(Pizza slices from €2/US$2.30, snacks €2.50/US$2.80; www.anticofornoroscioli.it)*

$$

Midrange
Pianostrada Offering vintage furnishings and a glorious summer courtyard, this bistro is a Roman essential. The cuisine is creative, seasonal and veg packed. *(Meals €40/US$45; www.facebook.com/pianostrada)*

$$$

Flush
Salumeria Roscioli Tables at this vaunted restaurant are set alongside the deli counter, which is laden with mouthwatering Italian and foreign delicacies. *(Meals €55/US$62; www.salumeriaroscioli.com)*

Timing

Visit early morning or in the late afternoon, when it's less crowded, cooler and the light is much better for taking photos.

On Good Friday, crowds gather at the Colosseum to witness the Pope lead the traditional Via Crucis procession.

The top three tiers and hypogeum are open by guided tour only. Visits, which cost €9/US$10 extra, require advance booking.

Inside the Colosseum crowds bayed for blood from gladiators and wild animals (note the pens below the arena).

Outside, work is under way to protect the construction from the hazards of a modern city.

A classic Piaggio Ape in a typical Roman street.

Best value itineraries

2–3 days
Start at the Colosseum, Rome's huge gladiatorial arena – try to get there early to avoid the queues. Then head down to the Palatino to poke around crumbling ruins and admire sweeping views. From the Palatino, follow on to the Roman Forum, an evocative area of tumbledown temples, sprouting columns and ruined basilicas. Venture out to Via Appia Antica to see the creepy catacombs and look out for the remains of an ancient racetrack at the nearby Villa di Massenzio. Wear comfy shoes as the ancient Roman cobblestones are murder on the feet and you'll be doing plenty of walking.

7–10 days
After exploring ancient Rome, catch the train up the coast to Renaissance Florence to see Michelangelo's *David* at the Galleria dell'Accademia and pick your favourite Botticelli at the Galleria degli Uffizi. Head out into the countryside for a few decadent days in Chianti, toasting the area's *vino* and indulging in lazy lunches and countryside cycling. Detour west to the attractive town of San Gimignano, with its 14 towers rising up like a medieval Manhattan. Conclude with a day trip to Gothic Siena, home of the biannual Palio horse race.

1

© Suranga Weeratuna / Alamy Stock Photo

Blue Lagoon

In a magnificent black-lava field, the cyan Blue Lagoon spa is fed water from the futuristic Svartsengi geothermal plant; with its silver towers, roiling clouds of steam and people daubed in white silica mud, it's an otherworldly place.

Iceland's unofficial pastime is splashing around in its surplus of geothermal water. You'll find 'hot-pots' everywhere, from downtown Reykjavík to the isolated peninsular tips of the Westfjords. Not only are they incredibly relaxing, they're the perfect antidote to a hangover and a great way to meet the locals (this is their social hub, the equivalent of the local pub or town square). But the Blue Lagoon is the big cheese. Those who say it's overly commercial and overly crowded aren't wrong, but you'll be missing something special if you don't go.

The superheated water (70% seawater, 30% fresh water, at a perfect 38°C) is rich in blue-green algae, mineral salts and fine silica mud, which condition and exfoliate the skin – it sounds like advertising speak, but you really will come out as soft as a baby's bum.

Travel

International
Keflavík is Iceland's main international airport, 30 miles (48km) southwest of Reykjavík. Reykjavík Domestic Airport deals with mostly internal flights, and those to Greenland and the Faroes. Smyril Line operates a pricey but popular weekly car ferry, the Norröna, from Hirtshals (Denmark) through Tórshavn (Faroe Islands) to Seyðisfjörður in East Iceland.

Regional
The lagoon is 29 miles (47km) southwest of Reykjavík and 14 miles (23km) southeast of Keflavík International Airport. The complex is just off the road between Keflavík and Grindavík. Frequent bus services run year-round from town and from the airport, as do tours (which sometimes offer better deals than a bus ticket plus lagoon admission).

Stay

Shoestring
Reykjavík Downtown Hostel Top dorm digs or private rooms in this HI hostel offer some of the best bargains in the city centre. (*Dorms from 5700kr/US$47, doubles from 18,400kr/US$148; www.hostel.is*)

Midrange
Galtafell Guesthouse Four one-bedroom apartments and three double rooms in a historic mansion are within easy walking distance of the city centre. (*Doubles from 24,600kr/US$201, apt from 29,000kr/US$237; www.galtafell.com*)

Flush
Consulate Hotel Reykjavík Hilton's new hotel is housed in a tasteful conversion of a 1900s department store, combining antique flourishes and modern comforts. (*Doubles from 44,700kr/US$365; www.curiocollection3.hilton.com*)

Eat

Shoestring
Grandi Mathöll A former fish factory turned into a pioneering street-food hall, this place has long trestle tables sitting beside stalls loaded with lamb, fish and veggie delights. (*Mains from 1200kr/US$9.65; www.grandimatholl.is*)

Midrange
Snaps This bistro is a perennial favourite with Reykjavikers. The secret is simple: perfectly cooked seafood and bistro mains – think steak or *moules frites* – at decent prices. (*Lunch mains from 2000kr/US$16; www.snaps.is*)

Flush
Dill Exquisite 'New Nordic' cuisine at a Michelin-starred bistro. Friends with Copenhagen's Noma, the owners take Icelandic cuisine to heady heights. (*Five courses 11,900kr/US$97; seven courses 13,900kr/US$114; www.dillrestaurant.is*)

Timing

Pre-booking is essential year-round; evenings tend to be quieter.

If you just want to take a look and a few snaps of the lagoon you can use the free short pathway around the complex.

The lagoon has an enormous complex of changing rooms, restaurants, a hotel, spa, steam rooms, sauna, bar and gift shop. A VIP section has its own interior wading space, lounge and viewing platform.

The Blue Lagoon is filled with water from the nearby geothermal plant; there are extra-hot sections where the steam rises,

You shouldn't miss seeing some of Iceland's many waterfalls, such as Gullfoss.

The austere interior of the Hallgrimskirkja in Reykjavík is as mesmerising as the angular exterior.

Best value itineraries

3–4 days
Over a few days in Reykjavík you can explore the Old Reykjavík quarter, taking in the Ráðhús (town hall) and Alþingi (Parliament), then peruse the National Museum, Reykjavík Art Museum or the Settlement Exhibition, built around a Viking longhouse. Photograph the immense church, Hallgrímskirkja (for a perfect view, zip up the tower), and stroll Laugavegur, the main shopping drag. Head out on a whale-watching tour from the old harbour, visit the Reykjavík Art Museum and round things off with an otherworldly soak at the Blue Lagoon.

7–10 days
A week or more gives you time to explore the island. After landing at Keflavík, make a beeline for the Blue Lagoon to soak away the jet lag. Wander the Reykjanes Peninsula's steaming earth near Valahnúkur or Seltún before barrelling down the coast for seafood in Eyrarbakki or Stokkseyri. Base yourself near Hella or Hvolsvöllur for horse-riding or Northern Lights spotting (in the colder months). Take a super-4WD tour or amphibious bus to Þórsmörk, and head out on hikes around the valley. Returning west, visit the gushing cascades at Gullfoss, the spurting Geysir from which all others got their name, and the rift valley and ancient parliament site, Þingvellir National Park – the classic Golden Circle route. Wrap up your minibreak in Reykjavík.

BOSNIA & HERCEGOVINA

Stari Most

Arching high over the town of Mostar, Stari Most (Old Bridge) is the Balkans' most celebrated crossing.

Framed by medieval watchtowers, its swooping arch was originally built between 1557 and 1566 on the orders of Suleyman the Magnificent, but was tragically blown to smithereens by a Croat artillery attack in November 1993 during the civil war. The laboriously reconstructed bridge reopened in 2004 and is now a symbol of national pride, as well as a Unesco World Heritage Site. Spectacular enough by day, the bridge looks even more astounding as darkness falls, when its pale stone reflects the golden glow of sunset. As dusk sets in, the lights of numerous millhouse restaurants twinkle across gushing streamlets, and narrow Kujundžiluk ('Gold Alley') bustles joyously with trinket sellers. It's an enchanting scene.

The bridge is also famed for its daredevil bridge divers. In summer, young men honour a centuries-old tradition by plummeting more than 20m into the freezing cold Neretva River. It's a hilarious spectacle, involving much stretching, preening and posing in Speedos and cajoling the crowd for donations. Divers won't leap until 50 Bosnian marks have been collected (double that in winter). If nothing else, it makes bungee jumping look pretty tame by comparison.

© Domingo Leiva / 500px

1

Travel

International

The main gateway to Bosnia and Hercegovina by air is busy little Sarajevo International Airport, from where you can take a bus (2½ hours) or train (two hours) to Mostar. It is sometimes worth comparing prices on flights to Dubrovnik or Split in Croatia and taking the bus from there (three and four hours respectively). Mostar has its own airport, with fairly regular summer charters from Rome, Naples and Bari on Mistral Air, but the only year-round service is from Zagreb on Croatia Airlines.

Regional

Local buses will transport you around town, but the city is small and it's easily walkable. The bridge is unmissable in the centre of town.

Stay

$

Shoestring

Hostel Balkanarama Run by a creative Anglo-Bosnian, this excellent new hostel has become one of Mostar's most popular. Quirky features include a central kitchen table fashioned from beer crates and seats made from container pallets. *(Dorm 20-30KM/US$12-17; www.facebook.com/balkanaramahostel)*

$$

Midrange

Muslibegović House In summer, tourists pay to visit this late-17th-century Ottoman courtyard house, but it's also a charming boutique hotel. Rooms mix elements of Bosnian, Turkish and even Moroccan design. *(Doubles from €90/US$103; www.muslibegovichouse.com)*

Eat

$

Shoestring

Tima-Irma Expect queues at this insanely popular little grill joint that serves groaning platters of ćevapi (skinless sausage), pljeskavica (burger meat) and shish kebabs. *(Mains 5-11KM/US$3-6.50; www.cevabdzinica-tima.com)*

$$

Midrange

Šadrvan Situated on a corner shaded in vines and trees, this tourist favourite has tables set around a fountain made of old Turkish-style metalwork. The meat-free đuveč tastes like ratatouille on rice. *(Mains from 10KM/US$5.80; www.facebook.com/sadrvanmostar)*

Timing

The first week of September is ideal for a visit: high season has just finished but the autumn rains haven't yet set in.

April to June is a good time to beat the heat in Hercegovina and see blooming flowers in Bosnia.

Do stay into the evening to see the illuminated bridge without the summer hordes of day trippers.

1

Rebuilding of the bridge by Spanish and Portuguese military engineers under the command of the UN Protection Force began in 2001.

2

The arch is an example of Balkan Islamic architecture.

3

It remains a stage for the famed cliff jumpers to show their bravado.

Best value itineraries

4 days

Four days is enough to get a taste of the country's two key cities, their surroundings and turbulent histories. Devote your first two days to exploring Sarajevo, including a free city walking tour and a war-survivors' tour. On day three nip down to Mostar, peruse the bridge and sign up for a multi-stop tour for day four to regional gems Počitelj, Blagaj and the Kravice Waterfalls.

8 days

Given just over a week, you can transit all the way from Belgrade (Serbia) to Dubrovnik (Croatia). Take the bus from Belgrade to Višegrad to see its 16th-century bridge, river canyons and Andrić-themed pseudo-antique inner-city. Continue on to Sarajevo, soaking up the capital's mix of Turkish and Austrian historical influences. Jump on the bus to attractive Konjic. Assuming you've booked ahead and got the dates right, visit Tito's billion-dollar nuclear bunker or raft down the Neretva River. Continue south to Mostar and visit the bridge. Head to underrated Trebinje with its Mediterranean central square and walled Old Town. Then bus it to Dubrovnik.

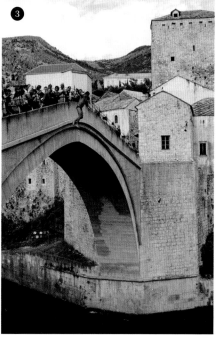

© Milosz Maslanka / Shutterstock

GREECE

Acropolis

The Acropolis is the most important ancient site in the Western world. Crowned by the Parthenon, it stands sentinel over Athens, visible from almost everywhere within the city. Its monuments and sanctuaries of white marble gleam in the midday sun and gradually take on a honey hue as the sun sinks, while at night they stand brilliantly illuminated above the city. A mere glimpse cannot fail to exalt your spirit.

Inspiring as these monuments are, they are but faded remnants of the city of Pericles, who spared no expense – only the best materials, architects, sculptors and artists were good enough for a city dedicated to the cult of Athena. It was a showcase of lavishly coloured buildings and gargantuan statues, some of bronze, others of marble plated with gold and encrusted with precious stones.

Explore it early in the morning or soak up the view from a dinnertime terrace; no matter how you experience the Acropolis, you will be mesmerised by its beauty, history and sheer size. Beyond the Parthenon, you can find quieter spots, such as the exquisite Temple of Athena Nike and the Theatre of Dionysos. Nearby, the Acropolis Museum showcases the surviving treasures of the Acropolis.

Travel

International
Athens' international airport, at Spata, 27km east of the capital, is a manageable single terminal with all the modern conveniences. It's served by many major and budget airlines as well as high-season charters. Most ferry, hydrofoil and high-speed catamaran services leave from the massive port at Piraeus, southwest of Athens. Intercity trains to central and northern Greece depart from the Larisis train station; all international trains in and out of Greece go via Thessaloniki.

Regional
Athens has a network of buses that go everywhere. The city's metro is fast and efficient and most useful for visitors. Taxis are genuinely affordable and very much part of the 'public transport' system. To get to the Acropolis by metro, get off at the Akropoli station, near the east entrance.

Stay

Shoestring
Athens Backpackers The rooftop bar with Acropolis views is a major draw at this Australian-run backpacker favourite. *(Dorms from €24/US$27; www.backpackers.gr)*

Midrange
Hera Hotel This elegant neoclassical hotel is based a short walk to the Acropolis and Plaka, and the rooftop Peacock restaurant and bar have fine views. *(Doubles from €170/US$192; www.herahotel.gr)*

Flush
Athens Was The location of this boutique property, a three-minute walk to the Acropolis east gate, simply couldn't be better. Suites on the 5th and 6th floors also have Acropolis views. *(Doubles from €230/US$260; www.athenswas.gr)*

Eat

Shoestring
Mikro Politiko Just the thing to stave off post-Acropolis slump: a quick souvlaki or falafel from this little place. *(Souvlaki €1.70/US$1.90)*

Midrange
Mani Mani This delightful modern restaurant specialises in herb-filled cuisine from the Mani region in the Peloponnese. *(Mains €15-20/US$17-23; www.manimani.com.gr)*

Flush
Tudor Hall On the 7th floor of the King George Hotel, this smart restaurant offers what is perhaps the most breathtaking window on the spotlit Acropolis. The menu here is gourmet Greek with a modern spin. *(Mains €25-49/US$28-55; www.tudorhall.gr)*

Timing

Visit first thing in the morning or late in the day. The east entrance, near the Akropoli metro, can be less crowded than the main entrance.

From November to March, admission is free on the first Sunday of the month. Check www.culture.gr for changing opening hours.

A combo ticket (€30/US$34) permits entry to the Acropolis and six other sites within five days. Buy this at a smaller site, to avoid the queues.

The Parthenon is at the heart of the Acropolis, which is dedicated to the goddess Athena.

The temple of the Parthenon, complete with its external frieze, the *metopes* (or panels), represents the best of Greek architecture.

For more amazing Greek architecture head to the Palace of Knossos on Crete and its illustrations of the Minotaur.

Best value itineraries

3–4 days
Head to the east entrance of the Acropolis early, to beat the crowds and the heat. Wind down the far side of the hill, passing by the Roman Agora with its Tower of the Winds and exploring the Ancient Agora, the centre of ancient Athens' civic life. From there, head to the Acropolis Museum and its masterpieces from the Parthenon. On subsequent days, watch the changing of the guard at Tomb of the Unknown Soldier on Plateia Syntagmatos, visit the Benaki Museum of Greek Culture and the National Archaeological Museum, and leave plenty of eating time for tavernas in Plaka, Kolonaki, Petralona or Monastiraki.

7–10 days
Athens makes an ideal launchpad for a longer tour of Greece's ancient sites and museums. After doing the Acropolis, day-trip to the sacred island of Delos for its fascinating ancient ruins, then hop on a ferry to spectacular Santorini to watch the sun sink from the dramatic cliffs of its volcanic caldera. Take another ferry to Crete's capital, Iraklio, to explore the nearby magnificent Minoan ruins of Knossos. Catch the bus to Hania with its charming harbour and labyrinth of backstreets, then trek through the famous Samaria Gorge, which spills out on to a beach lapped by the crystal-clear Libyan Sea.

British Museum

With more than six million visitors trooping through its doors annually, the British Museum in London is Britain's largest museum, and one of the oldest and finest in the world.

Originating in 1753 with a 'cabinet of curiosities' sold to the nation by royal physician Sir Hans Sloane, the collection mushroomed through acquisitions, bequests – and plundering the empire. It's now home to a truly vast, globe-spanning collection representing pretty much every civilisation in human history: Egyptian, Etruscan, Greek, Roman, European and Middle Eastern, among countless others.

As you wander through the maze of galleries, you get the impression you could spend a lifetime in this vast collection of artefacts, art and antiquity, and still make daily discoveries. To avoid being overwhelmed, focus on the must-see items. Don't miss the Rosetta Stone, the key to deciphering Egyptian hieroglyphics, discovered in 1799; the controversial Parthenon Sculptures, taken from the Parthenon in Athens by Lord Elgin (then the British ambassador to the Ottoman Empire); and the large collection of Egyptian mummies. Also be sure to visit the Anglo-Saxon Sutton Hoo burial relics and the Winged Bulls from Khorsabad, as well as the famous Great Court, restored and augmented by Norman Foster in 2000 with a spectacular new glass-and-steel roof.

Travel

International

Most people arrive in London at one of the city's five airports: Heathrow, which is the largest, to the west; Gatwick to the south; Stansted to the northeast; Luton to the northwest; and London City in the Docklands. An alternative is the Eurostar, a high-speed passenger rail service linking London St Pancras International with Paris, Brussels, Amsterdam and Lille.

Regional

The easiest way to get around is the London Underground ('the Tube'; 11 colour-coded lines supplemented by the Docklands Light Railway and Overground). London's double-decker buses afford great views, but the going can be slow. The rechargeable Oyster Card offers the best fares. Black cabs are ubiquitous but expensive, while Santander Cycles are great for shorter journeys.

Stay

Shoestring

YHA London Oxford St The most central of London's seven YHA hostels is also one of the most intimate with just 104 beds. (*Dorms from £18/US$23; www.yha.org.uk*)

Midrange

Hoxton Hotel In the heart of hip Shoreditch, this sleek hotel offers style and reasonable prices; book well ahead for the best rates. (*Rooms from £69/US$90; www.thehoxton.com*)

Flush

Zetter Townhouse Marylebone This boutique spot blends fusty style, kitsch and humour. Superior rooms have four-poster beds and coffee machines. (*Doubles from £210/US$273; www.thezettertownhouse.com/marylebone*)

Eat

Shoestring

Talli Joe Sharing plates of regional Indian dishes, including Keralan-style fish curry, Bohri chicken from Gujarat, and Kolkata five-spiced potatoes. (*Dishes £4-11.50/US$5.20-15; www.tallijoe.com*)

Midrange

Bon Vivant This bistro in Marchmont St, Bloomsbury, boasts an oh-so-Gallic menu of *bavette* (flank steak), *poulet farci* (stuffed chicken) and *magret de canard* (duck breast). (*Mains £10-17/US$13-22; http://bonvivantrestaurant.co.uk*)

Flush

Dinner by Heston Blumenthal A gastronomic tour de force, taking diners on a journey through British culinary history (with inventive new inflections). (*Three-course set lunch £45/US$58, mains £30-49/US$39-64; www.dinnerbyheston.co.uk*)

Timing

The museum is huge, so make a few visits if you have time and take advantage of the free tours. There are up to 15 free Eye-Opener Tours of individual galleries each day.

The museum also has free 45-minute lunchtime gallery talks, a 1½-hour highlights tour (£14/US$18) and free 20-minute spotlight tours on Friday evenings.

Audio and family guides (adult £7/US$9.10, child £6/US$7.80) in 10 languages are available.

The Standard of Ur, in the British Museum, is a small wooded box decorated with mosaic scenes dating from Mesopotamia in around 2500 BC.

The Great Court designed by Foster and Partners is a bright introduction to the museum.

Exhibits from the British Museum's ancient Greece collection.

Best value itineraries

3–4 days

Start out at the sprawling Tower of London, home to the red-coated Beefeaters, resident ravens and Crown Jewels. Cross the iconic Tower Bridge over the Thames, then hop on a double-decker bus for a full afternoon at the British Museum. Spend the next day wandering through Chinatown and Soho, shopping in Covent Garden and along Oxford St, visiting Westminster Abbey and Buckingham Palace, exploring the National Gallery on Trafalgar Square and having a picnic in Hyde Park. Factor in at least another day for the South Bank, including the Tate Modern and a performance at Shakespeare's Globe. Don't forget to aim your camera at St Paul's Cathedral on the far side of the elegant Millennium Bridge.

7–10 days

With more time you can explore the capital's more out-of-the-way neighbourhoods. Hop on a boat to Greenwich to see the Cutty Sark, National Maritime Museum and Royal Observatory. Allow another day for the East End, including Spitalfields Market, Brick Lane, Borough Market and the Olympic Park. On subsequent days, make trips to Kew Gardens and Hampton Court, and visit the museum district around Knightsbridge and South Kensington, home to the Victoria & Albert Museum, Natural History Museum and Science Museum. Finish up with shopping around Notting Hill and an evening at the über cool Electric Cinema.

© Matt Munro / Lonely Planet

© Niyazi Uğur Genca / 500px

TURKEY

Ephesus

The Greco-Roman world truly comes alive at Ephesus. After more than a century and a half of excavation, the city's recovered and renovated structures have made Ephesus Europe's most complete classical metropolis – and that's with 80% of the city yet to be unearthed!

As capital of Roman Asia Minor, Ephesus was once a vibrant city of more than 250,000 inhabitants, the fourth largest in the empire after Rome, Alexandria and Antioch. Adding in traders, sailors and pilgrims to the temples, these numbers were even higher, meaning that in Ephesus one could encounter the full diversity of the Mediterranean world and its peoples. So important and wealthy was Ephesus that its Temple of Artemis was the biggest on earth and one of the Seven Wonders of the Ancient World.

Only a few columns of the temple now remain, but many other well-preserved ruins give a true sense of the city, including complete streets, a three-tiered theatre, baths, latrines, a library and many other temples. It's also possible to see seven Roman homes built on three terraces. The colourful mosaics, painted frescoes and marble provide a breathtaking insight into the lost world of Ephesus and its aristocracy.

❷

Travel

International
İzmir's Adnan Menderes Airport is the closest airport, and is serviced by many domestic and international airlines. There are two terminals (one international, one domestic). Selçuk is a 90-minute train journey from the airport.

Regional
Selçuk is roughly a 2¼ mile (3.5km) walk from both entrances, with the Temple of Artemis and shade provided by mulberry trees en route to the Lower Gate. *Dolmuşes* (minibuses) run every half-hour in summer, hourly in winter, dropping off and picking up at the turnoff for the Lower Gate, about a 20-minute walk from the site. A taxi to or from either gate costs about ₺20/US$3.75.

Stay

$

Shoestring
Homeros Pension This longtime, family-run favourite offers 10 rooms in two buildings. Enjoy some of the best views in Selçuk on the roof terraces. *(Doubles from €17/US$19; www.homerospension.com)*

$$

Midrange
Hotel Bella A boutique hotel on a sloping street opposite the start of the aqueduct with 11 well-designed rooms with Ottoman flourishes in the decor. *(Doubles from €39/US$45; www.hotelbella.com)*

$$$

Flush
Casa Callinos The new boutique hotel opposite the Temple of Artemis offers excellent value for its standard and location, and is cobbled together from three buildings. *(Doubles from €50/US$57; www.casacallinos.com)*

Eat

$

Shoestring
Selçuk Köftecisi In a modern building by the fish market, this long-running local favourite serves *köfte* (meatballs) cooked to perfection and accompanied by salad, rice and onions. *(Mezes from ₺8/US$1.50; Şahabettin Dede Caddesi 10)*

$$

Midrange
Ejder Restaurant Next to the aqueduct in Selçuk, this outdoor restaurant offers lots of choices including *tavuk şiş* (roast skewered chicken) and homemade *sütlaç* (rice pudding). *(Mezes ₺6-10/US$1.15-1.95, mains ₺10-25/US$1.95-4.85)*

$$$

Flush
Seçkin & Firuze This lovely family-run eatery on Selçuk's 'restaurant row' serves grills and seafood dishes that taste just like *ana* (mum) makes. *(Mezes from ₺14/US$2.65)*

Timing

Visit early morning or late afternoon to avoid crowds and the midday sun (9.30am–1.30pm is busiest). If you can, avoid public holidays.

The softer morning light is best for photographing the ruins, but the site is generally quietest after 3pm, when the tour groups depart.

A visit to Ephesus takes at least two hours (add 30 minutes if visiting the Terraced Houses).

① Looking up at Celsus Library among the ruins of Ephesus.

② Looking down Curetes Way, lined with Roman ruins at Ephesus.

③ Take a *gulet* (boat) along the Aegean coast around İzmir.

④ A Roman statue on the ruin of the Library of Celsus.

Best value itineraries

3–4 days
After a few days in İstanbul, fly or bus to İzmir, spend a day or two exploring its museums and bazaar, and then catch the bus or train straight down to Selçuk. Time your visit to coincide with Selçuk's sprawling Saturday market and pair the magnificent ruins of Ephesus with a trip to the mountaintop village of Şirince.

7–10 days
After exploring Selçuk and Ephesus, travel to see the classical ruins at Hierapolis, an ancient spa city overlooking the village of Pamukkale from atop fascinating white limestone *travertines* (terraces). Nearby Afrodisias, once a Roman provincial capital, is equally incredible; you may have the 30,000-seat stadium to yourself. Add-ons could include Konya, its magnificent mosques recalling its stint as capital of the Seljuk sultanate of Rum, lakeside Eğirdir. with views of the Taurus Mountains, and Sagalassos, a ruined Greco-Roman city at an altitude of 1500m.

© Mark Read / Lonely Planet

© Mark Read / Lonely Planet

1

© Michael Abid / 500px

ITALY

Sistine Chapel

You've seen it a thousand times in pictures, but nothing can prepare you for your first up-close glimpse of the astonishing ceiling of the Sistine Chapel – Michelangelo's masterpiece, a triumph of Renaissance painting and, according to some, the greatest single work of art ever conceived by man.

Gazing upwards, you'll feel yourself drawn into a fabulous, technicolour world of scriptural imagery and larger-than-life biblical characters, recounting nothing less than the origin of man, the universe and everything.

Painted between 1508 and 1512, the 800 sq m ceilings centre around nine panels depicting stories from the book of Genesis. The scenes include the division of Light from Darkness, the creation of Adam and Eve and their subsequent banishment from the Garden of Eden, and the terrible tale of the Flood and Noah's Ark. For a 600-year-old artwork, it packs a powerful punch – you could spend hours peering into it and still find surprising new details. Indeed, some scholars have devoted their entire careers to interpreting it. On the west wall is Michelangelo's equally mesmeric *Giudizio Universale* (Last Judgment), showing Christ passing sentence over the souls of the dead as they are torn from their graves to face him.

Travel

International
Most people arrive in Rome by plane, landing at one of its two airports: Leonardo da Vinci, better known as Fiumicino; or Ciampino, the hub for European low-cost carrier Ryanair. Domestic flights connect Rome with airports across Italy. As an alternative to short-haul flights, trains serve Rome's main station, Stazione Termini, from a number of European destinations, including Paris (about 15 hours), as well as cities across Italy.

Regional
Public transport in Rome includes buses, trams, metro and a suburban train network. The main hub is Stazione Termini. Tickets are valid for all forms of transport. The nearest metro to the Vatican Museums is Ottaviano-San Pietro.

Stay

$

Shoestring
Colors Hotel This welcoming hotel impresses with its fresh, artful design and clean, colourful rooms. From June to August, dorms are available for guests under 38 years. *(Doubles from €62/US$72; www.colorshotel.com)*

$$

Midrange
Le Stanze di Orazio A friendly boutique B&B in the elegant Prati district that is a single metro stop from the Vatican. It has five bright, playfully decorated rooms. *(Doubles from €120/US$136; www.lestanzediorazio.com)*

$$$

Flush
Villa Laetitia Twenty rooms and mini-apartments in a riverside art nouveau villa are all individually designed by Anna Venturini Fendi of the famous fashion house. *(Rooms from €179/US$203; www.villalaetitia.com)*

Eat

$

Shoestring
Pizzarium This takeaway serves Rome's best sliced pizza, bar none. It belongs to Gabriele Bonci, the city's acclaimed pizza king. *(Pizza slices from €5/US$5.70)*

$$

Midrange
Il Sorpasso A bar-restaurant in the Prati area sporting vaulted stone ceilings, exposed brick and wooden tables, serving pasta, *trapizzini* (pyramids of stuffed pizza), cured meats and cocktails. *(Meals €20-35/US$23-40; www.sorpasso.info)*

$$$

Flush
Ristorante L'Arcangelo This informally styled bistro rightly enjoys a stellar reputation. Dishes are modern and creative yet still undeniably Roman, with traditional ingredients such as sweetbreads and *baccalà* (cod). *(Meals €50/US$57; www.larcangelo.com)*

Timing

● The Sistine Chapel is enormously popular; expect crowds and long queues. Get ahead by booking tickets online.

● Tuesdays and Thursdays are quietest; Wednesday mornings are good as everyone is at the Pope's weekly audience; afternoon is better than morning; avoid Mondays when many other museums are shut.

● The museums are free on the last Sunday of the month.

1 A view of Vatican City showing Ponte Sant'Angelo, built by Emperor Hadrian, and St Peter's Basilica.

2 The interior art of the Sistine Chapel, named after Pope Sixtus IV.

3 The unadorned brick exterior of the Sistine Chapel, part of the Pope's palace, from where it is accessed.

Best value itineraries

3–4 days
Once you've blown your mind at the Vatican Museums, head for St Peter's Basilica. If you have the energy, climb its Michelangelo-designed dome for fantastic views over St Peter's Square. Jump on the metro and cross the river to Piazza di Spagna. Plan your moves while sitting on the Spanish Steps, then push on to the Trevi Fountain, where tradition dictates you throw a coin into the water to ensure your return to Rome. On subsequent days, enjoy some market grazing in the Campo de' Fiori, boutique-hopping in Monti, a sunset on Piazza del Quirinale and late-night revelry in Trastevere.

6–7 days
With more time for your explorations of Roman art, add on a trip to the Museo e Galleria Borghese to marvel at amazing baroque sculpture. Afterwards, stroll through Villa Borghese down to La Galleria Nazionale for an injection of modern art. Then check what's going on at Rome's modernist cultural centre, the Auditorium Parco della Musica, before heading back to Piazza del Popolo and the Basilica di Santa Maria del Popolo, a magnificent repository of artworks. Conclude by browsing the flagship stores and designer boutiques in the upscale streets off Via del Corso.

© Vadim Bochkarev / Shutterstock

①

© Matt Munro / Lonely Planet

Grand Canal

Never was a thoroughfare so aptly named as the Grand Canal, reflecting the glories of a thousand years of Venetian architecture along its banks.

Venice's signature waterway is lined with 200 palaces that range from Venetian Gothic with Moorish flourishes (the Ca' d'Oro) to postmodern neoclassical (Palazzo Grassi), punctuated at either end by the double exclamation points of the Palazzo Ducale and Basilica di San Marco. Out on the canal itself, the water buzzes with cruise boats, passenger ferries and, of course, a chorus of crooning gondoliers, dressed in their customary uniform of stripy tops and straw boaters.

The best way to appreciate the show is to simply buy a ticket for the *vaporetto*, the small passenger ferry that buzzes up and down the length of the canal (a much better-value option than those overpriced, tourist-stuffed gondolas). Alternatively you can simply admire the view as you ride the *traghetto* (public gondola) across the Grand Canal for the princely sum of a couple of euros. Sunset is the premium time for sightseeing and photography on the Grand Canal – rush hour here really is something to behold.

Travel

International
Most flights land at Marco Polo Airport, 7½ miles (12km) outside Venice, east of Mestre. Ryanair and some other budget airlines also use Treviso Airport, a 16 miles (26km), one-hour drive from Venice. Direct intercity trains operate out of Venice to most major Italian cities, as well as points in France, Germany, Austria, Switzerland, Slovenia and Croatia.

Regional
Vaporetti (small passenger ferries) are Venice's main public transport. Single rides cost €7.50/US$8.50. Gondolas are strictly for tourists: day rates run to €80/US$91 for 40 minutes (six passengers max) or €100/US$113 for 35 minutes from 7pm to 8am, not including songs or tips.

Stay

$ Shoestring
Generator Generator rocks a sharp, contemporary interior including a fabulous kooky-kitsch bar-restaurant with crazy wallpaper, Murano chandeliers and a pool table. *(Dorms from €35/US$40; www.generatorhostels.com)*

$$ Midrange
Oltre Il Giardino This garden villa was the 1920s home of Alma Mahler, the composer's widow. Its six high-ceilinged rooms marry historic charm with modern comfort. *(Doubles from €180/US$204; www.oltreilgiardino-venezia.com)*

$$$ Flush
Hotel Palazzo Barbarigo Brooding, chic and seductive, Barbarigo delivers 18 plush guestrooms. Triple-windowed Room 10 has a Grand Canal view; whereas the standard rooms overlook Rio di San Polo. *(Doubles from €240/US$272; www.palazzobarbarigo.com)*

Eat

$ Shoestring
Snack Bar Ai Nomboli The Venetian answer to McDonald's serves crusty rolls packed with local cheeses, fresh greens, roast vegetables, salami, prosciutto and roast beef. *(Sandwiches €2/US$2.30, panini €6/US$6.80)*

$$ Midrange
CoVino Tiny CoVino has only 14 seats, but demonstrates bags of ambition with its inventive, seasonal, Slow Food menu inspired by Venetian terroir. *(Fixed-price menus lunch €27-36/US$31-41, dinner €40/US$45; www.covinovenezia.com)*

$$$ Flush
Bistrot de Venise Experience culinary time travel at this bistro, which has revived the recipes of Renaissance chef Bartolomeo Scappi so you can dine like a doge. *(Meals €47-78/US$53-89; www.bistrotdevenise.com)*

Timing

Sunrise and sunset are the best times to appreciate the full spectrum of colours on the Grand Canal.

Festivals to time your visit around include Carnival (February), with its elaborate costumes and a flurry of events; Vogalonga (May or June), a 'long row' show of endurance; Regata Storica (usually in early September), a historical procession along the Grand Canal; and Venice Glass Week (September), which showcases 1000 years of Venetian glassworking skills.

The Grand Canal hums with activity from dawn to night; there's always something to watch.

A gondolier passes the Basilica di Santa Maria della Salute at the entrance of the Grand Canal.

Prices for gondola rides are regulated and go up after dark.

Best value itineraries

3–4 days
Three or four days is enough for the big ticket sights: the Palazzo Ducale; the Byzantine blitz of golden mosaics inside Basilica di San Marco; the glorious artworks on show inside Gallerie dell'Accademia and the Peggy Guggenheim Collection; the produce-packed Rialto Market; and a waterborne trip along the Grand Canal. Alternatively, if you're just looking for a classic Venetian photo op, head for the Ponte dell'Accademia – Venice's only wooden bridge – before wandering past Squero di San Trovaso to glimpse gondolas under construction.

7–10 days
If you've a few more days, you'll have time to explore Venice's more out-of-the-way islands. Make your lagoon getaway on a *vaporetto* bound for green-and-gold Torcello and technicolour Burano. Follow the trail to Torcello's Byzantine Basilica di Santa Maria Assunta, where the apse's golden Madonna calmly stares down the blue devils opposite. Catch the boat back to Burano to admire extreme home-design colour schemes and handmade lace at Museo del Merletto. Move on to see the glass artisans at work in Murano's *fornaci* (furnaces) and see their finest moments at Museo del Vetro (Glass Museum). Hop back on the *vaporetto* to Giudecca for views of San Marco glittering across glassy waters.

1

© Andrey Omelyanchuk / 500px

CROATIA

Plitvice Lakes

Croatia's top natural attraction and the highlight of the Adriatic hinterland, this glorious expanse of forested hills and turquoise lakes is exquisitely scenic – so much so that in 1979 Unesco proclaimed it a World Heritage Site.

In fact, it's not so much the lakes that are the main attraction here, but the hundreds of waterfalls that link them. It's as though Croatia decided to gather all its waterfalls in one place and charge admission to view them. There are 16 crystalline lakes in all within this heavily forested national park, and a countless number of waterfalls and cascades. The mineral-rich waters carve through the rock, depositing tufa in continually changing formations. Clouds of butterflies drift above the 11 miles (18km) of wooden footbridges and pathways that snake around the edges and across the rumbling water.

It's best explored on foot: if you've got limited time, the upper lake section can be completed in two hours, or more like six if you want to see them all. Sadly, swimming is not permitted in any of the lakes.

Travel

International
Croatia has eight airports with direct flights from a variety of European and Middle Eastern cities year round: the best airports for the lakes are Zagreb (87 miles, 140km), Zadar (80 miles, 130km) and Split (151 miles, 243km). Zagreb is also Croatia's main train hub with direct international services from the country's neighbours.

Regional
Buses stopping at both park entrances run regularly from the main bus stations in Zadar (two hours), Zagreb (two hours, 20 minutes) and Split (3½-5½ hours). From Entrance 2, a shuttle bus travels to several locations around the lake.

Stay

$

Shoestring
Plitvice Backpackers Located in Jezerce, the nearest village to the lakes, this well-run hostel occupies a large house on the highway. Rooms are clean, lockers are big and there's a fully equipped kitchen. *(Dorms from 150KN/US$23, rooms from 340KN/US$52; www.plitvicebackpackers.com)*

$$

Midrange
House Župan With a welcoming hostess and clean, modern rooms, this is a superb choice in Rakovica, 6½ miles (11km) north of the lakes. *(Doubles from 370KN/US$56; www.sobe-zupan.com)*

$$$

Flush
Villa Lika These two large houses in the nearby village of Mukinje have shiny white rooms punctuated with brightly coloured curtains and tiles, all set around a landscaped pool. *(Rooms from 950KN/US$146; www.villa-lika.com)*

Eat

$

Shoestring
Vila Velebita Traditional meat grills are the speciality here, especially spit-roast lamb and suckling pig. It's worth the 8½ mile (14km) trip south from Entrance 2. *(Mains 55-110KN/US$8.40-17; www.vila-velebita.com)*

$$

Midrange
Restaurant Degenija Traditional treats at this upmarket hotel restaurant 2½ miles (4km) north of Entrance 1 include turkey on gnocchi-like dumplings and, in summer, veal and potatoes slow-cooked under a *peka* (traditional domed baking lid). *(Mains 55-140KN/US$8.40-21; www.hotel-degenija.com)*

$$

Midrange
Lička Kuća It's touristy and busy in high season, but it's minutes from Entrance 1 and the food is excellent. Specialities include slow-cooked lamb, dry-cured local prosciutto and mountain trout. *(Mains 70-195KN/US$10-30)*

Timing

The park is beautiful year-round, but spring and autumn are the best times to visit.

Winter is also spectacular, although snow can limit access and the free park transport doesn't operate.

The worst time to visit is in the peak months of July and August, when the falls reduce to a trickle, parking is problematic and the volume of visitors can turn the walking tracks into a conga line.

Plitviče's lakes are part of a National Park in central Croatia.

It's possible to tour the lakes on foot, although more adventurous hikes are possible deeper in the park.

Water cascades from lake to lake.

A fritillary butterfly photographed in the park.

Best value itineraries

1–2 days
You can see the park's classic sights in a day. From Entrance 2, it's an easy amble to Kozjak Lake, the largest lake. Follow the eastern shore to reach the lower lakes – with forests, grottos, steep cliffs and waterfalls – or take one of the regular free boats. Next is emerald Milanovac Lake, then the path runs below cliffs beside Gavanovac Lake. Above is the open-topped cavern of Šupljara and a viewpoint over Plitvice's lower reaches. A walkway cuts around reed-fringed Kaluđerovac Lake past two waterfalls. The second, the aptly named Veliki Slap, is the tallest in Croatia, with a 78m drop.

10 days
Take in the delights of Croatia's northern coastal stretches and wild hinterland. Start in Rijeka, a thriving port with a laid-back vibe and lively cafe scene. Add a day for the Belle Époque villas of seaside Opatija. Hop over to the Kvarner islands for two days – interconnected Cres and Lošinj are the most offbeat, while wilder, greener Cres has an off-the-radar feel. Back on the mainland, hike through the canyons of Paklenica National Park, head down to Zadar for Roman ruins and Habsburg architecture, then spend a day exploring Plitvice Lakes National Park.

© Mark Read / Lonely Planet

© koolimagesforyou / Getty Images

TURKEY

Nemrut Dağı

One man's megalomania echoes across the centuries atop the rugged summit of Nemrut Dağı, where a 1st-century BC Armenian king, Antiochus I Epiphanes, built himself a soaring mountain-top burial ground, filling it with colossal statues of himself and the gods.

This lonely, isolated peak rises to a height of 2106m in the Anti-Taurus Range in southeastern Turkey. When you stand on the summit in the chill of dawn, it seems as if Shelley's *Ozymandias* has been brought to vivid life. As the sun rises over the bare, wind-scoured mountain, a host of statues appear from the darkness, their colossal 2m-high heads toppled from their bodies by earthquakes, their features worn and weathered by centuries of exposure to the elements. They're scattered over two huge terraces, cut by hand straight into the mountainside and overlooked by a gravel-covered 50m-high burial cone that is said to cover the tombs of Antiochus himself (along with three female relatives). It's a bizarre, profoundly spooky sight – the pitilessly staring statues with their mutilated features make a haunting monument to the hubris of a king's ambitions.

Travel

International
Nemrut Dağı is located between the cities of Malatya to the north and Kahta to the south. The nearest domestic airports (accessible by bus) are Malatya, Adiyaman and Şanlıurfa, which receive flights from the international hubs of Ankara and İstanbul. Trains run to Malatya twice daily from Ankara.

Regional
The mountain is set within the 138 sq km Nemrut Dağı Milli Parkı (Mt Nemrut National Park). It's relatively easy to get to the summit with your own vehicle and it's also easy to take a tour from Kahta or Malatya. There are several accommodation options a few kilometres from the summit in the village of Karadut; most are reachable by public transport and will drive guests up to the summit. All nearby places to stay offer meals.

Stay & Eat

$ Shoestring
Çeşme Pansiyon The closest shut-eye option to the summit (5 miles, 8km; the owners will drive you there for ₺50/US$9.40 to ₺60/US$11). The rooms (all with private bathrooms) are basic but clean and campers will enjoy the shaded garden setting. Grilled trout is on offer for dinner; breakfast is ₺10/US$1.90. *(Rooms without meals ₺50/US$9.40, campsite ₺20/US$3.75)*

$ Shoestring
Karadut Pansiyon This pension, ½ mile (1km) up the road from Karadut village centre, is run by two amiable brothers and has 14 neat, compact rooms. Good meals are available (breakfast ₺10/US$1.90, dinner ₺20/US$3.75), along with wine or beer, in the alfresco terrace bar. *(Per person without meals ₺30-40/US$5.65-7.50, campsite ₺5/US$0.95)*

$$ Midrange
Nemrut Kervansaray Hotel One of Karadut's two larger hotels, the 22-room Kervansaray has small but attractive rooms with comfy beds, big glass-door showers and, in some, mountain views and private balconies. *(Doubles with half-board €64/US$73; www.nemrutkervansarayhotel.com)*

$$ Midrange
Hotel Euphrat This relatively large low-rise hotel offers good-sized, clean rooms with writing desks and glassed-in showers, plus a pool and spectacular views from the restaurant terrace. *(Doubles with half-board from ₺180/US$34; www.nemruteuphrathotel.com)*

Timing

Try to visit Nemrut between May and September, when the roads to the summit should be snow-free. They may be passable as early as mid-March and as late as mid-November, but this can't be guaranteed.

July and August are the warmest months, but even in high summer it will be chilly and windy on top of the mountain. This is especially true at sunrise, the coldest time of the day. Take warm clothing no matter when you go.

 1
The head of King Antiochus, an Armenian ruler of the Kingdom of Commagene.

 2
Antiochus, who started his own cult, demanded that his body be preserved after death in a tomb atop Mt Nemrut. His birthday and coronation were celebrated post-humously each month.

 3
Nemrut Dağı National Park: Antiochus' tomb was lost here until its rediscovery in 1883.

Best value itineraries

2 days
The easiest route to the mountain is to take an overnight trip from Şanlıurfa (depending on the current security situation, it may be safer to join a guided tour than to make your own way). Spend a few hours exploring the old pilgrimage town and the lively bazaar, then visit the ancient megaliths of Göbekli Tepe and the beehive houses of Harran. Overnight in Kahta, from where you can head up to Nemrut Dağı for the all-important sunrise. After exploring the mountain, head back to Kahta via the ruins of Arsameia, the ancient capital of the kingdom of Commagene. Make sure you visit the graceful Roman bridge at Cendere and the 1st-century burial mounds of Karakuş Tümülüsü, before returning to Şanlıurfa or Gazantiep.

7–10 days
Begin in Ankara, the Turkish capital. Visit the Anıt Kabir, Atatürk's hilltop mausoleum, and the Museum of Anatolian Civilisations, a restored 15th-century *bedesten* (covered market) packed with finds from the surrounding steppe. Leave three days to explore Cappadocia, staying in a cave hotel surrounded by valleys of fairy chimneys, rock-cut churches and underground cities. The next day, depart for Gaziantep – this fast-paced and epicurean city has about 180 pastry shops producing the world's best pistachio baklava. Then make your way to Şanlıurfa and follow the two-day itinerary above. Be sure to check the current security situation before you travel in this region.

© Justin Foulkes / Lonely Planet

GREECE

Meteora

Magnificent Meteora will leave you speechless. The massive pinnacles of smooth rock could be the setting for a futuristic science-fiction tale or an ancient one. The monasteries perched eyrie-like atop them add to the strange and beautiful landscape. Today this spectacular stone forest beckons pilgrims and rock climbers from around the world.

Soaring pillars of rock hoist the monasteries heavenward. Built as early as the 14th century, these were home to hermit monks fleeing persecution. The rope ladders that once enabled the monks to reach the top have long been replaced by steps carved into the rock, and six of the 24 monasteries remain open to resident monks and visitors alike.

The geological heart of Meteora is the Adrachti, or obelisk, a striking column visible from anywhere in Kastraki. Nearby, on the east-facing side of the Pixari rock face, look for the colourful cave chapel of Agios Andonios. To the left of the chapel, in the hollows and cavities of the rock face, are the Askitaria (Cave Hermitages), complete with hanging ladders and nesting doves. The Askitaria were occupied until the early 20th century by solitary monks and they remain a testament to the original spirit of Meteora.

Travel

International
Greece is easy to reach by plane or ferry. Athens' Eleftherios Venizelos International Airport lies near Spata, 17 miles (27km) east of Athens, and receives flights from all over Europe and the rest of the world. Second busiest is Makedonia International Airport, about 10½ miles (17km) southeast of Thessaloniki. From either city, it's easy to reach Meteora by car, bus or rapid intercity train service.

Regional
For those without a car, there are four daily buses that depart from the nearby villages of Kalambaka and Kastraki to Meteora and back, giving you enough time to visit at least three of the monasteries.

Stay

Shoestring
Alsos House The well-managed guesthouse has views of the rocks from the terrace and rooms. Owner Yiannis Karakantas knows as much about Meteora as the monks do about prayers. *(Doubles from €45/US$51; www.alsoshouse.gr)*

Midrange
Doupiani House The delightful Doupiani is just outside Kastraki village, providing a window to Meteora and one of the region's best panoramic views. *(Doubles from €60/US$68; www.doupianihouse.com)*

Flush
Monastiri Guest House Behind the station in Kalambaka, this stone mansion has views of the rocks and a small pool ringed by owner Dita's rose bushes. *(Doubles from €70/US$79; www.monastiri-guesthouse.gr)*

Eat

Shoestring
Taverna To Paramithi This Kalambaka taverna has grills, fresh pasta, seafood and classic Greek dishes dished up owner-cooks Makis and Eleni – often served with a side order of local music. *(Mains €5.50-9/US$6.20-10)*

Midrange
Taverna Gardenia Popular Kastraki taverna for excellent *mousakas* (shepherd's pie), *yemista* (stuffed peppers and tomatoes) and other *mayirefta* (ready-cooked meals), along with grilled and spit-roasted meats. *(Mains €7-11.50/ US$7.90-13)*

Flush
Taverna Panellinion Next to a fountain in Kalambaka, the antique-filled Panellinion serves traditional dishes such as *pastitsio* (macaroni and meat bake) and *briam* (mixed eggplant and veggies). *(Mains €6-11.50/US$6.80-13)*

Timing

Entry to each monastery is €3/US$3.40 and dress codes apply: no bare shoulders are allowed, men must wear trousers and women must wear skirts below the knee (wraparound skirts are provided at the entrances).

Double-check days and opening hours. They vary by both the day and the hour. Note that at least one monastery is closed each weekday. All six are open on weekends. Between November and March some monasteries might be closed for two days, not one.

❶
Moni Agias Varvaras Rousanou is one of the outstanding monasteries at Meteora.

❷
Its highlight is the beautiful coloured-glass-illuminated *katholikon* (principal church of a monastic complex).

❸
Of the 24 monasteries built here, six still function, home to monks or nuns.

❹
A nun at Moni Agiou Stefanou.

Best value itineraries

2–3 days
Using local buses allows enough time to explore at least three monasteries – Megalou Meteorou, Varlaam and Rousanou, for example. A popular option is to take the bus one-way to the top and then work your way down and around on foot, finishing at either Moni Agiou Nikolaou on the Kastraki side or at Moni Agios Triados on the Kalambaka side. On subsequent days, keen walkers can explore many other *monopatia* (monk paths) that thread through the region (about 800 at last count).

6–7 days
For a longer trip begin with a couple of days in cultured Thessaloniki to lose yourself in Ottoman-style architecture, Turkish sweets and a vibrant arts scene. Scale the slopes of Mt Olympus (2918m), Greece's highest peak, then visit the monasteries of Meteora, perched high on narrow pinnacles of rock. Your last stop is Ancient Delphi, former home of the mysterious Delphic oracle.

© Justin Foulkes / Lonely Planet

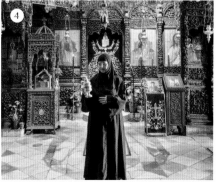

© Justin Foulkes / Lonely Planet

RUSSIA

St Basil's Cathedral

The candy-coloured onion domes and swirly spires of St Basil's Cathedral in Moscow are an unmistakeable symbol of Russia.

Red Square never ceases to inspire. This great cobblestone expanse, where so much of Russian history has unfolded, is perhaps the most storied patch of real estate in all of Russia. Backed by the imposing towers and buildings of the Kremlin, the seat of the nation's political power, it's also home to this ecclesiastical masterpiece – a crazy confusion of colours, patterns and shapes that is completely unique to Russian architecture. It's an electrifying ensemble, best seen at night when the square empties of crowds and the domes are awash in lights.

Commissioned in 1552 by Ivan the Terrible, and completed in 1561, the cathedral's apparent anarchy of shapes hides nine main chapels, each consecrated in honour of an event or battle in the struggle against Kazan. The tall, tent-roofed tower in the centre houses the namesake Church of the Intercession of the Mother of God, while the four biggest domes top four octagonal-towered chapels. In particular, look out for the icon depicting St Basil himself, with Red Square and the Kremlin in the background.

Travel

International
Most travellers arrive in Moscow by air, flying into one of the city's four international airports: Domodedovo, Sheremetyevo, Vnukovo or Zhukovsky. The vast majority of international flights go in and out of Domodedovo and Sheremetyevo, both of which are about an hour from the city centre by car or train. Rail riders will arrive at one of Moscow's central train stations. Kievsky or Belorussky vokzal if you're coming from Europe; Leningradsky vokzal if you're coming from St Petersburg.

Regional
Red Square is the heart of the city and easy to get to by public transport. The Moscow metro is cheap, efficient, interesting to look at and easy to use. The downside is that it's uncomfortably crowded during peak periods. The metro stop for St Basil's Cathedral is Ploshchad Revolyutsii. For fine views of the Kremlin, or just good, old-fashioned transport, a boat ride on the Moscow River is one of the city's highlights.

Stay

Shoestring
Loft Hostel 77 This sweet spot offers stylish dorm rooms equipped with lockers, individual lights, orthopaedic mattresses and privacy curtains. Exposed brick walls and leather furniture create an attractive shabby-chic atmosphere. *(Dorms from R1000/US$15; www.hostel-77.com)*

Midrange
Bulgakov Mini-Hotel Classy rooms, with high ceilings and *Master and Margarita*-inspired art, are as good as it gets in Moscow for this price, especially considering the location. *(Doubles from R4000/US$61; www.bulgakovhotel.com)*

Eat

Shoestring
Dukhan Chito-Ra One of the most revered Georgian eateries in town is also one of the cheapest. The object of worship here is *khinkali* (large, meat-filled dumplings). *(Mains from R300/US$4.55; www.chito-ra.ru)*

Midrange
Elardzhi Another of Moscow's standout Georgian restaurants. Sink into a sofa in the romantic dining room or on the light-filled porch for the house special, *elarji* (cornmeal with suluguni cheese). *(Mains from R600/US$9.10; www.ginza.ru)*

Timing

Stand-out seasons to visit Moscow are late spring and early autumn. Summer is also pleasant and long hours of sunlight bring out revellers. In winter, temperatures can drop to -15°C.

If you think Red Square is impressive by day, come back at night when the crowds are gone and the lights cast a magical glow.

If you're also planning on visiting the Kremlin, note that visitors are only allowed to enter the Armoury and Ivan the Great Bell Tower at specified times.

1

The unique outline of St Basil's Cathedral at the southern end of Red Square. It was completed in 1561 to mark Ivan the Terrible's capture of Kazan, a Tatar stronghold.

2

The cathedral contains nine chapels, each with an ornate interior.

3

The Tsar Cannon in Red Square, the largest in the world (by bombard) at almost 40 tonnes and 5m in length.

Best value itineraries

3–4 days
Arrive at the Kremlin ticket office at 9.30am, and dedicate your morning to inspecting the ancient icons and gawking at the gold and gems. Afterwards, stroll through Alexander Garden and catch the changing of the guard at the Tomb of the Unknown Soldier. Jump into the queue on Red Square for Lenin's Tomb before it closes at 1pm. Ogle the Kremlin spires and St Basil's domes, then visit the cathedral after lunch. Spend the rest of your time in Moscow strolling Gorky Park, visiting the Tretkayov Gallery and sightseeing on the Moscow River.

8–10 days
If you have more time, follow your Moscow itinerary with a few days in the historic and serene Golden Ring towns of Sergiev Posad, Suzdal and Vladimir. Then follow the Volga River north to Tver where Catherine the Great used to pause on her court's cross-country journeys. Make a side trip to serene Lake Seliger. Top up on big-city culture and fun in St Petersburg, then take the train to Petrozavodsk to access Lake Ladoga and the island of Valaam, home to a beguiling working monastery. Return to Petrozavodsk, where you can board a hydrofoil that will zip you across Lake Onega to the island of Kizhi, an architectural reserve that includes the astounding Transfiguration Church.

© javarman3 / Getty Images

SWITZERLAND

Matterhorn

You can sense the anticipation on the train from Täsch: couples gaze wistfully out of the window, kids fidget and stuff Toblerone into their mouths, people rummage for their cameras. And then, as they arrive in Zermatt, all give little whoops of joy at the pop-up-book effect of the Matterhorn, the hypnotically beautiful, one-of-a-kind peak that rises like a shark's fin above town.

Some 3000 alpinists summit the 4478m-high peak, Europe's most photographed, each year. You don't need to be superhuman to do it, but you do need to be a skilled climber (with crampons), be in tip-top physical shape (12-hour endurance performance) and have a week in hand to acclimatise beforehand to make the iconic ascent up sheer rock and ice. A much easier alternative is to ride Zermatt's Gornergat Bahn, the highest cogwheel railway in Europe, or the Matterhorn Glacier Paradise, the continent's highest-altitude cable car. Needless to say, the views of the mountain from both are quite simply out of this world.

Travel

International
Geneva is the most useful Swiss airport for accessing the Valais area, including Zermatt and the Matterhorn, although Zurich and Milan are alternative gateways. You could also pop through the Tunnel du Grand St Bernard from Italy (bus or car only) to Martigny; take the Simplon Pass and Tunnel to Brig from Domodossola in Italy, or arrive from Chamonix in France into Martigny by train or vehicle.

Regional
Zermatt is easily reached by train or car from Geneva. Direct trains to Zermatt depart hourly from Brig, on the main rail line between Geneva and Milan. Trains also access Valais by tunnel from Zurich, Bern and Spiez to Visp, where you can change trains to all parts of the region. Zermatt itself is car-free (motorists must to take the shuttle train from Täsch), and dinky, nearly noiseless electro-taxis zip around town (and often take pedestrians by surprise – watch out!).

Stay

Shoestring
Zermatt Youth Hostel At this impeccably clean hostel, rooms split across two houses are bright and modern, and the four-course evening meal is unbeatable value. *(Dorms from Sfr42/US$42; www.youthhostel.ch/en/hostels/zermatt)*

Midrange
Hotel Bahnhof Opposite Zermatt's train station, these budget digs have comfy beds, spotless bathrooms and family-perfect rooms for four. *(Doubles from Sfr120/US$120; www.hotelbahnhofzermatt.com)*

Flush
Kulmhotel Gornergrat At 3100m, Switzerland's highest hotel is located at the top of the Gornergrat cogwheel railway, and has glorious wraparound mountain panoramas. *(Doubles from Sfr295/US$295; www.gornergrat-kulm.ch)*

Eat

Shoestring
Bayard Metzgerei Join the queue for a street-grilled sausage (pork, veal or beef) and chunk of bread to down with a beer on the hop. *(Sausage Sfr6/US$6; www.metzgerei-bayard.ch)*

Midrange
Whymper Stube This cosy bistro, attached to the Monte Rosa Hotel, is legendary for raclette and fondues. *(Raclette Sfr9/US$9, fondue from Sfr25/US$25; www.whymper-stube.ch)*

Midrange
Chez Vrony Ride the Sunnegga Express funicular to 2288m for dried meats, homemade cheese and sausage from Vrony's cows. *(Mains from Sfr25/US$25; www.chezvrony.ch)*

Timing

The Swiss snow season generally runs from roughly October to April or late May.

Cable cars and viewing platforms sometimes close in bad weather, so check the weather forecast.

Avoid peak season (school holidays in winter and summer) for better deals on accommodation.

Looking towards the Matterhorn from Zermatt. Each face of the mountain faces in a cardinal direction.

Dawn over Zermatt, one of Europe's highest ski resort, with snow available all year round.

Because Zermatt centre is car-free, arriving by train is the best option and the approach affords some amazing views.

Best value itineraries

3 days
A couple of days is enough to explore Zermatt, but three or four is even better (especially given the unpredictable mountain weather). Factor in the Matterhorn Museum and Mountaineers' Cemetery on day one, and an afternoon riding the Matterhorn Glacier Paradise cable car. On day two ride the Gornergratbahn to 3883m and gawp at 14 glaciers and 38 mountain peaks over 4000m from the Panoramic Platform, then head back into town for some warming fondue. On day three, hike the dramatic Matterhorn Glacier Trail (two hours, 4 miles/6.5km) from Trockener Steg to Schwarzsee.

8 days
The 180 mile (290km) Glacier Express train journey is a fantastic way to see the Swiss mountains. Board the cherry-red train in St Moritz and overnight in Graubünden's quaint capital, Chur. Travel through the Rhine Gorge, Switzerland's Grand Canyon, climb over the Oberalp Pass (2044m) and stop in ski resort Andermatt. Traverse the Furka Pass via Switzerland's highest Alpine tunnel and stay in the gorgeous car-free resort of Bettmeralp. Spot the icy tongue of the Aletsch Glacier, then travel along the Rhône Valley into Valais, stopping at Brig for its onion-domed castle, wine-producing Visp and – drum roll – final destination Zermatt, where the Matterhorn makes a fitting finale.

© Jaro68 / Shutterstock

SPAIN

Sagrada Família

Fanciful and profound, inspired by nature and barely restrained by a Gothic style, Barcelona's quirky temple soars skyward with an almost playful majesty. The improbable angles and departures from architectural convention will have you shaking your head in disbelief, but the detail of the decorative flourishes on the Passion Facade, Nativity Facade and elsewhere are worth studying for hours.

The modernista brainchild of Antoni Gaudí, La Sagrada Família remains a work in progress more than 90 years after its creator's death. Work began in 1882 and is hoped (perhaps optimistically) to be completed in 2026. Unfinished it may be, but it attracts about 2.8 million visitors a year and is the most visited monument in Spain. Gaudí devised a temple 95m long and 60m wide, able to seat 13,000 people, with a central tower 170m high above the transept (representing Christ) and another 17 towers of 100m or more. Demonstrating his characteristic dislike for straight lines (there were none in nature, he said), Gaudí gave his towers swelling outlines inspired by the weird peaks of the holy mountain Montserrat outside Barcelona, and encrusted them with a tangle of sculpture that seems an outgrowth of the stone.

Travel

International
Most travellers enter Barcelona via El Prat Airport, 10½ miles (17km) southwest of Plaça de Catalunya. Some budget airlines use Girona-Costa Brava airport or Reus airport. Train is the most convenient overland option for reaching Barcelona from major Spanish centres such as Madrid and Valencia. Barcelona is well-connected by bus to other parts of Spain, as well as to major European cities.

Regional
Barcelona has abundant options for getting around town. The excellent metro can get you most places, with buses and trams filling in the gaps. Taxis are the best option late at night. Metros run from 5am to midnight, Sunday to Thursday. A hop-on, hop-off Bus Turístic, from Plaça de Catalunya, is handy for those wanting to see the city's highlights in one or two days. To get to the cathedral by metro, take Línia 2 or 5 to the Sagrada Família stop.

Stay

Shoestring
Casa Gràcia The hip Casa Gràcia has raised the budget bar. Common spaces include a terrace, library nook, arty lounge, restaurant and DJ-fuelled bar. *(Dorms from €31/US$35; www.casagraciabcn.com)*

Midrange
The 5 Rooms This first-floor apartment actually has 12 rooms between L'Eixample and Barcelona's old centre. *(Doubles from €160/US$181; www.thefiverooms.com)*

Flush
The One Barcelona A stunning five-star property with 89 light-filled rooms, some of them displaying original works by Chilean artist Fernando Prats. *(Doubles from €230/US$260; www.hotelstheone.com)*

Eat

Shoestring
Tapas 24 Hotshot chef Carles Abellán runs this basement tapas haven known for its gourmet versions of old faves. *(Tapas €2.20-12/US$2.50-14; www.carlesabellan.com)*

Midrange
Auto Rosellon With cornflower-blue paintwork and fresh produce on display, Auto Rosellon utilises organic ingredients sourced from small producers and its own garden. *(Mains €12-18/US$14-20; www.autorosellon.com)*

Flush
Disfrutar At this gastronomic temple run by alumni of Ferran Adrià's El Bulli restaurant, nothing is as it seems. *(Tasting menus €120-185/US$136-209; www.disfrutarbarcelona.com)*

Timing

The completed sections and museum may be explored at leisure. Guided tours (50 minutes, €24/US$27) are available. Online tickets give a discount and allow you to skip queues.

An extra €14/US$16 will get you into lifts that rise up inside the towers in the Nativity and Passion facades; these tower tours must be pre-booked online.

Hats and revealing clothing are not permitted.

1
Slow progress: construction of the Nativity facade was finished under the supervision of Gaudí himself as he knew he wouldn't live to see the cathedral completed and wanted to leave a template.

2
Looking out over Barcelona from the Gaudí-designed Parc Güell.

3
The vaulted interior of La Sagrada Familia is as wondrous as the exterior.

Best value itineraries

3–4 days
Start with La Sagrada Família, Gaudí's wondrous work in progress and also view it from his Parc Güell. Explore more of the great modernista buildings on L'Eixample's Passeig de Gràcia. Have a look at the three most famous buildings that make up the Manzana de la Discordia. Then visit one of Gaudí's house museums, either Casa Batlló or La Pedrera. On subsequent days, explore the medieval lanes of the Barri Gòtic, wander down La Rambla, admire the architectural treasures of La Ribera, and visit the Museu Picasso inside conjoined medieval mansions.

7–10 days
When you can tear yourself away from Barcelona, rent a car and head north, passing through Tossa de Mar and its castle-backed bay, then Calella de Palafrugell and Tamariu, two beautiful coastal villages, before heading inland to Girona. The next day is about Salvador Dalí, from his fantasy castle, Castell de Púbol, to his extraordinary theatre-museum in Figueres, and then his one-time home, seaside Cadaqués. Leave the Mediterranean behind and drive west in the shadow of the Pyrenees. Your reward for the long drive is Taüll, gateway to the Parc Nacional d'Aigüestortes i Estany de Sant Maurici. A loop south via Lleida then east brings you back to Barcelona.

SCOTLAND

Skara Brae

There's a magic to Orkney that you begin to feel as soon as the Scottish mainland slips astern. An archipelago of mostly flat, green-topped islands stripped bare of trees and ringed with red sandstone cliffs, it's famous for having some of Europe's oldest and most important ancient monuments – and none is more extraordinary than Skara Brae.

This is northern Europe's best-preserved Neolithic village – pre-dating Stonehenge and the Pyramids of Giza. When visiting ancient sites it can be difficult to bridge the gulf of years or feel a sense of connection with the people who built them, but Skara Brae has an immediate impact, with its carefully constructed fireplaces, beds, cupboards and water cisterns offering a superb glimpse of everyday Stone Age life. It was hidden until 1850, when waves whipped up by a severe storm eroded the sand and grass above the beach, exposing the houses underneath, but it can feel as though the inhabitants have just slipped out to go fishing and could return at any moment.

It's one of several outstanding prehistoric monuments in the area, including the 5000-year-old Maeshowe, a Stone Age tomb that was built from enormous sandstone blocks, and the impressive stone circles known as the Ring of Brodgar and the Standing Stones of Stenness.

© Pecold / Shutterstock

Travel

International
Scotland has four main international airports: Aberdeen, Edinburgh, Glasgow and Glasgow Prestwick, with a few short-haul international flights landing at Inverness. London is the main UK gateway for long-haul flights. Loganair flies daily to Kirkwall in Orkney from Aberdeen, Edinburgh, Glasgow, Inverness and Sumburgh (Shetland), and in summer from Manchester, Fair Isle and Bergen (Norway). Northlink Ferries run from Scrabster to Stromness, and from Aberdeen and Lerwick on Shetland to Kirkwall. Pentland Ferries run from Gills Bay to South Ronaldsay, and John O'Groats Ferries has a passenger-only service to South Ronaldsay, with connecting buses to Kirkwall.

Regional
The regular bus service between Kirkwall and Stromness is good for accessing several of the ancient sites, though not Skara Brae. It's possible to walk along the coast from Stromness to Skara Brae (9 miles/14.5km), or it's an easy taxi or cycle from Stromness. The south coast and Birsay are also serviced by buses.

Stay

Shoestring
Birsay Hostel In a former activity centre and school turned hostel, the two- or four-bedded dorms are the most spacious. There's a big kitchen and a grassy camping area. *(Dorms from £19/US$25; https://orkney.campstead.com)*

Midrange
Orkneylodge This old seaplane base makes a comfortable spot if you've got a car, and has a conservatory lounge and bar. It's right beside the Houton ferry terminal. *(Doubles from £65/US$84; www.orkneylodge.com)*

Eat

Shoestring
Birsay Bay Tearoom A pleasant spot with sweeping views over green grass, black cows and blue-grey sea, this cafe serves tea, coffee, home baking and light meals. *(Light meals £3–8/US$3.90–10; www.birsaybaytearoom.co.uk)*

Midrange
Orkney Brewery This brewery creates delicious Orcadian ales and also runs regular tours of its facilities. The Tasting Hall cafe-bar serves burgers and sharing platters. *(Mains from £8.95/US$12; www.orkneybrewery.co.uk)*

Timing

Visit in June, July or August for plenty of summer sunlight and Scotland's longest daylight hours.

Check www.orkneyharbours.com for cruise-ship arrivals – places such as Skara Brae get very busy when a big boat is in town.

The Orkney Explorer Pass covers sites including Skara Brae, the Broch of Gurness and the Brough of Birsay. It lasts for 30 days and is available from April to October.

Skara Brae: imagine the life of hunters, fishers and farmers in this Neolithic village.

The Ring of Brodgar has enchanted visitors since the 60 massive stones were first erected 5000 years ago (36 still stand).

A chamber inside the cairn of Maeshowe; the entrance is aligned with the midwinter sun to light enters.

Best value itineraries

3 days
If you only have time and budget to visit one area of Orkney, Mainland is the place to choose: it's where most of the major sites are located and is easily accessed by plane or ferry. The Heart of Neolithic Orkney is a Unesco World Heritage Site and consists of four standout archaeological sites, all of which can be visited in a couple of days: Skara Brae, Maeshowe, the Standing Stones of Stenness and the Ring of Brodgar. If you have more time, other lesser-known sites such as the Barnhouse Neolithic Village and the Broch of Gurness are also worth a visit.

7–10 days
It's easy to incorporate Orkney into a wider tour of Scotland's Highlands. Start out in activity-focused Aviemore, then take a trip to see the ancient forests of the Cairngorm National Park. Head west to Fort William. Overnight here, then spend a morning exploring Glen Nevis before heading north along the Great Glen to see Urquhart Castle and Loch Ness – leave time for a monster-spotting cruise – and finish up in Inverness. From Inverness, continue around the mainland coast through the gorgeous wilderness of Coigach and Assynt, and on via Cape Wrath and Durness to Thurso, where the ferry to the Orkney Islands awaits.

GERMANY

Schloss Neuschwanstein

As you approach Schloss Neuschwanstein the turrets and gables appear through the forested mountaintops like a mirage and you can understand how it became the inspiration for Walt Disney's *Sleeping Beauty* castle.

King Ludwig II planned this fairy-tale pile himself, with the help of a stage designer rather than an architect. He envisioned it as a giant set on which to recreate the world of Germanic mythology, inspired by the operas of his friend Richard Wagner. Work started in 1869 and, like so many of Ludwig's grand schemes, was never finished. For all the coffer-depleting sums spent on it, the king spent just over 170 days in residence.

Step inside to experience the fairy tale for yourself. The most impressive room is the Sängersaal (Minstrels' Hall), where frescoes depict scenes from the opera *Tannhäuser*. Other completed sections include Ludwig's Tristan and Isolde–themed bedroom, dominated by a huge Gothic-style bed crowned with intricately carved cathedral-like spires; a gaudy artificial grotto (another allusion to *Tannhäuser*); and the Byzantine-style Thronsaal (Throne Room), which has an incredible mosaic floor containing more than two million stones. And don't forget to look outside: almost every window provides tour-halting views across the plain below.

Travel

International
Munich is Bavaria's main transport hub, second only to Frankfurt in flight and rail connections. Rail is the best way to reach Munich from other parts of Germany and the best means of getting from the Bavarian capital to other parts of Bavaria. Without your own set of wheels in eastern Bavaria and the Alps, you'll have to rely on bus services, which peter out in the evenings and at weekends.

Regional
If you want to do the castle in a single day from Munich, you'll need to start very early. The first train leaves Munich at 4.48am (change in Kaufbeuren), reaching Füssen at 6.49am. Otherwise, stay overnight in Füssen: direct trains leave Munich once every two hours throughout the day. RVO buses 78 and 73 leave at least hourly from Füssen train station for the castle (eight minutes).

Stay

$

Shoestring
Bavaria City Hostel The BCH is a colourful, well-run place created out of a part of the Zum Goldenen Posthorn Hotel. Dorms hold four to six people and, though bright, their themes will be a touch 'in your face' for some. *(Dorms from €18/US$21; www.hostelfuessen.com)*

$$

Midrange
Hotel Sonne This favourite in Füssen's Old Town offers an unexpected design-hotel experience within. Themed rooms feature everything from swooping bed canopies to big-print wallpaper, huge pieces of wall art to sumptuous fabrics. *(Doubles from €90/US$103; www.hotel-fuessen.de)*

Eat

$

Shoestring
Vinzenzmurr The Füssen branch of the Munich butcher and self-service canteen offering no-nonsense portions of meatloaf, goulash soup, bratwurst and schnitzel. *(All dishes under €6/US$6.85)*

$$

Midrange
Zum Franziskaner This popular restaurant specialises in *Schweinshaxe* (pork knuckle) and schnitzel, prepared in more varieties than you can imagine. *(Mains €6.50-18/US$7.40-21)*

Timing

● Avoid overcrowded July and August if you possibly can; come in autumn for wonderful woodland colours.

● For the postcard view of Neuschwanstein and the plains beyond, walk 10 minutes up to Marienbrücke (Mary's Bridge), which spans the spectacular Pöllat Gorge over a waterfall just above the castle.

1 Snow adds to the fairy-tale magic of Neuschwanstein.

2 The castle's name translates as 'new swan stone' and it was commissioned 1868 to recreate King Ludwig II of Bavaria's childhood home, Hohenschwangau Castle.

3 The Throne Hall is where King Ludwig II would have lived out his regal fantasies but in reality Bavaria had been conquered by Prussia in 1866.

Best value itineraries

4 days
From April to October a Romantic Road Coach (www.romantischestrasse.de) runs daily along Germany's most popular holiday route. The entire journey takes about 12 hours, but there's no charge for breaking the journey and continuing the next day. As such, you can use it to hop between the major sights: Würzburg and its stately Residenz, the pretty towns of Rothenburg ob der Tauber and Dinkelsbühl, dramatic Schloss Harburg, elegant Augsburg and the mighty Wieskirche, near Wies. Wherever you stop along the way, Füssen and Schloss Neuschwanstein make unforgettable end points.

8 days
Make a study of Munich for a few days, folding day trips to Schloss Neuschwanstein and up the Zugspitze into your itinerary. Continue west to Lake Constance, where stops should include enchanting Lindau and picture-perfect Meersburg. Revel in the youthful university spirit of ancient Freiburg for a day, then steer north for scenic drives through the Black Forest, ending in Baden-Baden for the night. Relax in the town's thermal spas before moving on to Heidelberg, with its ancient student taverns and charismatic ruined castle.

© Andrew Montgomery / Lonely Planet

© Sean Pavone / Shutterstock

Sintra

All rippling mountains, dewy forests thick with ferns and lichen, exotic gardens and glittering palaces, the town of Sintra is like a page torn from a fairy tale. It's the must-do side trip from Lisbon and its Unesco World Heritage–listed centre, Sintra-Vila, is dotted with pastel-hued manors folded into hills that roll down to the blue Atlantic.

The star of Sintra-Vila is the Palácio Nacional, with its iconic twin conical chimneys and lavish, whimsical interior. It is a mix of Moorish and Manueline styles, all arabesque courtyards, barley-twist columns and 15th- and 16th-century geometric *azulejos* (hand-painted tiles). Another highlight is Quinta da Regaleira, a neo-Manueline extravaganza dreamed up by Italian opera-set designer Luigi Manini, under the orders of Brazilian coffee tycoon António Carvalho Monteiro, aka 'Monteiro dos Milhões' (Moneybags Monteiro). The villa is surprisingly homely inside, despite its ferociously carved fireplaces, frescoes and Venetian-glass mosaics.

Don't miss a hike up to Castelo dos Mouros, a ruined 10th-century Moorish castle looming above the forest. When the clouds peel away, the vistas over Sintra's palace-dotted hill and dale, and across to the glittering Atlantic are, like the climb, breathtaking.

Travel

International
The ultramodern Aeroporto de Lisboa is accessible via direct flights from North and South America, Africa and numerous European capitals. Lisbon can also be easily reached by train from Madrid, and by bus from Madrid and Paris.

Regional
Comboios de Portugal runs trains half-hourly between Lisbon's Rossio station and Sintra (hourly on weekends), and every 20 minutes from Lisbon's less-convenient Oriente station (half-hourly on weekends). If arriving by train, go to the last stop – Sintra – from where it's a pleasant, sculpture-peppered ½ mile (1km) walk into the village.

Stay

$ Shoestring
Moon Hill Hostel This minimalist newcomer outshines the competition. Rooms have colourful reclaimed-wood headboards and wall-covering photos of Sintra forests, and there's a Portuguese-fusion restaurant. *(Dorms from €19/US$22, doubles from €55/US$62; www.moonhillhostel.com)*

$$ Midrange
Sintra 1012 Run by a young Portuguese-American couple, this superb four-room guesthouse hunkers behind medieval walls. In Roman times, it was Sintra's first theatre. *(Doubles from €65/US$74; www.sintra1012.com)*

$$$ Flush
Villa Mira Longa This restored 1898 villa offers comfy rooms (the best with panoramic views) and beautiful common areas (an antique-filled dining room and manicured garden). *(Doubles from €115/US$130; www.villamiralonga.com)*

Eat

$ Shoestring
Cafe Saudade A former bakery with cherub-covered ceilings and a rambling interior. It's a fine spot for pastries (the massive scones are a highlight) and lighter fare. *(Mains from €5.50/US$6.25; www.facebook.com/cafesaudade)*

$$ Midrange
INcomum Chef Luis Santos specialises in modern upgrades to Portuguese cuisine, served amid the muted greys and greens of his dining room. *(Mains from €12.50/US$14, tasting menu €37.50/US$43; www.incomumbyluissantos.pt)*

$$ Midrange
Nau Palatina Congenial owner Zé's creative tapas are as off-centre as his location, a 1km walk from Sintra centre in São Pedro de Penaferrim. Spice Route undertones are weaved throughout the tasty menu of tidbits. *(Tapas from €1.50-11.90/US$1.70-13; www.facebook.com/barnaupalatina)*

Timing

Sintra has become popular and it's hard to escape the tourist masses (especially in summer). Midweek, go early in the day to escape the worst of the crowds.

Parques da Sintra – Monte da Lua (www.parquesdesintra.pt), which runs tours to most of Sintra's greatest hits, offers discounted combined tickets for its attractions. Discounts range from 5% (two sights) to 15% (six sights).

Palácio Nacional da Pena is just one of several historic sites in Sintra that are within walking distance of each other.

The Quinta da Regaleira is an enchanting villa with gardens about an hour's stroll from Palácio Nacional.

Lisbon's historic trams – this one dates from the 1930s – are an authentic way to see the city.

Best value itineraries

3 days
Start in Lisbon, spending two days exploring the city's enchanting neighbourhoods, fado-filled taverns, atmospheric cafes and restaurants, and late-night street parties. Take vertiginous tram rides, and visit the hilltop castle and viewing points, museums and historic sites. On day three, head to beautiful Sintra for quaint village life amid woodlands and palaces.

11 days
After the three-day itinerary, enjoy two days exploring fascinating Évora and its nearby megaliths. From there, go south and spend a day in peaceful Tavira, one of the Algarve's prettiest towns, and then take the ferry out to car-free Ilha de Tavira. Continue west to beach- and nightlife-loving Lagos. Keep going west until you hit laid-back Sagres, where you can visit its dramatically sited fort and surf the waves. Then drive north to Tomar, a sleepy river town that's home to the staggering Convento de Cristo. Book two nights in the venerable university town of Coimbra, wandering the old quarters and visiting medieval convents and churches. Spend your last two days in Porto, Lisbon's rival in beauty.

© Justin Foulkes / Lonely Planet

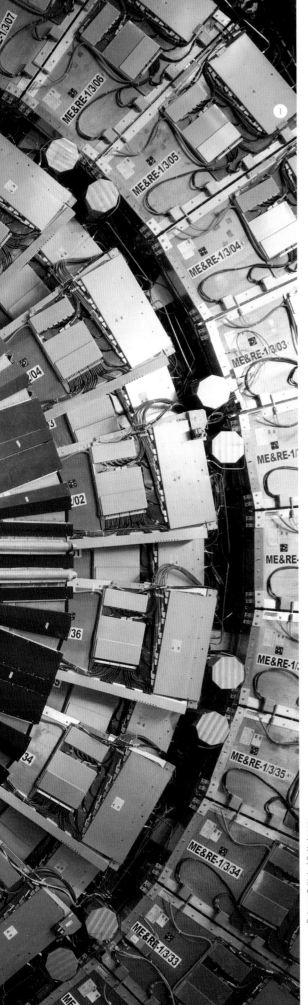

SWITZERLAND

CERN

From the outside, the CERN (Conseil Européen pour la Recherche Nucléaire) laboratory doesn't look like much: a complex of drab 1960s buildings with as much visual appeal as a municipal car park. But it's what lies hidden 100m under the mountain that makes this a wonder of the world – a 27km circular tube called the Large Hadron Collider, the biggest machine ever built by humans.

Founded in 1954 just outside Geneva, CERN stands at the cutting edge of particle physics. It accelerates protons down the tube at close to light speed, colliding them to create new matter. In the process, scientists gain new insights into the worlds of quantum physics and subatomic particles, and ultimately hope to be able to answer some of humankind's most vexing questions regarding the origins of the universe. And no – despite what you may have read, it's not going to make us fall into a black hole, travel through time or step through a portal into a parallel universe.

Several fascinating exhibitions and brain-boggling guided tours shed light on the centre's work. Unfortunately, the LHC is off-limits, but you can trace its outline above ground on an interactive bike circuit called 'The Passport to the Big Bang'.

Travel

International
Geneva (Cointrin) Airport, 2½ miles (4km) northwest of the town centre, is served by a wide variety of Swiss and international airlines. More-or-less-hourly connections run from Geneva's central train station, Gare CFF de Cornavin, to most Swiss towns and cities, and many others across Europe. Gare Routière de Genève operates buses across the border into neighbouring France.

Regional
The easiest way to get to CERN is to take tram 18 from Gare CFF de Cornavin. Tickets for buses, trolleybuses and trams are sold at dispensers at stops and at the main ticket office inside the central train station.

Stay

Shoestring
Geneva Youth Hostel The vast open-plan lobby of this hostel has an industrial air to it. It spans several floors; the best rooms are the four-bedders and there's a big terrace on the first floor. *(Dorms from Sfr36/US$36; www.genevahostel.ch)*

Midrange
La Cour des Augustins With a selection of bright, playful guestrooms, suites and long-stay apartments, this funky design hotel on the fringe of the Old Town is very popular. *(Doubles from Sfr168/US$168; www.lacourdesaugustins.com)*

Flush
Mandarin Oriental This luxury waterfront hotel has a choice of classically furnished Superior rooms, River View rooms, spacious Mandarin rooms and sumptuous suites. *(Doubles from Sfr655/US$655; www.mandarinoriental.com/geneva)*

Eat

Shoestring
Buvette des Bains Meet Genevans at this earthy beach bar – rough and hip around the edges – at the Bains des Pâquis lakeside pool and sauna complex. *(Mains from Sfr14/US$14; www.bains-des-paquis.ch)*

Midrange
Les 5 Portes The Five Doors is a fashionable Pâquis port of call. Its Sunday brunch is a particularly buzzing affair. *(Dinner mains Sfr28-44/US$28-44; www.les5portes.com)*

Flush
Le Petit Lac Take an afternoon boat tour from Jardin-Anglais or Genève-Pâquis to Corsier for an early dinner at this superb lakefront seafood restaurant. *(Three-course set menu Sfr52/US$52; www.lepetitlac.ch)*

Timing

June to August is the best time to visit, when temperatures rise. From March to May and September to November, Geneva is a hotbed of global conferences and trade shows – hotels fill up and prices soar.

Winter, with its December festivals and nearby skiing, is a real charmer.

Tours often fill up months ahead. Access the online booking portal here: http://visit.cern/tours/guided-tours-individuals.

1 The CMS (Compact Muon Solenoid) is part of the Large Hadron Collider (LHC) at CERN and is designed to detect extra dimensions and dark matter.

2 Although the LHC isn't open to the public, the Globe of Science and Innovation at CERN can be visited.

3 Geneva and its lake add to the appeal of a scientific sojourn in Switzerland.

Best value itineraries

3 days
Begin your exploration in Geneva's Old Town, climbing the bell towers of Cathédrale St-Pierre. Visit Musée International de la Réforme or Musée d'Art et d'Histoire. Next head down to the Jardin Anglais on Lake Geneva for iconic views of the Horloge Fleurie, a giant flowery clock face, and the Jet d'Eau, Geneva's mammoth lakefront fountain. On day two, get to know Geneva's international organisations, taking a United Nations tour at Palais des Nations or learning the history of the Red Cross at Musée International de la Croix-Rouge. Spend another day lounging in the Bains des Pâquis baths and investigating particle physics at CERN.

10 days
This Geneva-to-Zürich trip is eminently doable by car or public transport. Explore Geneva, including CERN, then trundle along the shore of Europe's largest Alpine lake to bustling Lausanne. Continue along the Swiss Riviera to the Lavaux wine region, past lakeside Château de Chinon, to Montreux. Head north next to Gruyères, land of châteaux, cheese, cream and pearly white meringues. Further north, cross the French–German language frontier to the Swiss capital Bern, then visit the lakeside towns around Interlaken for skiing and hiking. Detour via Lucerne to Switzerland's most hip and happening city, Zürich.

age fotostock / Alamy Stock Photo

Lucas Vellecillos / Alamy Stock Photo

CZECH REPUBLIC

Klementinum

The Klementinum is a complex of beautiful baroque and rococo halls in which sooty stone saints glare down at Charles Bridge and the trams and tourists on Křížovnické náměstí. Originally a Jesuit college, it became part of Charles University in 1773 and is now mostly occupied by the Czech National Library.

You can wander freely through the courtyards or take a guided tour to view the most impressive buildings. The baroque Library Hall (1727), magnificently decorated with ornate gilded carvings and a ceiling fresco depicting the Temple of Wisdom, houses thousands of theological volumes dating back to 1600. The Meridian Hall was used to determine the exact time of noon, using a beam of sunlight cast through a hole in one of the walls. Containing an exhausting 172 steps, the Astronomical Tower, which was used as an observatory until the 1930s, houses a display of 18th-century astronomical instruments and offers a 360-degree view of Prague.

The Chapel of Mirrors also dates from the 1720s and is an ornate confection of gilded stucco, marbled columns, fancy frescoes and ceiling mirrors – baroque on steroids. Perhaps the best way to transport yourself to the 18th century is to attend a classical music concert in the chapel, listening to the swelling sounds of an organ once played by Mozart.

Travel

International
Prague is well served by air, road and rail. Václav Havel Airport Prague, 10½ miles (17km) west of the city centre, is the main international gateway to the Czech Republic and hub for the national carrier Czech Airlines. Prague is well integrated into European rail networks. Train travel makes the most sense travelling from Berlin and Dresden to the north or Vienna, Kraków, Bratislava and Budapest to the east and south. Most domestic and all international trains arrive at Praha hlavní nádraží, Prague's main station.

Regional
Central Prague, where the Klementinum is located, is easily managed on foot (though wear comfortable shoes). For longer trips, the city has a reliable public-transport system of metros, trams and buses. The system is integrated, meaning that the same tickets are valid on all types of transport and for transfers between them. The tram network is extensive and the best way to get around shorter distances; the metro is good for visiting outlying areas or covering longer distances.

Stay

$ Shoestring
Sophie's Hostel There's lots of contemporary style on offer here, with oak-veneer floors, minimalist decor and 'designer' showers, which have autographed glass screens and huge rainfall showerheads. *(Dorms from 380Kč/US$17; www.sophieshostel.com)*

$$ Midrange
Domus Henrici This historic building, which is located in a quiet corner of Hradčany, has eight spacious and stylish rooms, all with polished wood floors, large bathrooms, comfy beds and fluffy bathrobes. *(Doubles 3600Kč/US$158; www.domus-henrici.cz)*

Eat

$ Shoestring
Lokál A classic Czech beer hall with excellent *tankové pivo* (tanked Pilsner Urquell) and a daily-changing menu of Bohemian dishes. *(Mains from 155-265Kč/US$6.80-12; www.lokal-dlouha.ambi.cz)*

$$ Midrange
Sansho British chef Paul Day champions Czech farmers by sourcing all his meat and vegetables locally. There's no menu as such – dishes depend on the day's market produce. *(Mains 200-250Kč/US$8.80-11; www.sansho.cz)*

Timing

High season in Prague generally means April to June, September and October, plus the Christmas and New Year holidays; the Prague Spring festival in May is the busiest time of year. July and August are midseason and the rest of the year is low season, when hotel rates can drop by as much as 30% or 40%.

1 Atlas bears the celestial sphere on his shoulders at the top of the Astronomical Tower.

2 The Klementinum's baroque Library Hall contains about 20,000 theological titles in one of the world's most beautiful libraries.

3 The Gothic spires of Church of Our Lady Before Týn dominate Prague's Old Town Square.

Best value itineraries

3–4 days
Wander the courtyards of Prague Castle before the main sights open, then spend the day visiting St Vitus Cathedral, the Old Royal Palace, the Lobkowicz Palace, exploring Malá Strana and admiring the baroque beauty of St Nicholas Church. As day fades, stroll across Charles Bridge in the evening light. Day two is for the Staré Město (Old Town). Stroll the Old Town Square, watch the Astronomical Clock do its thing, climb the Old Town Hall Tower, visit the Prague Jewish Museum and tour the Klementinum. On days three and four, explore Nové Město (New Town) and pay a visit to Vyšehrad Citadel.

7–10 days
Begin with three or four days in Prague, and take day-trips to Karlštejn Castle and heart-rending Terezín, a former concentration camp for European Jews. Head west to the spa town of Karlovy Vary to sample the sulphurous spring waters. Day-trip to picture-postcard Loket with its riverside castle. Allow a morning for the spa town of Mariánské Lázně before continuing southeast to Plzeň, where Pilsner Urquell is made. Continue the beer theme at České Budějovice, home of the Budvar brewery, finishing in Český Krumlov, with a day for its picturesque streets and castle, and a second for boat trips along the Vltava River.

© Luciano Mortula - LGM / Shutterstock

Széchenyi Baths

Budapest sits on a crazy quilt of almost 125 thermal springs and 'taking the waters' is a part of everyday life here. Széchenyi Baths is the crown jewel – it's the largest medicinal bath in Europe, with an astonishing 15 indoor pools and another three outdoors.

Some of Budapest's baths date from Turkish times, others are art nouveau marvels and still others are spick-and-span modern establishments that boast all the mod cons. Which one you choose is a matter of taste and what exactly you're looking for – be it fun, a hangover cure or relief for something more serious – but a visit to the stately Széchenyi Baths is essential.

The gigantic wedding cake of a building in City Park dates from just before the outbreak of WWI, but the hot-water spring was discovered while a well was being drilled in the late 19th century. Feel your cares melt away in the thermal pools; the water, high in calcium, magnesium and hydrogen carbonate, is said to be good for pains in the joints, arthritis, blood circulation and disorders of the nervous system. Perhaps best of all, the baths are open year-round, and there aren't many places on the planet where you can watch people playing chess on floating boards while it's snowing.

Travel

International
Ferenc Liszt International Airport is Budapest's global gateway. Minibuses (including the MiniBUD shuttle), buses and taxis travel to central Budapest from the airport. Most international trains (and domestic traffic to/from the north and northeast) arrive at Keleti train station, though a few also arrive at Nyugati and Déli stations.

Regional
The baths are located in City Park in Pest, 15 minutes from the centre of town and easily accessible by metro and trolleybus. The metro is the quickest but least scenic way to get around. Trams are faster and more pleasant for sightseeing than buses. Travel passes are valid on all trams, buses, trolleybuses, suburban trains and metro lines.

Stay

Shoestring
Maverick City Lodge Modern, warehouse-style hostel with great facilities and three floors of dorms and private rooms decked in bold colours and beanbags. *(Dorms from €10/US$11, doubles from €40/US$46; www.mavericklodges.com)*

Midrange
Casati Budapest Hotel The art-adorned reception area sets the tone at this classy hotel, situated in an 18th-century building with many original features. *(Rooms from €90/US$103; www.casatibudapesthotel.com)*

Flush
Hotel Palazzo Zichy This hotel was the 19th-century home of the aristocratic Zichy family. The 80 rooms, all charcoals and creams, are enlivened by red-glass-topped desks. *(Rooms from €125/US$143; www.hotel-palazzo-zichy.hu)*

Eat

Shoestring
Culinaris A restaurant? A cafe? A gourmet food shop? Apparently all three, with a chaotic selection (pork vindaloo, Mexican beef chilli, Moroccan lamb pita). *(Mains 1990-2490Ft/US$7.05-8.85; www.culinaris.hu)*

Midrange
Seller Bistro There's a warm welcome at this candlelit cellar. The Hungarian home cooking includes dishes such as grey beef, duck leg, oxtail and lamb's knuckle. *(Mains from 3600Ft/US$13)*

Flush
Onyx This Michelin-starred eatery has set out to modernise Hungarian cuisine, with a six-course 'Hungarian Evolution' tasting menu. One for romancing your sweetie. *(Tasting menus from 29,900Ft/US$106; www.onyxrestaurant.hu)*

Timing

Spring is glorious in Budapest. Summer is festival season. Autumn is beautiful, particularly in the Buda Hills.

For a cheaper bathing experience, visit after 5pm. Come back on a Saturday night for a raucous, wet'n'wild 'sparty'.

You're not supposed to stay in the hottest thermal pool for more than 20 minutes at a time for health reasons.

The thermal bath at Széchenyi, one of the largest in Europe, contains sulphate, calcium, magnesium, bicarbonate and a lot of bathing bodies.

Admiring the Art Nouveau decor.

Bathing at Széchenyi is a social experience, with regulars catching up on a game of chess.

Best value itineraries

3–4 days
Spend your first morning in Budapest on Castle Hill, taking in the views from the Royal Palace and establishing the lay of the land. Visit either the Hungarian National Gallery or the rebranded Castle Museum, then make your way to the Király Baths for a soak. On your second day, cross the Danube and see Pest at its finest by walking up leafy Andrássy út, which will take you on your way to Heroes' Square, past architectural gems like the Hungarian State Opera House and New Theatre, and wonderful cafes including Művész Kávéház and Lotz Terem Book Cafe. Conclude with a walk around City Park, a visit to the Budapest Zoo and a swansong soak at the wonderful Széchenyi Baths.

7–10 days
For a longer trip, from Budapest make your way north to the towns of the Danube Bend: picture-postcard Szentendre, royal Visegrád and holy Esztergom. The road continues west along the Danube to Sopron, Hungary's finest medieval city, replete with worthwhile museums and churches. Travel south to Lake Balaton and recharge your batteries at Keszthely and nearby Hévíz, which boasts its own thermal lake. Pécs, Hungary's 'Mediterranean' town, is a treasure trove of early Christian and Turkish sites.

Trolltunga

A slender spur of rock projecting into the void above Lake Ringedalsvatnet, Trolltunga (the Troll's Tongue) is one of Norway's most photographed features and one of the country's most popular hiking targets. You definitely won't be alone at the top – it's possibly the most Instagrammed sight in all of Norway – but standing on the edge of the rock and staring out into thin air is worth every gruelling step to the top.

The hike is usually doable from late May to early September, depending on snowfall, but it's tough going: 14 miles (23km), or 10 hours return, from the trailhead at Skjeggedal, 8 miles (13km) northeast of Odda. The trail is well marked from the car park, with distance markers along the route outlining the distance left to the summit – but the ascent is brutal in places, covering a total climb of about 1000m, so make absolutely sure that you're in adequate shape and have the proper gear before you decide to tackle it. En route, watch out for the Tyssestrengene waterfall (646m).

If you continue on a little way beyond Trolltunga you will reach another fine vantage point, Preikestolen (Pulpit Rock), a smaller version of the much more famous lookout of the same name overlooking Lysefjord, near Stavanger.

Travel

International
Oslo is well linked to other European countries by air, with a usual flying time of two hours from London or Paris, and a little shorter from Berlin. There are regular bus and rail services to Oslo from neighbouring Sweden, with a three- to four-hour journey from Gothenburg. Car and passenger ferries also connect the city's ports with Denmark, Sweden and Germany. Flying to the handsome fjord town of Bergen is another possible option.

Regional
The nearest town is Odda, 43 miles (70km) south of Eidfjord. Buses link the town with Oslo (seven hours, changing at Seljestad), Eidfjord (1½ hours) and Voss (two hours).

Stay

Shoestring
Odda Camping Campsites, rooms and huts occupy a pleasant spot on Sandvinvatnet's lakeshore. *(Camping from 150kr/US$18, cabins from 590kr/US$71; www.oddacamping.no)*

Midrange
Trolltunga Hotel A simple but proper hotel, with dorms and rooms attractively finished in fjord-blue tones. It's worth upgrading for lake views. *(Dorms from 450kr/US$54, doubles from 1045kr/US$125; www.trolltungahotel.no)*

Flush
Tyssedal Hotel Built in 1913, the art deco Tyssedal Hotel has terrific rooms with parquet floors and stylish fittings – Eidfjord artist Nils Bergslien is said to haunt the corridors. *(Doubles from 1690kr/US$202; www.tyssedalhotel.no)*

Eat

Midrange
Trolltunga Hotel There are good-value evening meals available from 5pm in the restaurant here. *(Mains from 189kr/US$23; www.trolltungahotel.no)*

Midrange
Tyssedal Hotel This grand hotel restaurant is Odda's best, serving mainly Norwegian staples. *(Mains from 199-329kr/US$24-39; www.tyssedalhotel.no)*

Timing

The main time for tackling the Trolltunga is in summer, usually from May to September. Snow covers the trail the rest of the year; make sure you confirm local conditions before setting out.

If you do want to tackle the walk earlier in the season, Trolltunga Active (www.trolltunga-active.com) offers guided hikes in the shoulder months, depending on the weather and snowpack.

A mountain farm at Kjeåson, high above Hardangerfjord. A road didn't reach the settlement until 1974.

The Troll's Tongue sticks out over Lake Ringedalsvatnet.

Glacial scenery around Eidfjord near Odda makes hiking here a joy.

© Justin Foulkes / Lonely Planet

© Julian Love / Lonely Planet

Bay of Kotor

Gorgeous, breathtaking, majestic, divine; however hefty your thesaurus, the mind-blowing beauty of the Bay of Kotor will leave you struggling for superlatives.

Hemmed in by commanding cliffs and shape-shifting between rippling gulfs and sparkling straits, the cobalt cove even manages to defy geographic description: is it a fjord? A submerged canyon? It seems there's only one way to define Boka Kotorska: unmissable.

Scattered with photogenic medieval towns admiring their reflections in peacock-blue inlets, the compact bay – or 'Boka', as it's known in local parlance – is stitched together by a series of scenic, serpentine roads, making it easy to explore. As if determined to prove the 'good things come in small packages' adage, the region crams in everything from island monasteries and show-stopping citadels to adventure sports and extraordinary eateries, where waterfront views induce as much drooling as the fresh seafood. Whatever your bliss, you'll find it at Boka.

Travel

International
The closest airport is at Tivat, on the bay and 5 miles (8km) from Kotor town. Flights arrive from around Montenegro, Europe and the Middle East, with connections to further afield. There are buses from Budva and Podgorica (which has an international airport) to towns around the bay, with some services from as far as Sarajevo and Belgrade. Buses head to Kotor from Dubrovnik six times a day, via Herceg Novi.

Regional
A road wends its way around the coast. From Kotor the main road takes a tunnel and comes out near Tivat airport. A car ferry crosses back and forth between Kamenari and Lepetane at the bay's narrowest point. There are three main bus routes in the Boka. Frequent services take the coastal road from Herceg Novi to Kotor, stopping at all the villages along the way. In summer, taxi boats are useful.

Stay

Shoestring
Old Town Hostel Sympathetic renovations at this 13th-century palazzo-turned-hostel in Kotor have brought the place to life, and the stone walls echo with the chatter of travellers. *(Dorms from €12/US$14, doubles from €28/US$32; www.hostel-kotor.me)*

Midrange
Palazzo Drusko Filled with antiques, this 600-year-old palazzo is a memorable place to stay in Kotor's Old Town. *(Doubles from €80/US$91; www.palazzodrusko.me)*

Flush
Hotel Hippocampus The owner of this boutique hotel is an architect and it shows: every inch is elegant and evocative. *(Doubles from €140/US$159; www.hotelhippocampus.com)*

Eat

Shoestring
Kotor Market Stock up at this farmers' market under the town walls and try free samples of local *pršut* (air-dried ham), cheese, olives and strawberries. *(Food from €1/US$1.15)*

Midrange
Restoran Galerija This bustling Kotor waterfront restaurant excels in meat and seafood. Try the seafood in sauce (a blend of olive oil, wine, garlic and spices). *(Mains from €7-20/US$7.90-23; www.restorangalerija.com)*

Flush
Galion Upmarket Galion gazes directly at Kotor's Old Town across the millionaires' yachts in the marina. Fresh fish is the focus, but you'll also find steaks and pasta. *(Meals from €12-23/US$14-26)*

Timing

May is dry, with mild temperatures and fragrant Mediterranean foliage in bloom. June is the best month, when temperatures are around 28°C, rainfall is low and prices are off-peak. July and August are the hottest and driest months – but also the busiest and most expensive.

Take your own photo from this viewpoint by climbing up to the fort above town.

Perast is a small town of 16 churches and 17 formerly grand palazzi on the shores of the Bay of Kotor.

3

Ostrog Monastery, clinging to a cliff 900m above Zeta Valley, is the most important site in Montenegro for Orthodox Christians

Best value itineraries

2 days
From the pretty town of Herceg Novi, wind your way around the bay by bus towards Kotor, stopping at Perast en route. All three bayside towns are filled with old churches and marbled squares. Kotor's Stari Grad, or Old Town, is a wanderer's delight, with its warren of lanes, squares and handsome palazzi. Take a boat trip around the bay and hike up to cliff-top St John's Fortress at sunset for sweeping bay views.

8–10 days
Kotor is a great base for further Montenegrin adventures – but ideally you'll need your own car. Take the dazzling drive up and over the mountains through Lovćen National Park, stopping to visit the Njegoš Mausoleum on the way. Explore Montenegro's former royal capital, Cetinje, which zings with museums and galleries by day, and lively cafe-bars by night. Next day, head up to the mountainside Ostrog Monastery before sweeping south to Podgorica to roam the small city and sample its up-and-coming bar scene. On day four, continue to Virpazar for a chilled-out two-hour cruise on Lake Skadar, then carry on down to Sveti Stefan and beachy Budva.

© Dmitry V. Petrenko / Shutterstock

Java Sea

Arafura Sea

TIMOR-LESTE

Savu Sea

Timor Sea

Gulf of Carpentaria

INDONESIA

INDIAN OCEAN

Northern Territory

AUSTRALIA

Uluru
☆

Western Australia

South Australia

Great Australian Bight

Oceania

SOLOMON ISLANDS
SOUTH PACIFIC OCEAN
VANUATU
Daintree Rainforest
Coral Sea
Great Barrier Reef
FIJI
NEW CALEDONIA
Queensland
Norfolk Island (AUSTRALIA)
Lord Howe Island
New South Wales
Australian Capital Territory
Victoria
Tasman Sea
Tasmania
NEW ZEALAND
Milford Sound
Stewart Island

①

© superjoseph / Shutterstock

AUSTRALIA

Great Barrier Reef & the Daintree Rainforest

Despite the obvious effects of the changing climate, there's something special about visiting the largest living thing on earth.

The coral ribbons, reefs and shoals that make up the Great Barrier Reef stretch for a staggering 1430 miles (2300km) along the northeastern coast of Australia. One of the world's top playgrounds for divers and snorkellers was a hazard for early mariners, who regularly holed their vessels on its coral outcrops. Old timers may reminisce that the colours were more vivid before coral bleaching, but the reefs still teem with life, from tiny crustaceans to mighty megafauna such as dolphins, turtles and sharks.

This magnificent marine world is mirrored by a similarly rich ecosystem on land, the astonishing Daintree Rainforest, the last remnants of the primordial forest that once covered Australia. Split days between reef, beach and jungle and you'll be living the tropical dream, swimming in a world of carpet sharks, dugongs and giant clams, and pushing back rainforest vines in search of tree kangaroos, cassowaries and saltwater crocodiles.

Travel

International

Cairns is the top gateway for both the Barrier Reef and the Daintree, attracting legions of divers, nature fans and party-oriented backpackers. Direct flights serve Bali, Singapore, the Philippines and Japan, with easy connections on to Europe, the Middle East, Australia and beyond, while local carriers whoosh to every corner of Australia. For the full reef'n'rainforest experience, head 87 miles (140km) north to Cape Tribulation, where reefs, sands and rainforest combine into a perfect package.

Regional

From Cairns, buses zip north into the Daintree along the sealed road to Cape Tribulation, but to penetrate deeper into the rainforest along the bumpy Bloomfield Track, you'll need a 4WD. En route from Cairns you can drop into chichi Port Douglas, croc-stalked Daintree Village and foliage-choked Mossman Gorge. The reef is easily reached from Cairns, but if you head off from Cape Tribulation, you can return to a shoreline of white sand backed by swaying palms.

Stay

Shoestring

Cape Trib Beach House This presents the Daintree experience as you've imagined it – a secluded rainforest location, a lovely beach and a lively bar and restaurant to unwind in. (*Dorms from A$29/US$21, cabins from A$150/US$108; www.capetribbeach.com.au*)

Flush

Daintree Eco Lodge & Spa Cabins are perched high in the canopy at this exquisite ecoresort near Daintree Village, where even the restaurant uses responsibly sourced rainforest ingredients. (*Treehouses from A$325/US$110; www.daintree-ecolodge.com.au*)

Eat

Shoestring

Turtle Rock Café Burgers, tacos and wraps fly fast from the kitchen at this canopy-covered cafe in the middle of Daintree Village – well worth walking out for. (*Mains from A$7/US$5.15*)

Flush

Julaymba Restaurant The atmospheric eatery at the Daintree Eco Lodge will take you on a jungle journey. A profusion of rainforest nuts, berries and flowers make it onto the menu. (*Mains from A$28/US$21; www.daintree-ecolodge.com.au*)

Timing

Far North Queensland has a tropical climate, with a strong chance of torrential rain between November and April. Stinging jellyfish deter visitors from the beaches from November to May, so the best time for water babies is the dry high season from June to September, which also offers peak visibility on the reef. Visitor numbers and prices drop in the short shoulder seasons from April to May or October to November, which just avoid the stinger season.

The reef and its hundred of islands offer a home to 10% of the world's fish species and six types of turtle.

Buttressed roots of tropical trees in the Daintree rainforest.

You can't mistake the colours (and helmet) of a cassowary, Queensland's formidable (if flightless) avian giant.

© Torsten Pursche / Shutterstock

NEW ZEALAND

Stewart Island

New Zealand's third island feels a million miles from the North and South Island. Named Stewart Island by colonial settlers, and Rakiura ('glowing skies') by the original Maori inhabitants of the area, this sparsely populated island has just one town, few roads and just a few hundred inhabitants, which explains why it offers your best chance of spotting a kiwi in the wild.

Most of the island is protected by a 1400 sq km national park, where you can get far from the nearest human being and imagine New Zealand as it might have been before homo sapiens first tramped on to the scene. While you explore its silent beaches, muddy swamps, ribbon-like inlets and fern-filled forests, look out for chance encounters with kiwis, which wander at will in this predator-free sprawl of hills. At points along the shoreline, you can gaze out over empty waters that stretch, uninterrupted, all the way to Antarctica, beneath a curtain of lights from the aurora australis, and feel just a hint of the lonely freedom of the fishermen who have moored here across the centuries. Afterwards, reset your sense of perspective with a pint at the South Sea Hotel, the southernmost pub in New Zealand.

Travel

International
It's often said that visitors to Stewart Island have a choice between 10 minutes of terror or an hour of torture. Wind-tossed flights connect the island's only town, Oban, to Invercargill on the South Island, or you can brave the ocean for an hour-long ferry crossing from Bluff over the notoriously choppy Foveaux Strait. Flights connect Invercargill to Dunedin International Airport, but the only international flight from here is to Brisbane, so you many need to connect through Auckland or Christchurch.

Regional
Stewart Island has only one town, which is where almost everyone arrives, and most of the island's 12½ miles (20km) of roads link Oban to surrounding bays outside the national park area. To penetrate deeper into the interior, you have to walk, but water taxis can drop you off at remote bays around the national park so you can start your tramp in pristine nature. Sea kayaks are another popular way to explore, but most paddlers stay close to Oban in Paterson Inlet.

Stay

Shoestring
Bunkers Backpackers A handy central location in Oban and a sunny garden add to the appeal at this small, cosy backpacker hostel in an old wooden villa. *(Dorms from NZ$34/US$23, rooms from NZ$80/US$55; www.bunkersbackpackers.co.nz)*

Flush
Observation Rock Lodge Perfectly positioned for views of sea, sunset and aurora, this small, graceful lodge has a bush setting and luxurious rooms with private decks. *(Rooms from NZ$395/US$272; www.observationrocklodge.co.nz)*

Eat

Shoestring
South Sea Hotel This iconic pub – the southernmost in New Zealand – is an essential Oban stop for cold beer by the quart, fish and chip suppers and great bar banter. *(Mains from NZ$18/US$12; www.southseahotel.co.nz)*

Flush
Church Hill Restaurant & Oyster Bar Local oysters, salmon and crayfish dominate the menu at this hilltop heritage villa, serving Oban's best sit-down dinners. *(Mains from NZ$38/US$26; www.churchhill.co.nz)*

Timing

Stewart Island edges into the roaring forties so rain falls regularly year-round and its muddy trails are often waterlogged.

The cool winter from June to August is best avoided for camping, but there's more competition for space in overnight huts from December to February.

Ferry crossings from Bluff to Oban are reduced from May to September, but this is the best time to catch the aurora australis.

The Stewart Island kiwi (or tokoeka) is one of New Zealand's largest varieties and forages throughout the island at night (and sometimes by day).

Shale formations in New Zealand's newly designated national park, Rakiura National Park on Stewart Island.

Pause at a pier on the Rakiura Track, one of New Zealand's 'Great Walks'.

Best value itineraries

4 days
Four days is really the minimum if you want to get into the interior of Stewart Island. The glorious Rakiura Track takes three days to loop around the isthmus inland from Oban, offering prime kiwi-spotting opportunities en route, with accommodation in trekkers' huts or campsites along the trail. On the way you'll walk lonely beaches with hardly a footprint on the sand and forest trails dripping with fern fronds, taking in stunning views across the island and ocean. At the end there's a day for exploring tiny, friendly Oban and the surrounding bays or kayaking on Paterson Inlet.

7–10 days
With up to 10 days, you can really leave the masses behind and get far from humanity on the north or western coasts of the island. The easier Southern Circuit offers a six-day transect across the centre of Stewart Island from Halfmoon Bay or the Freshwater boat landing, following forested valleys to Mason Bay with hut accommodation for each overnight stop. You'll need nine days or more for the tougher North West Circuit, linking a string of trekkers' huts around the north end of the island, passing dune-backed beaches, rocky headlands and ferny forests.

© slyellow / Shutterstock

AUSTRALIA

Uluru

First to the important business: Australia's most famous landmark is called Uluru, not Ayers Rock. The Anangu people, the traditional custodians of the rock, have never accepted the name imposed by British colonial settlers. In the *tjukurpa*, the moral and social code handed down through generations of Anangu people, Uluru was created by ancestral spirits when the world was young and it's easy to see why this magnificent hunk of stone has such massive spiritual significance.

In the saturated light of early morning or late afternoon, Uluru seems to glow from within, as if a piece of the spirit realm is pushing through into the physical world. Technically, Uluru is an inselberg, all that remains of a mighty mountain range that was ground to dust by millennia of erosion, and two-thirds of the outcrop is hidden below the desert sands, adding to the sense that something mysterious lurks just out of sight. View it at dawn or dusk and you'll get a sense of the Australia that could have existed if the outside world had chosen not to intervene. Tourists once clambered willy-nilly over Uluru, but these days most respect the beliefs of the Anangu people and view Uluru from ground level, tramping around the base to admire its ancient curves.

Travel

International
Uluru is five hours by road from the nearest population centre at Alice Springs, but you can get within a few miles of the sacred site by air. Diminutive Ayers Rock Airport (it has yet to catch up with the preferred local name) is just 20 minutes by road from Uluru at Yulara on the outskirts of Uluru-Kata Tjuta National Park. Flights arrive here from Alice Springs, Cairns, Brisbane, Melbourne and Sydney, connecting with international flights from almost everywhere.

Regional
Having dropped on to the dusty tarmac at Ayers Rock Airport, you'll need to decide how you want to approach Uluru – by tour bus, by hire car, by bike, or even by air on a scenic fly-by. Yulara is 11 miles (18km) from Uluru, and 34 miles (55km) from the Kata Tjuta rock formations, so walking is only for the committed and well prepared. Prices for trips out of Yulara are steep considering the small distances, so many prefer to come by hire car from Alice Springs.

Stay

Shoestring
Ayers Rock Resort Campground Accommodation comes at a premium in Yulara, but the campsites are a saviour for budget travellers, with free barbecues, a camp kitchen and pool. *(Camping from A$43/US$32, cabins from A$184/US$135; www.ayersrockresort.com.au)*

Flush
Desert Gardens Hotel The swishest part of the Ayers Rock Resort offers sleek, Scandinavian-style hotel rooms. The best of them have rock or desert views. *(Rooms from A$360/US$264; www.ayersrockresort.com.au)*

Eat

Shoestring
Ininti Café The Anangu-run cafe at Uluru's Cultural Centre is the best bet for light, inexpensive meals, in a prime location overlooking the rock. *(Meals from A$20/US$15)*

Flush
Sounds of Silence It doesn't get much more romantic than Champagne, canapes and fine dining at tables set up under the outback sky near Uluru – a top-end experience served up by the Ayers Rock Resort. *(Set dinners A$210/US$154; www.ayersrockresort.com.au/sounds-of-silence)*

Timing

Consider the desert climate when planning a trip to Uluru. Sensible travellers visit between May and September, when daytime temperatures fall to manageable levels and the colours are at their most saturated. Mad dogs and Englishmen who visit in the hot months from December to February must compete with daytime highs of 36°C – park officials recommend only walking before 11am to avoid overheating.

Sunset at Uluru: there are several viewing platforms, including Talinguru Nyakunytjaku, the most popular.

Check out the sheer rock walls – safely! – at Kings Canyon.

Camels were introduced to Australia in the 1840s to aid desert exploration; today you can ride one on a camel tour of Uluru.

Best value itineraries

3–4 days
Three to four days is an ideal duration for Uluru, giving yourself time to get there and to appreciate Uluru's changing moods. Reserve day one for the bone-rattling drive from Alice Springs, and roll into Yulara in time to set up camp and order a beer to wash away the trail dust. Day two and three are Uluru days – block out time for a dawn and sunset view, and allow half a day for the 6 mile (10km) walk around the base of the massif. On day four, head 22 miles (35km) west to Kata Tjuta (formerly the Olgas), exploring the mysterious boulders on the 4½ mile (7½km) Valley of the Winds walk.

7–10 days
Due to Uluru's remote location, it helps to have time to cover the distances. Kick off with a few days in Alice Springs to enjoy the creature comforts before hitting the Lasseter Highway, then high-tail it to Yulara and devote three or four days to exploring Uluru and Kata Tjuta on foot, by camel or by rented bike. For a scenic route back to Alice, stop off at Curtin Springs, leaping-off point for the flat-topped plateau of Mt Conner, then follow the Luritja Rd to Kings Canyon, a natural chasm in wildlife-filled Watarrka National Park.

© Matt Munro / Lonely Planet

1

2

AUSTRALIA

Lord Howe Island

Travellers seeking the perfect pirate island need look no further than Lord Howe.

Floating like a crab's claw in the middle of the Tasman Sea, this pinprick on the map is 373 miles (600km) from the nearest landfall on mainland Australia. Access is by one of the country's most expensive domestic flights, which puts most things on the island at a premium, except of course the pristine nature, served up free to every visitor. The crumbled remains of a vanished volcano, Lord Howe is the whole island package: blinding sand beaches, a coral-reef-filled lagoon, tropical jungle covering the interior like a green blanket and, at either extremity, soaring mountains climbed by rugged trails through frond-filled forests plucked straight from *Jurassic Park*.

Away from the informal 'town' at the north end of the island, this is a place to live all your *Robinson Crusoe* fantasies, as you clamber to reach rocky lookouts where you can cast your eye over the entire island and feel like king of all you survey. Lord Howe even has its own flag, depicting exactly what anyone imagining a pirate island would choose – a palm tree, a beach and Lord Howe's two highest mountains, Mt Lidgbird and Mt Gower.

Travel

International
For a tiny tropical island far out in the Tasman Sea, Lord Howe is well connected. Planes land here year-round from Brisbane and Sydney, joined by flights from Port Macquarie, the nearest point on the mainland, from February to June and September to December. Both Sydney and Brisbane have excellent connections to Asia and the Middle East, with onward flights to almost everywhere on the globe.

Regional
Having stepped on to the tarmac at tiny Lord Howe Airport, the first choice for getting anywhere is on foot. The island measures just 10km by 2km at its widest point, so you can walk to every corner of the island, though you may have to pick your way through the rainforest on the way. Bikes are handy for exploring the flat bits, but the trails to the summits of Mt Lidgbird and Mt Gower are for hiking only.

Stay

Shoestring
Beachcomber Lodge Winter prices at this centenarian bungalow on the hill above 'downtown' are perhaps the cheapest on the island, and there are kitchens here for self-caterers. *(Apartments from A$170/US$125; www.beachcomberlhi.com.au)*

Flush
Pinetrees Lodge The lack of wi-fi and mobile phone signal is a blessing at this sublimely relaxing Lord Howe institution, in business since 1842 and famed for its restaurant and service. *(Rooms from A$710/US$521; www.pinetrees.com.au)*

Eat

Shoestring
Coral Café There's a globe-trotting menu at the museum cafe, with everything from sushi to roast meats to keep hungry island-hoppers satisfied. *(Mains from A$8/US$5.90)*

Midrange
Anchorage Restaurant Modern Australian is the name of the game at this respected eatery, popular for breakfast coffee and sit-down fine dining at night. *(Mains from A$30/US$22; www.earlsanchorage.com)*

Timing

The Australian summer brings perfect tropical weather to Lord Howe – warm but never too hot for comfort – but also the top prices for flights and accommodation. Spring and autumn are good times to visit, with seasonal flights covering the shorter trip from Port Macquarie from February to June and September to December. To cut costs, visit in winter, from June to August; prices dip and daytime temperatures still reach a respectable 19°C.

With around 170 avian species, Lord Howe is an important nesting site for birds, like this sooty tern.

Lord Howe Island is the crescent-shaped remnant of a volcano, with these two peaks at the southern tip.

The coral reefs around the island are also remarkably rich in life.

Best value itineraries

3–4 days
Due to the high price tag, four days may be all you can manage on Lord Howe, but there are enough thrilling experiences here to make it worth every penny. Devote a day or two to the beaches – Ned's Beach near town has tame fish and good snorkelling, but it's worth hiking to North Beach for more privacy and the company of nesting sooty terns. Allow another day for mountain climbing – it takes eight strenuous hours to reach the top of Mt Gower and return, but the summit views are stupendous. Leave day four for an excursion on the water. Bird-watching and climbing trips run to Ball's Pyramid, the remote stack 20km offshore, and there's excellent scuba-diving on the world's southernmost coral reef.

7–10 days
If you have 10 days to spare, there'll be time to fit in some detours on the mainland before you fly to Lord Howe. Bookend a week on the island with a few days surfing Port Macquarie's breaks, venturing out into the bay to spot whales, and finding quiet stretches of sand on the track between Tracking Point Lighthouse and Sea Acres National Park. On Lord Howe, take your time exploring. Spend some laid-back days on the beaches and out on the water, then tackle the Mt Gower climb. Leave another day for the vertiginous scramble to the summit of Mt Lidgbird, where Goat House Cave affords epic views over the island.

NEW ZEALAND

Milford Sound

New Zealand has a full hand of epic landscapes, from mountain glaciers to fern-filled forests, but even in this company, Milford Sound – Piopiotahi to the indigenous people of South Island – stands out.

Dominated by the soaring buttress of 1692m Mitre Peak, this dramatic inlet was carved by glaciers during the last ice age. When the ice sheets retreated some 10,000 years ago, they left behind an almost supernatural landscape of sculpted mountains rising sheer from the mirrored surface of the fjord. Viewed from the cruise ships that navigate the calm waters of the sound, the peaks rise like breaching humpback whales, isolating the inlet from the outside world.

When it rains, which it does often in this corner of the South Island, foamy cascades surge downhill into the sound, slowing to a trickle when the skies clear again. Stirling and Lady Bowen falls are the most reliable performers, kicking up rainbows of spray when the sun emerges after rain. To fully appreciate the scale of the landscape, you need to get down to water level. Trade the cruise ships for a guided kayak tour or don scuba gear and explore the remarkable terrain below the water – a playground for octopus, seals, penguins and dolphins.

①

②

Travel

International

Tourist flights drop into tiny Milford Sound Airport from Queenstown, Wanaka and Te Anau, but Queenstown has the only airport with international connections. A handful of airlines serve Sydney and the east coast of Australia, but for connections to Asia and further afield, you'll need to fly first to Dunedin or Christchurch. Buses run to the sound from Queenstown and Te Anau, but many visitors prefer to come here on self-drive campervan trips.

Regional

Most people visit Milford Sound from Queenstown or Te Anau as this natural wonder has limited infrastructure and places to stay, apart from the Milford Sound Lodge and berths on visiting cruise ships. Buses and tourist flights run daily from both cities, making day trips a popular option. Self-drivers should fill up before leaving Queenstown or Te Anau as prices are elevated at the lone pump in the sound.

Stay

Shoestring

Te Anau Lakefront Backpackers The lakefront location ensures lovely views from this popular hostel in Te Anau, which offers a choice of simple bunkrooms or smarter private rooms. *(Dorms from NZ$20/US$14, rooms from NZ$88/US$61; www.teanaubackpackers.co.nz)*

Flush

Milford Sound Lodge Rustic chic is the watchword at this rural lodge providing everything from wow-factor chalets to pocket-friendly dorms, as well as jaw-dropping views. *(Dorms from NZ$40/US$28, chalets from NZ$415/US$285; www.milfordlodge.com)*

Eat

Shoestring

Sandfly Café Locals and outsiders come together at this lively Te Anau hangout, great for morning coffee, hearty breakfasts and light lunches. *(Mains from NZ$7/US$4.80)*

Flush

Public Kitchen & Bar This lakeside Queenstown eatery makes full use of meat and produce from local farms; come for a slap-up dinner after a day trip to the sound. *(Mains from NZ$12/US$8.25; www.publickitchen.co.nz)*

Timing

Milford Sound is famously green and pleasant – credit for this goes to the abundant rains, which swell the waterfalls year round, most spectacularly in December and January. The weather is drier from June to August, but temperatures dip and the waterfalls thunder a little less dramatically. The shoulder seasons from March to May and September to November strike a happy compromise, with fewer visitors, but plenty of waterworks.

Milford Sound receives a mean annual rainfall of 6000mm, meaning that it's one of the wettest places in the world – and has lots of waterfalls.

The Darran Mountains reflected in Lake Marian, one of many lakes in Fiordland National Park.

Take the plunge from Kawarua Bridge near Queenstown.

Best value itineraries

3–4 days

Due to the limited accommodation available on the sound, most visitors come on day trips from Queenstown or Te Anau, so consider an itinerary linking all three places, leaving room for some adventure activities on the side. Start with a couple of days in Queenstown, reserving one day for rafting, tramping, paragliding, bungee-jumping, canyoning or climbing in the fabulous countryside outside town. On day three, head off early for the sound and immerse yourself in the stunning scenery – both on arrival and along the route – before overnighting at Milford Sound Lodge. Continue on day four to Te Anau, which serves up its own set of stunning lakeside landscapes.

7–10 days

With a week to spare, it would be a shame to enjoy the wonders of the sound for just a day. The legendary Milford Track runs from Glade Wharf on Lake Te Anau to Milford Sound in four scenery-filled days, passing towering waterfalls, lofty mountain passes, plunging glacial valleys and pockets of rainforest. Boats zip trekkers from Te Anau to Glade Wharf, but visitor numbers are strictly controlled and the route is booked out within days of opening to tourists each year. Head onward to Queenstown to enjoy the food and party mood, then continue the fun at Wanaka for a more low-key vision of lakeside living.

Index

A

abandoned & ancient
  settlements
  22–23, 24–27,
  72–75, 76–77,
  116–119, 126–129,
  178–181, 234–237,
  290–293
Abu Simbel, Egypt 34–37
Acropolis, Greece
  284–287
Alhambra, Spain 238–241
Amazon rainforest 92–95
ancient monuments
  & ruins 10–13,
  14–17, 24–27,
  34–37, 72–75,
  76–77, 110–111,
  116–119, 126–129,
  160–163, 174–177,
  178–181, 206–209,
  218–221, 234–237,
  242–243, 244–
  247, 272–275,
  284–287, 290–
  293, 306–307,
  322–325
Angel Falls, Venezuela
  124–125
Angkor Wat, Cambodia
  160–163
Antarctica 112–115
Antelope Canyon, USA
  56–57
architecture 48–51,
  136–139, 156–159,
  164–167, 230–233,
  252–253, 280–
  283, 298–301,
  312–315, 318–321,
  336–337
Argentina
  Iguazú Falls 102–105
Australia
  Great Barrier Reef
    & Daintree
    Rainforest
    350–353
  Lord Howe Island
    360–361
  Uluru 356–359
Aya Sofya, Turkey
  254–257

B

Bay of Kotor, Montenegro
  344–347
Belize

Blue Hole 70–71
Bhutan
  Punakha Dzong 216–217
  Taktshang Goemba
    200–201
Blue Hole, Belize 70–71
Blue Lagoon, Iceland
  276–279
Bolivia
  Salar de Uyuni 96–99
Bordeaux wine region,
  France 258–261
Borobudur, Indonesia
  218–221
Bosnia & Hercegovina
  Stari Most 280–283
Botswana
  Okavango Delta 38–41
Brazil
  Amazon rainforest
    92–95
  Iguazú Falls 102–105
British Museum, England
  288–289
Burj Khalifa, United Arab
  Emirates 136–139

C

Calakmul, Mexico 76–77
Cambodia
  Angkor Wat 160–163
Canada
  Haida Gwaii 52–55
  Lake Louise 78–81
  Niagara Falls 86–89
Caño Cristales, Colombia
  100–101
Cappadocia, Turkey
  230–233
CERN, Switzerland
  332–335
Chile
  Marble Caves 120–123
  Moai, Easter Island
    110–111
China
  Forbidden City 182–185
  Great Wall of China
    164–167
  Terracotta Army
    174–177
  Zhāngyè Dānxiá
    Geopark 212–215
cities & urban landmarks
  48–52, 132–135,
  136–139, 156–159,
  182–185, 254–257,
  270–271, 272–275,

284–287, 312–315,
  318–321, 338–341
Colombia
  Caño Cristales 100–101
Colosseum, Italy 272–275
Croatia
  Plitvice Lakes 302–305
culture & people
  ceremonies &
    gatherings
    188–191, 202–205,
    338–341
  food & drink 258–261
  museums & libraries
    82–85, 226–229,
    254–257,
    262–265,
    270–271, 288–289,
    294–297, 336–337
Czech Republic
  Klementinum 336–337

D

Davit Gareja, Georgia
  244–247
Dead Sea, Jordan/Israel
  & the Palestinian
  Territories
  196–199
Door to Hell,
  Turkmenistan
  168–169

E

Ecuador
  Galápagos Islands
    106–109
Egypt
  Abu Simbel 34–37
  Pyramids of Giza 14–17
England
  British Museum
    288–289
  Stonehenge 242–243
Ephesus, Turkey 290–293
Ethiopia
  Lalibela 10–13

F

Forbidden City, China
  182–185
France
  Bordeaux wine region
    258–261
  Louvre 270–271
  Mont St-Michel
    252–253

G

Galápagos Islands,
  Ecuador 106–109
Geirangerfjord, Norway
  248–251
Georgia
  Davit Gareja 244–247
Germany
  Schloss Neuschwanstein
    326–327
Ghats of Varanasi, India
  202–205
Giant's Causeway,
  Northern Ireland
  266–269
Golden Temple, India
  170–173
Grand Canal, Italy
  298–301
Grand Canyon, USA
  58–61
Grand Palace, Thailand
  132–135
Great Barrier Reef &
  the Daintree
  Rainforest,
  Australia 350–
  353
Great Wall of China
  164–167
Great Zimbabwe 24–27
Greece
  Acropolis 284–287
  Meteora 308–311
Guatemala
  Tikal 126–129
Gunung Mulu National
  Park, Malaysia
  150–153

H

Haida Gwaii, Canada
  52–55
Halong Bay, Vietnam
  186–187
Hang Son Doong,
  Vietnam 144–145
Hawai'i Volcanoes
  National Park, USA
  63–65
Hermitage Museum,
  Russia 226–229
Himeji Castle, Japan
  210–211
Hungary
  Széchenyi Baths
  338–341

I

Iceland
  Blue Lagoon 276–279
  Northern Lights
    224–225
Iguazú Falls, Brazil/
  Argentina 102–105
India
  Ghats of Varanasi
    202–205
  Golden Temple 170–173
  Meghalaya Tree Bridges
    192–195
  Taj Mahal 146–149
  Temples of Hampi
    206–209
Indonesia
  Borobudur 218–221
Iran
  Naqsh-e Jahan Square
    156–159
Israel & the Palestinian
  Territories
  Dead Sea 196–199
  Temple Mount 140–143
Italy
  Colosseum 272–275
  Grand Canal 298–301
  Pompeii 234–237
  Sistine Chapel 294–297

J

Japan
  Himeji Castle 210–211
  Sakura 188–191
Jordan
  Dead Sea 196–199
  Petra 178–181

K

Klementinum, Czech
  Republic 336–337
Kolmanskop, Namibia
  22–23

L

Lake Louise, Canada
  78–81
Lalibela, Ethiopia 10–13
Lord Howe Island,
  Australia 360–361
Louvre, France 270–271

M

Machu Picchu, Peru
  116–119
Madagascar
  Tsingy de Bemaraha

30–33
Malaysia
Gunung Mulu National Park 150–153
Marble Caves, Chile 120–123
Matterhorn, Switzerland 316–317
Meghalaya Tree Bridges, India 192–195
Mesa Verde, USA 72–75
Meteora, Greece 308–311
Mexico
Calakmul 76–77
Milford Sound, New Zealand 362–365
Moai, Easter Island, Chile 110–111
Montenegro
Bay of Kotor 344–347
Mont St-Michel, France 252–253
Mt Everest, Nepal 154–155
Mt Kilimanjaro, Tanzania 8–9

N
Namibia
Kolmanskop 22–23
Naqsh-e Jahan Square, Iran 156–159
national parks 8–9, 30–33, 44–47, 52–55, 62–65, 66–69, 78–81, 92–95, 100–101, 124–125, 150–153, 212–215, 302–305, 354–355
natural wonders
forest, jungle & other flora 52–55, 66–69, 92–95, 124–125, 126–129, 144–145, 150–153, 188–191, 192–195, 360–361
geological phenomena 30–33, 44–47, 56–57, 58–61, 96–99, 120–123, 144–145, 150–153, 168–169, 186–187, 212–215, 230–233, 266–269, 308–311, 342–343, 356–359

mountains & volcanoes 8–9, 18–21, 44–47, 62–65, 78–81, 154–155, 316–317, 362–365
Northern Lights 224–225
oceans & coasts 70–71, 186–187, 344–347, 350–353, 360–361, 362–365
rivers & lakes 38–41, 48–51, 78–81, 86–89, 92–95, 96–99, 100–101, 102–105, 120–123, 124–125, 150–153, 196–199, 202–205, 248–251, 276–279, 280–283, 298–301, 302–305
waterfalls 28–29, 44–47, 86–89, 102–105, 124–125, 248–251
wildlife 18–21, 38–41, 52–55, 92–95, 106–109, 126–129, 150–153, 350–353, 354–355
Nemrut Dağı, Turkey 306–307
Nepal
Mt Everest 154–155
Netherlands
Rijksmuseum 262–265
New York Harbor, USA 48–51
New Zealand
Milford Sound 362–365
Stewart Island 354–355
Ngorongoro Crater 18–21
Niagara Falls, Canada/USA 86–89
Northern Ireland
Giant's Causeway 266–269
Northern Lights, Norway/ Iceland 224–225
Norway
Geirangerfjord 248–251
Northern Lights 224–225
Trolltunga 342–343

O
Okavango Delta,

Botswana 38–41

P
palaces, castles & temples 132–135, 140–143, 146–149, 156–159, 160–163, 170–173, 182–185, 200–201, 206–209, 210–211, 216–217, 218–221, 238–241, 252–253, 254–257, 294–297, 308–311, 312–315, 318–321, 326–327, 328–331
Peru
Amazon Rainforest 92–95
Machu Picchu 116–119
Petra, Jordan 178–181
Plitvice Lakes, Croatia 302–305
Pompeii, Italy 234–237
Portugal
Sintra 328–331
Punakha Dzong, Bhutan 216–217

R
Redwoods, USA 66–69
Rijksmuseum, The Netherlands 262–265
Russia
Hermitage Museum 226–229
St Basil's Cathedral 312–315

S
sacred sites 10–13, 132–135, 140–143, 160–163, 170–173, 200–201, 202–205, 206–209, 216–217, 218–221, 252–253, 308–311, 356–359
Sagrada Família, Spain 318–321
Sakura, Japan 188–191
Salar de Uyuni, Bolivia 96–99
Schloss Neuschwanstein, Germany 326–327

Scotland
Skara Brae 322–325
Sintra, Portugal 328–331
Sistine Chapel, Italy 294–297
Skara Brae, Scotland 322–325
Smithsonian Institution, USA 82–85
Spain
Alhambra 238–241
Sagrada Família 318–321
Stari Most, Bosnia & Hercegovina 280–283
St Basil's Cathedral, Russia 312–315
Stewart Island, New Zealand 354–355
Stonehenge, England 242–243
Switzerland
CERN 332–335
Matterhorn 316–317
Széchenyi Baths, Hungary 338–341

T
Taj Mahal, India 146–149
Taktshang Goemba, Bhutan 200–201
Tanzania
Mt Kilimanjaro 8–9
Ngorongoro Crater 18–21
Temple Mount, Israel & the Palestinian Territories 140–143
Temples of Hampi, India 206–209
Thailand
Grand Palace 132–135
Tikal, Guatemala 126–129

Trolltunga, Norway 342–343
Tsingy de Bemaraha, Madagascar 30–33
Turkey
Aya Sofya 254–257
Cappadocia 230–233
Ephesus 290–293
Nemrut Dağı 306–307
Turkmenistan
Door to Hell 168–169

U
Uluru, Australia 356–359
United Arab Emirates
Burj Khalifa 136–139
USA
Antelope Canyon 56–57
Grand Canyon 58–61
Hawai`i Volcanoes National Park 62–65
Mesa Verde 72–75
New York Harbor 48–51
Niagara Falls 86–89
Redwoods 66–69
Smithsonian Institution 82–85
Yosemite Valley 44–47

V
Venezuela
Angel Falls 124–125
Victoria Falls, Zimbabwe/ Zambia 28–29
Vietnam
Halong Bay 186–187
Han Son Doong 144–145

Y
Yosemite Valley, USA 44–47

Z
Zambia
Victoria Falls 28–29
Zhāngyè Dānxiá Geopark, China 212–215
Zimbabwe
Great Zimbabwe 24–27
Victoria Falls 28–29

October 2019
Published by Lonely Planet Global Limited
CRN 554153
www.lonelyplanet.com
10 9 8 7 6 5 4 3 2 1
Printed in Singapore
ISBN 978 1 78868 2329
© Lonely Planet 2019
© photographers as indicated 2019

Managing Director, Publishing Piers Pickard
Associate Publisher Robin Barton
Commissioning Editor Jessica Cole
Art Director Daniel Di Paolo
Editor Bridget Blair
Proof Reader Liz Granirer
Print Production Nigel Longuet
Written by Oliver Berry (Europe), Joe Bindloss (Asia,
Oceania), Mark Johanson (South America, Polar),
Matt Phillips (Africa & the Middle East),
Karla Zimmerman (North America)

Lonely Planet Offices

Australia
The Malt Store, Level 3,
551 Swanston St, Carlton, Victoria 3053
T: 03 8379 8000

USA
124 Linden St, Oakland,
CA 94607
T: 510 250 6400

Ireland
Digital Depot, Roe Lane (Off Thomas Street)
The Digital Hub,
Dublin 8, D08 TCV4

Europe
240 Blackfriars Rd,
London SE1 8NW
T: 020 3771 5100

STAY IN TOUCH lonelyplanet.com/contact

Cover photo © Matt Munro / Lonely Planet